IRQ, DMA & I/O

• •

Resolving and Preventing
PC System Conflicts, 2e

D1004550

IRQ, DMA & I/O

Resolving and Preventing
PC System Conflicts, 2e

by Jim Aspinwall

A Division of Henry
Holt and Co., Inc.

First Edition—1997

Printed in the United States of America.

Library of Congress Cataloging-in-Publication Data

Aspinwall, jim.
    IRQ, DMA & I/O / by Jim Aspinwall. — 2nd ed.
        p.   cm.
    ISBN 1-55828-565-2
    1. Microcomputers.   2. Software configuration management.
QA76.5.A77432   1997   97–30985
004.165—dc21   CIP

10 9 8 7 6 5 4 3 2 1

MIS:Press books are available at special discounts for bulk purchases for sales promotions, premiums, fund-raising, or educational use. Special editions or book excerpts can also be created to specification.

For details contact: Special Sales Director
                                MIS:Press
                                a Division of Henry Holt and Company, Inc.
                                115 West 18th Street
                                New York, New York 10011

Associate Publisher: Paul Farrell

Managing Editor: Shari Chappell   **Production Editor:** Kitty May
Editor: Rebekah Young   **Copy Edit Manager:** Karen Tongish
Technical Editor: Bud Paulding   **Copy Editor:** Gwynne Jackson

To Kathy
With Love

Acknowledgments

There are dozens of people to thank for their assistance along the way since I've become exposed to various technologies, absorbed them, been challenged by them, and found ways to share them:

- My parents, Bill and Joan, for everything

- My favorite user, Kathy, to whom I've dedicated this edition, for her love and patience

- To Kevin, Kathy's son, for testing a lot of what I know, and how well I could or could not share it

- Many close friends and supporters in and out of the computer trade

- My friends in amateur radio, past, present, and future, for pioneering and bringing technology to the masses before computers became popular

- My employers and co-workers at Curtin Call, Hycel, Finnigan, DiagSoft, CMG, LSI Logic, TuneUp.com, and others for the opportunities to work on so many different things and gather the experience so critical to the topics in this book

- My first PC mentors and fellow authors, for their help, insight, and contributions to PC users and their PCs

- Leslie, Paul, Gloria, Rebekah, Bud, and everyone at M&T Books and MIS:Press for helping to make our words into something useful and presentable

- Dozens of on-line friends, acquaintances, and readers far and wide who have helped make all of my writing efforts and especially this book so worthwhile and for making this hobby fun

- Ron and his students at 'B40' Junior High for the inspiration to convey knowledge of and access to computers to an inspiring generation of new computer users so they can carry on and exceed us

- The dozens of people I've come to know in the computer industry, from system board makers to disk drive engineers—they have constantly challenged and constantly exceeded all my expectations of quality and performance

- All of my customers and the millions of PC users who need and want more knowledge and information to get through their lives and workdays

My first computer experience was wiring prototypes of Intel 8088 systems for telephony and communications applications from 1972–1976. From there I moved on and learned to use and fix LSI Alpha-16 minicomputers, programmed with switches and paper tape. I moved on to LSI-2 systems, and then on to Data General Nova minicomputers, all hooked up to some amazing scientific research systems. My first personal computer was an Apple IIc. It did its job and got me away from the typewriter, but I knew there had to be more. After I spent six months of reading everything I could find about PCs and consulting friends, my first XT clone appeared, its cursor winking ominously and uselessly until we breathed shareware and fire into it (and me) one weekend in 1986.

Since that weekend, there seemed to be no stopping the encounters with the on-line world, new applications, database programming, and trying to figure out ways to simplify things and help others enjoy the same positive experiences. Not until 1991 and my first Pascal course had I ever written a real program, and with only two courses of Pascal and one of C, I don't think I'll be making a career of computer programming.

Thanks to an enlightened acquisitions editor at M&T Books, my first co-authors and I made it into print—first in 1989 with *The PC User's Survival Guide,* and again in 1991, 1994, and 1996 with *Troubleshooting Your PC.* We got the words out and they seemed to help quite a few people. Challenged by the ever-present need to help people understand and optimize their PC configurations, this project came about as much by coincidence as foresight and imagination. Success with this work and the ever present challenges imposed by new hardware, operating systems, technicians, and users pushes us further along.

This is all a labor of love and appreciation of both technology and the written word—and making good use of them both. After all, sharing our curiosities and our knowledge is the whole point.

My most sincere thanks and appreciation to everyone!

Jim Aspinwall

e-mail: jim@raisin.com

WWW: http://www.raisin.com

CONTENTS

Contents

Chapter 8: System Configuration Tools and Utilities............................229

INTRODUCTION

Welcome to the not-quite-pocket-sized guide to quickly and easily creating and maintaining a clean, high-performance PC configuration. The focus of this book is avoiding, or if needed, resolving resource conflicts within your system.

At least half of the PCs I hear about or am asked to support, whether as a favor to a family member or friend, through e-mail from readers, or as a primary career responsibility, are configured improperly. That's a *lot* of broken PCs. Ten percent would be a lot. Twenty percent would be a nuisance. Fifty percent is inexcusable.

Whether or not you believe me, the sad thing is that most users and support people may not be aware of this situation, have intentionally set up their systems improperly, or fail to associate some unusual system or application behavior problems with the possibility of a misconfiguration.

This is much like driving a car with the Service Engine or Oil light glaring from the dashboard, and not associating the indicator with the symptom of smoke coming out from under the hood or the engine dying in the middle of rush-hour traffic. At least cars have warning lights. In the case of PCs, we have to dig a little further to see what might be wrong. Digging into your PC's configuration is what this book is all about.

What's Here

You'll be reading through a lot of information you probably wish you had a long time ago that confirms your suspicions of one technical thing or another, or that you really didn't want to know but now have to know to survive life with your PC.

Since we'll be discussing them a lot, they are the title of this book, and they are the root of the PC configuration evil we face, let's define some basic system resource names:

- **IRQ (Interrupt Request Signals).** IRQs are signal lines connected between a variety of devices, both external (through add-in cards) and internal to your system board (containing the central processing unit *(CPU),* or main computer chip, and the connections for built-in and external devices.) An IRQ assignment is expressed simply as *IRQ3* or something similar. Via IRQ signals, devices such as the serial (COM) port, keyboard and disk drives, and some internal computer functions signal the computer that an activity on that device needs the CPU's attention quickly in order to move data or handle an error situation.

  In PC and XT-class systems there are only eight IRQ lines. A couple are reserved for internal system board use, leaving only IRQ 2, 3, 4, 5, and 7 to work with. In AT and higher-class systems there are 16 IRQ lines. Again, a few are reserved for internal system board use, leaving only IRQ 2, 3, 4, 5, 7, 9, 10, 11, 12, 14, and 15 to work with. IRQ 2 may or may not be useable, although it is available on the system bus because it is used to tie the second IRQ controller chip to the first. IRQ 9 may or may not be useable, though it is available on the system bus, as it is the replacement for the otherwise occupied IRQ 2 line.

  As a practical example, let's say an IRQ is signaled for every block of data that is received into a serial/COM port, letting the CPU know that it needs to fetch this data before it is lost and new data replaces it. A *lot* of IRQs occur during on-line e-mail and Web page loading.

• **DMA (Direct Memory Access Signals).** A DMA channel is a set of two signal lines, one line for *DMA request* (DRQ) and the other for *DMA acknowledgment* (DACK), assigned in corresponding pairs (as simply one DMA assignment), and is expressed simply as *DMA3* or something similar. DMA channels are available with devices that have the ability to exchange data directly with system memory without going through the CPU (many disk drive functions and multimedia cards use DMA to speed data throughput.)

With a DMA channel, a device signals the computer or the CPU signals a device about the need for or status of direct access between two devices, one of which is usually system memory. DMA data transfer is performed under the control of the devices themselves. It is very fast—much faster than if the CPU and software handled the operation, although it does cause the CPU to stop processing memory operations for a short time, so DMA cannot control the system indefinitely.

In PC and XT-class systems there are only four DMA lines. One is reserved for diskette drive use, leaving only DMA 0, 1, and 3 to work with. In an AT or higher-class systems there are eight DMA lines. One is reserved for diskette drive use, leaving only DMA 0, 1, 3, 5, 6, and 7 to work with. (DMA 4 is usually not useable or because it is used to link the second four DMA lines to the first DMA controller chip.) DMA 2 is always dedicated to diskette drives only.

As a practical example, sound files sent to your PC's sound card and speakers use DMA to transfer large amounts of data from memory into the sound card, filling the sound card with information that it translates into smooth music, sounds, or voices. If your system cannot satisfy a lot of DMA activity, either because it has a slow CPU or more data needs to be moved than there is allowable DMA time for, the audio will stutter and sound choppy.

- **I/O (Input/Output Addresses).** These are numerical representations of actual memory locations that are used for the *data bus* (the 8-, 16-, or 32-bit data lines that interconnect devices within the computer) or system RAM memory (from DOS or low memory, through the first 640 Kbytes of RAM, to the upper memory areas through any and all extended memory.)

Appearing most often in the form *378h*, indicating address 378 expressed in hexidecimal format, I/O addresses are used to uniquely identify the places in your system where data and control information can be written to or read from for the interactions between devices, the CPU, and system memory. Each device, such as a serial port or disk drive, is said to occupy a specific *address* or (location), in memory. Only data or commands specific to the device that occupies a particular address should be sent to or expected from its location.

The PC or XT-class system address ranges from 0 to 1 MB (0–1024 Kbytes, or 1,024,000 addresses), but relatively few addresses in the 100h–500h range are available for use by physical I/O devices, and the upper memory range from A000h–FFFFh is reserved for video, disk, and other accessory adapter data and ROM BIOS uses.

In practice, a device such as a serial or COM port really uses more than one full-byte address. While COM1's base address is 3F8h, it also uses every address inclusive from 3F8h to 3FFh (8 memory locations) for various data and control information. Some devices use only 1 address, others 4, still others use 16 or 32 addresses.

From this, it may be obvious that we don't have many system hardware resources. We're left with only 11 IRQ lines, and nearly every device in your system needs an IRQ line. This is the most common issue we'll have to deal with. When you start adding scanner adapters, modems, network cards, CD-ROM adapters, mice, and printers, you can see how resources can get scarce quickly. Even with the increasingly common presence of Plug and Play, the relatively new PCI bus, and other advances, we have to pay attention to how we use these limited resources. Still, it is possible to manage all of them and have a nicely running system.

IRQ, DMA, and I/O are mutually exclusive in that one is not dependent upon another (except for a few specific cases), and that they don't conflict with one another (IRQ1 doesn't conflict with DMA1, for example). Nevertheless, these three items can be closely related, as we will discuss in Chapter 2.

We'll also use other terms to refer to actual RAM memory, BIOS addressing, and configuration items. All of these various technical terms and more are the language of PC configuration, and as they come along we'll give them ample explanation.

Overview

In this book, we'll discuss the practice of configuration management and how to use it to determine the current status of your system; how to avoid conflicts that can cause crashes, errors, or lost functionality; how to optimize your system for its current use or the addition of new devices; and how to make sure that you can successfully install and use the latest operating systems and software. This may sound a bit strident, but the goal is a proper, reliable system setup.

In the two years since the first edition of this book was published, Plug and Play systems and devices, Windows 95, Windows NT, and their registry files, have received considerable attention as much for their successes as for their failures.

It is hoped that Microsoft and the system and device manufacturers have learned or been reminded of the same things I have—that Plug and Play (PnP) often doesn't, thus making us rethink and adjust some of the methods we use when configuring new PCs or adding options to existing ones. The logic of PnP is not perfect.

Most of us still have "legacy," or non-PnP devices, in our systems. With or without a mix of legacy and PnP devices, we're still required to obey the rules of the original and subsequent PC configuration designs and methods. Even when only PnP devices are in our systems, problems can arise. We'll talk about those problems and how to work around them as we go along.

The information provided in this book applies as much to the one- or two-user systems in the home or small office as it does to multisystem environments. With this book, you will learn how to:

- Determine your PC's present configuration
- Use the configuration information to determine what, if anything, to change
- Verify that your configuration is correct and functioning properly

Through this you will be able to:

- Save several hours of frustration over each potential PC problem

- Avoid loss of productive time
- Avoid costly technical support calls
- Enhance the performance of your system
- Prepare your system for IBM's OS/2 or Microsoft's Windows 95 or NT

This is a do-it-yourself guide. No complex tools, technologies, or skills are required to quickly and easily establish, upgrade, and maintain your PC system configuration. All of the resources you need, with the possible exception of a common screwdriver or two, are contained within your system and this book, aided by whatever information you can gather from your PC system board and add-in devices.

You may get a lot of information that you never wanted to be concerned with before. After all, computers and software are supposed to be more powerful than ever before—and they are. PCs in fact do a lot of things a lot faster than they used to, but faster does not mean smarter or better unless the system is configured properly, and proper configuration requires information.

Perfect Toast

I tell a lot of people that if you want to make toast, you have to know something about the toaster. While you may not want to design the toaster or make the bread or jam, you need to know that the toaster needs to be plugged in, where to put the bread, how to make the toaster heat up, and since my toaster does not have a setting for "Jim's Perfect Toast" (nor can it learn what that is on its own), then you need to know how to adjust it so the toast doesn't burn.

A toaster isn't much different from your PC. You should

know what the pieces are, be able to get it hooked up, confirm that the pieces are what they say they are, and that the pieces are working properly. Unlike "Jim's Perfect Toast," my PC can't be set any way I might like it and still come out okay. Rather, I've learned that the computer must be set up to conform to many others' standards of PC perfection.

The toaster analogy is a bit oversimplified, but I use it to illustrate that neither using PCs nor making toast are things we "just know" as part of life. Neither are natural, instinctive functions. Both take a little learning and some trial-and-error until we get the results we want or need.

Configuration management includes collecting and using information from your system and from your hardware and software manuals. Without accurate information, maintaining your system will be difficult at best. But often, the information is missing or misleading.

We've included a valuable piece of software, PC-Doctor from Watergate Software, which will help you identify your system's hardware resources, and help uncover many unknowns and possible conflicts that could be preventing the most efficient use of your investment.

DISK

The Properly Configured PC

A properly configured PC is one in which there are no interdevice conflicts among the limited set of resources we're given to work with. These resources, as you'll see over and over again, are the IRQ, DMA, and I/O address items mentioned earlier, in addition to, or rather than, just the amount of RAM, free disk space, or resources left by the operating system and software.

This proper configuration and proper use of these

resources depends on following established standards, and in some cases, making legitimate preferential choices for some devices working within the standards.

A proper configuration is for the most part defined by original and subsequent PC system designs. These designs specify which system resources a particular device must or in some cases, can or should, use. Variances are not tolerated for most devices, but they may be allowed, with sufficient awareness and accommodations, in others.

A conflict within your PC system can be any occurrence of hardware and, in some cases, software that is configured in such a way that it is trying to use the same system resources as another device or program. Hardware may conflict by being set up to use the same interrupt request (IRQ) signal, direct memory access (DMA) channel, or I/O address as another piece of hardware. Any one of these resources can be the cause of a conflict.

One symptom of a hardware conflict is the failure or inability to use one device coincident with the use of another. In such cases, either the entire system or just one or both devices may cease to operate. In some cases you may receive an error message from your software or from Windows indicating that some device you expect to be functioning properly is unavailable for use.

Software may conflict with other software or the system by trying to use the same area of memory as another piece of software, which may result in overwriting the other program's data or program space. Software may also contain unknown or unresolved bugs or conflicts with DOS, Windows, or device drivers, which might cause the software to try to issue a command for an illegal or untimely operation to the microprocessor. Software may also be limited to working only within predefined rules, and otherwise acceptable variances may not be tolerated by a particular program.

Software conflicts may be signaled by error messages

indicating insufficient memory, Exception 13, or Windows' infamous General Protection Fault dialog box. Exception errors and General Protection Faults are indicated by memory management software or Windows, both of which monitor and attempt to maintain tight control over the computer's operations. If software tries to circumvent or improperly control these operations, Windows or the memory manager may warn you—or may simply appear to freeze the system's operation.

While this is, strictly speaking, an operating system or environment configuration issue, software might be improperly set up to use the wrong device or the wrong address or IRQ or DMA channel for a device, consequently indicating a failure to locate or control a specific piece of hardware such as a sound board, COM port, or printer.

NOTE

Memory management configuration and conflict issues are best left to the software and other reference materials dedicated to the subject. We will maintain this book's focus on hardware issues, and when we use the words *system* and *device*, we are referring to hardware (and the software or drivers that enable specific hardware; a *system* is the combined and cooperative interworkings of both software and hardware).

Toward the primary goal of avoiding conflicts, we will take a step at a time—one device, file, or piece of software at a time—and work with the reference information you have and that which is provided here. You can and will become comfortable with and confident about your system, even if you need to address an issue only once so that you can get on with using your PC.

We'll also discuss the standards and assumptions that affect the configuration of your PC, since these are the reference points by which all PC items are developed, perhaps improved upon, and implemented. We'll discuss the PC and its components as they were, as they are, and as they may be in the future.

PC Standards and Their Evolution

There is a lot of history, tradition, logic, and reason packed into the design and development of the PC and its various pieces. We are still using many items that were state-of-the-art technology circa 1981–1990. These items are the legacy of early PC development, and are called *legacy devices* and *legacy systems*. Over time, PCs have become a hodgepodge of old and new technologies and various attempts to create standards that have been poorly or only partially implemented as work-around methods to try to fill in addresses or BIOS functions that IBM may have intended to use later on.

Here's a basic reference list of the technical documents, standards, and issues that have affected the PC so far:

- *The IBM PC Technical Reference Manual*
- *The IBM PC/XT Technical Reference Manual*
- *The IBM PC/AT Technical Reference Manual*

These documents form the functional and legacy foundation for all PCs to date.

- The PC, XT, and AT industry standard architectures in general
- IBM's MicroChannel PC system architecture
- EISA system architecture
- PCMCIA (PC Card) bus

- VESA Local Bus
- PCI system architecture

These are subsequently accounted for and affected by:

- Video Electronics Standards Association
- Plug and Play BIOS and hardware specifications
- Desktop Management Task Force
- Automatic Power Management and Energy Star
- Microsoft's PC95 and PC97 initiatives

Considerable information may be obtained about the post-ISA architectures from on-line or membership sources referenced in the back of this book. The IBM reference manuals may be very hard to come by unless you find someone who is throwing out a set. They weren't cheap at $150 apiece.

All of these issues and developments affect the present-day PC to some extent. While VESA Local Bus is rarely if ever used in production systems these days, the VESA Video BIOS Extensions (VBE) are still quite important to video system compatibility. Of all of these, only ISA and PCI really concern us where PC hardware configuration resources are concerned, and often as not, PCI is not an issue because it uses different signals from ISA devices.

The current but now almost outdated standard for the interworkings of hardware and software involves Microsoft's PC95 strategy. Microsoft and equipment vendors are now working toward new PC97 goals. PC95 and PC97 are technical specifications that hardware makers are expected to build into their products and software creators should accommodate. These standards encompasses many aspects of the PC industry's Plug and Play specification, the PCI and PCMCIA/PC Card system bus, Intel's Pentium technology, new media and connection methods, and the functions of Microsoft's Windows family of PC operating systems.

To be effective, Plug and Play technology must be built into a PC's system BIOS (Basic Input/Output System software, which controls the booting up of your system), as well as into all devices connected to a PnP-compliant PC and then used with a PnP-compliant operating system, such as Microsoft's Windows 95 or IBM's OS/2. (Windows NT up to and including version 4.0 does not support PnP.)

PnP must take into account and support both legacy and PnP–compliant hardware devices.

Plug and Play exists in all new PC systems, and many systems built as early as 1994 (although systems built back then may not support the latest release 1.0a of the PnP specification).

NOTE

The latest Plug and Play specifications are available from http://www.microsoft.com/spain/windows/thirdparty/ hardware/pnpspecs.htm (URL accurate as of July 1997).

PnP is intended to detect and resolve, if not eliminate, PC configuration problems by providing automatic legacy and PnP device detection, and automatic configuration of PnP-compliant hardware devices. PnP can only detect but not reconfigure legacy or non-PnP devices, so it is our responsibility to properly configure the legacy devices ourselves.

PnP does its job by detecting non-PnP hardware first. Then it works around the items it cannot change, fitting PnP-devices into what's left of system resources to provide an optimum configuration. Some of this PnP work is done during boot-up, some of it occurs while the operating system is loading, and some of it is done as we use various programs and devices. PnP is not really an implementation of artificial intelligence, and sometimes it seems to be a reverse evolution because it won't "unlearn" or change its behavior when things change.

The introduction of IBM OS/2, Microsoft Windows 95, Windows NT, multimedia, and general networking connectivity into the world of IBM-compatible personal computers presents us all with more system conflict challenges. While both OS/2 and Windows 95 provide significant improvements in simplifying first-time installation of these powerful-yet-complex environments, they still do little to help you detect hardware, report exacting device conflicts, and most important, offer solutions to any problems encountered.

Since most of us are not fortunate enough to be able to scrap our existing systems, peripherals, and software and invest in all new PnP-compliant tools, we will have to learn, know more about, and deal with both old and new hardware issues.

The Old–Fashioned Way

Even with Plug and Play, we are still faced with the problems of setting up our existing PC hardware and software "by the numbers" that represent existing resources we are given. These numbers, or resources, include the addressing of input/output (I/O) devices, and the interrupt request (IRQ) and direct memory access (DMA) assignments common to all add-in devices. A detailed definition of each of these is provided in Chapter 1.

To help you get your work done in the gap between legacy items and total PnP compatibility, there are many books, software tools, and old hands at this PC trade. You will be introduced to the information and foundation for them, and learn how to find the information you need, select which information is applicable, and make the most of it.

You will encounter a lot of discussion of both the jumpers and switches (hardware) of a typical PC configuration and the configuration files (software). These items are the implementation of the configuration rules and conflicts we are destined to work with until every PC system, peripheral device, and software application uses Plug and Play or better technology.

There are aspects of PC configurations and hardware that you simply may not want to deal with. If you find this to be the case, this book will help you recognize that this is the case and then wisely seek out the right kind of help from a friend, a service shop, or a technical-support phone call. If you find this book to be the long-awaited respite from your PC nightmares, so much the better.

All of this information is primarily to your benefit, and secondarily, perhaps, to the benefit of jammed tech-support phone lines. There are a few secrets tucked away in here, and we hope to leave you wondering why this book and the tools and information within it aren't packaged with every piece of hardware and software you buy. We could also hope for an unsung thank you from the developers of those hardware and software packages for giving their tech support folks a much-needed break. The next time you have to make a tech-support call, ask them if they've seen this book!

The first chapter introduces you to the topic of configuration management, the basic steps, and where you fit into the process. As you read further, you will be able to learn about old and new configurations and standards, and the tools that are used in the process. You'll be alerted to inherent limitations of hardware, software, and technology implementations. All of the chapters are rich in reference information and experience, from the original IBM PC to the latest in high-speed Pentium technology, new data bus features, Plug and Play, and the Windows Registry.

The ultimate goal is for you to get the most out of your personal computer through understanding the discipline involved in having a smooth-running PC system.

Over the course of the next few years, the PC industry will be working to eliminate all non-Plug and Play, or legacy, devices. We can't wait—or can we? To redesign the PC the industry will have to refine and follow its own standards very closely. Until then, and probably even when that day arrives, we will have to make our current tools perform the jobs we have to do today.

CHAPTER 1

CONFIGURATION MANAGEMENT: What It Is and How to Do It

Topics covered in this chapter:

- PC configuration management defined

- Why manage your PC's configuration

- Backing up your configuration

- System inventories

    - Physical devices

    - Software items

    - System information

- Making and recording configuration changes

Configuration management is the process of planning, implementing, organizing, and even changing a variety of factors that affect the hardware and software in your system. Simply put, it is keeping track of what is in your system, what changes have been made, and why, so the changes can be undone, if necessary—all while trying to keep your system running smoothly.

Establishing your initial system configuration usually occurs at the time your PC is designed and built, by a manufacturer or yourself. *Managing* the configuration begins with the person who installs the system and sets it up for use. The process involves detailed information about every aspect of your system: the installed hardware, the *system setup* values (also known as the *CMOS setup*), disk partitioning and formatting, and the operating system and applications software. Through these steps we can discover, resolve, and prevent system conflicts.

Properly managing your system configuration is done (or is often left undone) every time a change is made to your system setup, the DOS **CONFIG.SYS** file (the first system and DOS configuration file the computer encounters at startup) and **AUTOEXEC.BAT** file (usually the first DOS configuration file encountered after DOS loads at system startup), or any of your batch files or device parameters; or within Microsoft Windows 3.x, Windows 95, Windows NT, OS/2, or other operating environments.

If changes are made to your hardware by adding or removing an option card, memory, cache chips, or CPU, or by changing the address on a network or other card, you are dealing with the details of your system configuration. Some of these details will concern the address, IRQ, or DMA assignments for one or more hardware devices. With Plug and Play, the system BIOS and operating system try to help you manage the configuration automatically. This process may or may not work correctly; it varies by system BIOS and device type.

Other details involve device drivers, either generic or vendor-specific, which are somewhat outside the scope of this book. What you do to keep track of these details sets the level of configuration management you practice with your system.

Why a PC System Configuration Should Be Managed

Configuration management is important to anyone using or supporting a PC system. It is critical to all end users who want a reliable, stable, properly functioning PC system—whether you maintain the system yourself or rely on others to do so for you. It is especially critical when more than one PC system or group of support people is involved, as in an office or corporation.

Some of the more significant benefits of configuration management are:

- Reliability
- Easier servicing
- Loss prevention (equipment auditing and tracking)
- Equipment amortization and tax purposes
- Software licensing and copyright compliance

Your goal may be as simple as getting all of the components in your system to operate together correctly with stability and maintainability. Some software installations alter your configuration files or the settings of your modem, video card, or software-configured devices, and this changes the way things worked before. You should also see benefits in ensuring that you can reconstruct your system and get back to work efficiently in case something fails or becomes corrupt—recoverability.

Stability, maintainability, and recoverability are three very important issues for any user. If you share your system with other users, or if someone else is responsible for maintaining your system with or without your presence or immediate awareness, stability and recoverability cannot be overemphasized.

If you have dozens or hundreds of PCs in a workgroup or corporation, getting and keeping them all the same or similar—and at least properly configured and documented—saves a considerable amount of time and money when you need to repair or upgrade one or more systems.

Most PC systems sold today are preconfigured at the factory, but many of us still buy components and build our own systems. Even after obtaining a factory-built system, we find ourselves replacing, adding to, or upgrading one or more system components with off-the-shelf items purchased from the local computer store or by mail order. Replacement components sent by system manufacturers usually need some additional configuration.

Considering that many users and companies will be upgrading to higher-performance components and operating software at some time, it is important to know if existing PC systems are capable of all the tasks required of them, if software or hardware upgrades are warranted, or if they are even possible. If you don't have a handle on the configurations of all of your PCs, implementing the move or operating system upgrade of these systems will either be impossible, or at the least excessively time consuming, while you custom-tailor each system move or upgrade.

For a small 10–to–30–system office, where only a few systems may be used differently than most (and thus likely configured differently to suit a different set of tasks), keeping track may be fairly simple. Maintaining the configuration of hundreds of systems by more than one or two people is a significant task that requires planning, sound procedures, and discipline. The fewer systems you have that perform different functions, with few or no specialized configurations to suit those functions, the easier it is to maintain them.

Fortunately, configuration management for any number of systems consists conceptually of just a few basic procedures. The user considering IBM's OS/2 or Microsoft's Windows 95 or Windows NT will save a lot of time and frustration knowing what components are in the system, how they are configured, whether the system is properly configured, and how to correct configuration problems. This way, any upgrade work can proceed smoothly and successfully.

You should only trust the operating system and applications software so much, within limits, and be able to determine for yourself if it has misidentified or failed to identify a critical component in your system. Even systems running Windows 3.x or plain old DOS can benefit from a properly configured system. You cannot fix a bad configuration by upgrading a DOS or Windows 3.x system to Windows 95 or NT. Often as not, you will not be able to perform the upgrade if the system is misconfigured.

Both the beauty and the curse of PC-compatible systems is that they are so flexible and easily reconfigured by the user. This provides us many opportunities for interesting and unique working situations, and just as many opportunities for things to go wrong. Managing the configuration by locking the covers on the box and write-protecting critical files is one method that has been used, but it does not do enough, especially if the system is locked down in an improper configuration.

System configurations are managed first by the steps you take to ensure the integrity and recoverability of the hardware, software, and configuration file items within your system. This includes system inventories and frequent and regular backups. The original configuration should be recorded and saved for future reference.

Then, as you make changes to the system (such as upgrading or adding components), record these changes. With this information you can trace the changes and reestablish the original configuration, if need be.

Backing Up Configuration-Critical Files

Before any work is done on your system, you should make backup copies of all files applicable to your system configuration. As changes are made to your system, these files may also be changed, and it's possible that one or more configuration changes will fail. Recovering from such failures is much easier if you can go back to a set of configuration files that allowed the system to work properly. These copies may be kept on the system's hard disk, or on a diskette dedicated specifically to this purpose. If you keep these files on a diskette, you should format the diskette to be a bootable (or system) diskette. This makes it easier to access DOS if you encounter problems with your hard disk during reconfiguration. Ideally, you should maintain complete and current backups of all files on your system's hard drives on tapes or diskettes.

The minimum set of files for which you should keep backups is:

- **CONFIG.SYS** (found in the Root directory of your C: drive)

- **AUTOEXEC.BAT** (found in the Root directory of your C: drive)

- **WIN.INI** (found in your Windows subdirectory)

- **SYSTEM.INI** (found in your Windows subdirectory)

- **PROGMAN.INI** (found in your Windows subdirectory)

- **CONTROL.INI** (found in your Windows subdirectory)

- **SYSTEM.DAT** (for Win95/NT, found in your Windows subdirectory)

- **USER.DAT** (for Win95/NT, found in your Windows subdirectory)

Include with the **CONFIG.SYS** and **AUTOEXEC.BAT** files any device driver or program files that are necessary to boot up and run your system at least at the DOS level.

You may also wish to keep copies of all of your Windows .**INI** files (those files with the extension of **INI** after their filename) and your Windows Program Group files (those with the extension of **GRP** after their filename.) The INI files are used by Windows and applications to store a variety of configuration information that defines how Windows or its applications appear on screen and function. The GRP files define each of the major folders on your Windows desktop and contain application and file references.

NOTE While GRP and INI files are used to maintain compatibility with some older 16-bit (Windows 3.x) applications under Windows 95 and NT, you should back them up along with all of the new INI files created by Windows 95. Much of this old information is moved to and contained in the Registry (SYSTEM.DAT and USER.DAT) and Shortcut (.LNK) files, but if a system crashes, these older files may help you get your system back together faster.

NOTE For Windows NT, two files can be critical to system recovery: The file(s) **NTUSER.DAT** exist under both the \WINNT\Profiles\Administrator, and the \WINNT\Profiles\[user name] sub-directories. The file **USER.DMP** is in the \WINNT directory. These files contain information about the user and system setup information with which the system was last run.

NOTE If you are in a networked environment that uses DOS-based networking software (typically Windows 3.x environments), you may also wish to keep a copy of your network configuration file (typically **NET.CFG**) with your backup files so you can recover network protocol and address information. This information may also be stored in yet another (non-Windows) INI file specific to the network software.

Taking Inventory

The most important step you can take is to inventory your system. This includes both a physical inventory and a configuration inventory, covering these items:

- A list of all your hardware items
- A log of how your hardware is configured
- A list of all your software and configuration files
- All of the manuals for your hardware and software stored together in a convenient place
- Hardware-specific software and data files (on their respective diskettes) gathered together

This inventory allows you to establish a baseline indicating the present condition of your system. In the process, you may discover items that are misconfigured (according to standards or certain rules that apply to PCs).

- In multiple-system situations, inventory may also be taken by the system administrator or computer support department where you work. Some of this information can be retrieved automatically during routine system and network maintenance. It is in everyone's best interests to maintain system inventories, for all of the reasons stated earlier as well for network management.

Physical Inventory

A hands-on, physical inventory of your system and system configuration information should be performed when you first buy, unpack, or build your system. You should have a written or data-file record of all the makes, models, versions, serial numbers, descriptions, and technical support numbers of the components in and around your system. This includes everything from the power supply to the mouse, hard drive adapter to sound to multimedia cards.

For your system board and add-in cards, note the numbers printed on any labels that are attached to the tops of chips or the boards. These numbers likely reflect revisions of *BIOS* (Basic Input/Output System) for the system, for *SCSI* (Small Computer System Interface) host adapters, video adapters, and sound cards (some of these are visible on-screen during system startup, or appear on a label on the boards themselves).

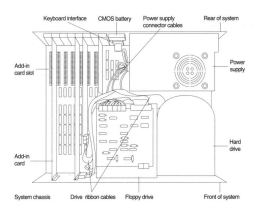

Figure 1.1 Your particular system configuration may differ from the AT-style desktop system shown here, but the general appearance of the boards, power supply, cables, and disk drives is basically the same in all systems.

A typical physical inventory list might look like this:

System Make/Model: homemade
System Board: clone w/ Intel 430VX chipset
System BIOS: Award 4.51G
Power Supply: 250-watt AT-desktop style
CPU: Intel Pentium-90

RAM:	4 ea. 4M 32/36-bit 70nSec SIMMs
Hard Drive Adapter:	On-board IDE
SCSI Adapter:	Adaptec 1542B
Hard Drive:	Quantum Lightning 1 gigabyte IDE
CD-ROM:	Toshiba 3301 SCSI
Diskette Drives:	Sony 3.5″ 1.44M
Diskette Controller:	On-board
Video Adapter:	Diamond SpeedStar 24x, VESA BIOS 1.1
Video Monitor:	Panasonic PanaSync C1381i
Ports:	COM1 (on-board, 2nd port disabled); COM2, (clone add-in w/ 16550 UAR/T)
LPT1 (on-board):	Connected to Canon BJ-200ex printer
Mouse:	Logitech Trackman Marble, serial interface to COM1
Network Card:	Clone NE1000-compatible, BNC connector
Modem:	USRobotics Sportster 28.8/ Fax on COM2, Internal Version #: DSP Version #:
Keyboard:	Northgate OmniKey/Plus

OTHER REFERENCE

Additional modem-specific information may be obtained by using software to look inside the modem. A program such as Hank Volpe's Modem Doctor, which is available from many BBSs and on-line services, or nearly any communications software (Qmodem, or even Windows' Terminal) can be of great help identifying your modem, especially if it is an internal model.

KEYBOARD

With your communications software off-line, running in *direct* or *terminal mode,* if you key in the command **AT13[Enter]** and wait for a response, then **AT17[Enter],** you should see a display similar to the following:

```
at13[Enter]
Sportster 28800/Fax V6.0
OK
at17[Enter]

Configuration Profile...
Product type            US/Canada External
Options                 V32bis,V.FC,V.34
Fax Options             Class 1/Class 2.0
Clock Freq              20.16Mhz
EPROM                   256k
RAM                     32k
Supervisor date         11/30/94
DSP date                11/29/94
Supervisor rev          6.0.4
DSP rev                 1.0.5
OK
```

The first line after the **AT13** command usually returns the modem's model number. The last four lines shown here, not including the **OK**, are typical pieces of information that the modem manufacturer may ask you for during a support call. Major manufacturers such as Hayes, USRobotics, Supra, Practical Peripherals, Intel, and AT&T provide these internal facilities to help with either manual or automatic identification of modems, which can be very useful during automatic setup of communications and facsimile programs. Clone or no-name "white box" modems may not be as helpful.

In addition to identifying the various devices in your system you should also record the settings or positions of the jumpers and switches present on these devices. This is another part of any recovery process you may need to invoke later on if you have to change something to resolve a conflict.

It's also a good idea to clearly label each device and all of its settings. Using a non-conductive, self-adhesive, removable paper label attached directly to the device is an excellent way to keep a convenient and accurate record.

System Information

To properly manage a PC configuration, you need at least three types of information about the devices in your PC. So key are these to configuration management that this book's title is based on them—**IRQ, DMA,** and **I/O**.

Let's refresh ourselves with some basic definitions:

- **Interrupt ReQuest (IRQ) assignments.** These are signal lines connected between a variety of devices, both external (through add-in cards) and internal to your *system board* (containing the *central processing unit [CPU]* or main computer chip, and the connections for built-in and external devices).

  Devices such as the serial (COM) port, keyboard and disk drive, and some internal computer functions use IRQs to signal the computer that an activity on that device needs the CPU's attention to move data or handle an error situation.

  Two devices cannot share or use the same IRQ line. Because there is no indication of what device may have generated an IRQ signal, these assignments must be unique, pre-assigned and known per device by the operating system and software.

- **Direct Memory Access (DMA) channel assignments.** A DMA channel is a set of two signal lines, one line for DMA *request* (DRQ) and the other for DMA *acknowledgment* (DACK). These are assigned in corresponding pairs as simply one DMA assignment to devices that have the ability to exchange data directly with system memory without going through the CPU (many disk drive functions and multimedia cards use DMA to speed data throughput).

With a DMA channel, a device signals the computer or the CPU signals a device about the need for (or status of) direct access between two devices, one of which is usually system memory. These lines must also be unique and known for each device that uses them.

- **Input/Output (I/0) addresses.** These are numerical representations of actual memory locations that are used for the *data bus* (the 8, 16, or 32 bit data lines interconnecting devices within the computer) or system RAM memory (from DOS or low memory, through the first 640 Kbytes of RAM, to the upper memory areas through any and all Extended Memory).

  I/O addresses are used to uniquely identify the places in your system where data and control information can be written to or read from for the interactions between devices, the CPU, and system memory. Each device, such as a serial port or disk drive, is said to occupy a specific address or location in memory. Only data or commands specific to the device that occupies a particular address should be sent to or expected from its location.

You may also need to know the memory location of a particular device's internal BIOS, known as the *BIOS address* (which may also be referred to as the *ROM address* or *ROM BIOS address*). This information is usually standardized, though there can be a lot of variables, typically for SCSI host adapters used to connect disk, tape, scanner, and CD-ROM devices.

If you think technology should take care of itself, that you have no need for the technical details of your system, and that utility tools such as the Norton Utilities are for someone more technical, the time has come to reconsider. Ready or not, you are in the market for some diagnostic or utility software.

Gathering System Information

To get the IRQ, DMA, and I/O information you need requires one or more pieces of software for gathering information from your system. It also might entail a closer physical inspection of the hardware to find labels or legend markings, with the manuals for your system and add-in cards as critical references to help you isolate and make note of these items.

Even Microsoft, one of the world's largest software companies, saw the need for a technical information tool to help with software support. In an attempt to fill this need, Microsoft created MSD, the Microsoft Diagnostics. It's intended to be used by any user to give a basic snapshot of generic system hardware by device type (See Figures 1.2 and 1.3). MSD is no longer in wide distribution. Microsoft now relies on the automatic device detection capabilities of Windows 95 to figure out what's there, and the Device Manager displays under Control Panel's System applet, to tell you what it found.

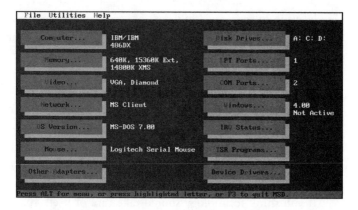

Figure 1.2 Microsoft's MSD program's basic information screen.

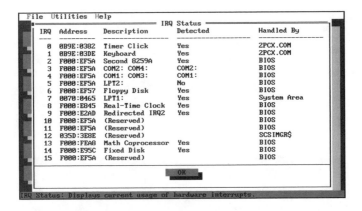

```
 File  Utilities  Help
========================= IRQ Status =========================
  IRQ   Address    Description      Detected           Handled By
  ---   --------   -----------      --------           ----------
   0   0B9E:0382   Timer Click      Yes                2PCX.COM
   1   0B9E:03DE   Keyboard         Yes                2PCX.COM
   2   F000:EF5A   Second 8259A     Yes                BIOS
   3   F000:EF5A   COM2: COM4:      COM2:              BIOS
   4   F000:EF5A   COM1: COM3:      COM1:              BIOS
   5   F000:EF5A   LPT2:            No                 BIOS
   6   F000:EF57   Floppy Disk      Yes                BIOS
   7   0070:0465   LPT1:            Yes                System Area
   8   F000:E845   Real-Time Clock  Yes                BIOS
   9   F000:E2AD   Redirected IRQ2  Yes                BIOS
  10   F000:EF5A   (Reserved)                          BIOS
  11   F000:EF5A   (Reserved)                          BIOS
  12   035D:3E8E   (Reserved)                          SCSIMGR$
  13   F000:FEA8   Math Coprocessor Yes                BIOS
  14   F000:E95C   Fixed Disk       Yes                BIOS
  15   F000:EF5A   (Reserved)                          BIOS

                        [    OK    ]

 IRQ Status: Displays current usage of hardware interrupts.
```

Figure 1.3 Microsoft's MSD program's IRQ information screen.

OTHER REFERENCE

MSD is available with many Microsoft product packages, or from on-line services such as CompuServe and America Online. Microsoft wants you to have this program to make its own technical support life easier. That a software company found itself needing hardware information to support software packages should tell us something about the tremendous universal need for technical information about our PC systems. Unfortunately, as you may discover, MSD is not complete nor entirely accurate in its detection and reporting of system details.

A preconfigured PC system may come with some form of diagnostic, information, or support software. Well-defined hardware add-in kits, such as multimedia adapters and network adapters, embed system information utilities such as these into their installation programs.

OTHER REFERENCE

If your system did not come with diagnostic or utility software, after-market programs such as Symantec/Norton's SYSINFO and Quarterdeck's MANIFEST are available as part of other utility software packages (Norton Utilities and Quarterdeck's QEMM respectively—see Figures 1.4 and 1.5). Still others may be found in online system libraries as public domain software or shareware by searching for the terms such as *sysinfo*. These all provide basic configuration information.

Figure 1.4 The Norton Utilities system information screen.

The complexity of systems and the variety of add-in devices available causes many of the commonly available utilities to miss or simply not provide important details, or they give erroneous or assumed information. You might have to use more than one of these programs to ensure that most or all of the devices in your system are properly detected, and to confirm any possible irregularities.

For a more accurate and complete identification of system hardware and resource usage than many other programs provide, an evaluation copy of Watergate Software's PC-Doctor program for DOS and an IRQ and DMA specific utility (RCR) by Doren Rosenthal are included with this book.

Figure 1.5 Quarterdeck's Manifest system information screen.

DISK

PC-Doctor is developed and frequently updated in close cooperation with many PC device and system manufacturers, often at their request, for their own uses. This program, accompanied by the specific details in your add-in device manuals and a physical inspection of the hardware, will give you a complete picture of the existing system, and of changes as they are made. See Figures 1.6 through 1.9.

Figure 1.6 Watergate Software's PC-Doctor program—the first system information screen.

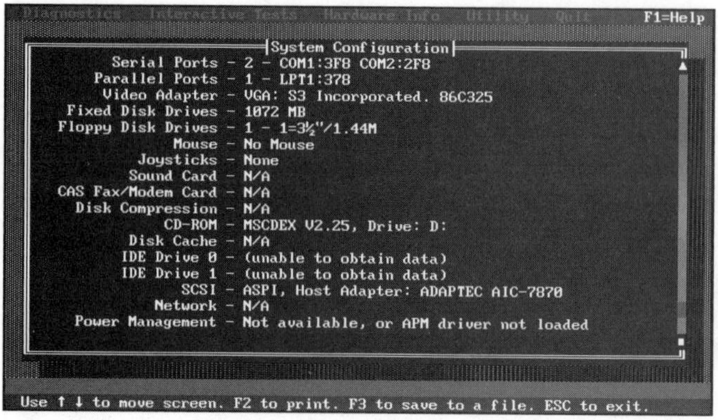

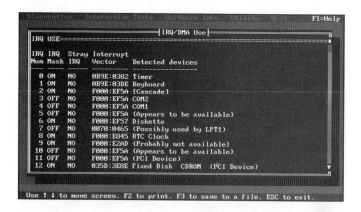

Figure 1.7 Watergate Software's PC-Doctor program—the second system information screen.

Figure 1.8 Watergate Software's PC-Doctor program—the first IRQ information screen.

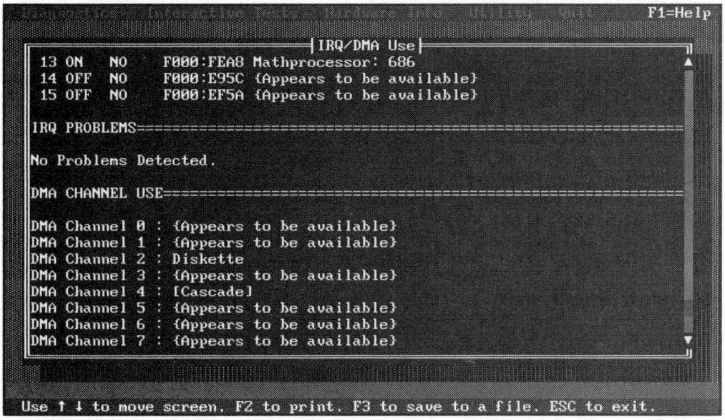

Figure 1.9 Watergate Software's PC-Doctor program—the second IRQ and DMA information screen.

Any utility or system information program can only report on the presence and configuration of the devices they are designed to identify (by extensive research). This occurs only if they are functional enough to be identified by any program as existing in your system. You will get a report of the functioning devices that exist and the resources they use. Software cannot report on devices that physically exist but are defective or functionally inactive. Nor can they report conclusively on whether or not a resource is available, unused, or otherwise unoccupied.

Only by process of review and elimination will you be able to summarize the resources (I/O addresses and IRQ and DMA assignments) that remain available to you, but we'll be helping with that process as we go along.

People who support multiple systems will likely use network management–specific tools to perform many of these inventory and tracking functions, but if you are supporting only one system, you can get by with PC-Doctor.

Using at least one of these programs, you should gather and record all of the information you can get about your system. Most programs such as these provide the ability to print the information or store the information in text files on disk. Keep this information with your physical inventory and settings records.

Compare the information you collect with the "rules" and information provided in this book. From this comparison, you will have the information you need to assess your present configuration and correct it if necessary. You will also (by process of elimination) have information about the resources available for any changes you want to make to your system by adding a new hardware feature or converting your system to use Windows 95 or OS/2.

TIP

You can gather some information about your system from the initial boot-up screen that appears when your system starts, and from system's CMOS setup program. During boot-up you can press the **Pause** key to read the screens as they come up. Pressing any key will resume the boot-up process. Entering your CMOS setup program varies between systems. Sometimes you are prompted during boot-up to press the **Del** key to enter setup; for other systems you may have to use the **F1**, **F2**, **F10** or **Esc** key at just the right time in the boot-up process. For still others, you may have to use a combination of keys such as **Ctrl-Alt-S**, **Ctrl-Alt-Esc**, or use a special program sent with your system after the system has booted up into DOS.

WARNING

The CMOS setup program screens for many systems may contain and allow you to change some very tricky technical settings that are not applicable to the configuration of IRQ, DMA or I/O addresses for your hardware. Be wary of what you might change, and avoid changing anything until you have analyzed and determined that you need to make configuration changes. Then, do so only for specific I/O devices, as needed.

Cleaning Up Existing Conflicts

If, in the process of gathering the physical and "soft" inventories of your system, you encounter any configuration questions or conflicts, now is the time to correct them. (Indeed, the purpose of this book is to help you do that.) Many references toward a proper configuration are contained throughout. These references also exist in numerous hardware and software manuals. Most of the corrective processes also require you to refer to drawings and tables that may be found only in the original documentation, on-line help, or downloadable support files from the maker of a system component.

There are after-market books and support files that contain references to many common PC components, such as system boards, disk drives, disk drive adapters, and video adapters. These may be your only source of reference for some components, though there are as many or more no-name, generic, or "white box" components that have no alternative documentation sources and no easy means to obtain replacement documentation from the original manufacturer.

Such clone devices and those of off-shore origin are plentiful and have provided us with a steady flow of inexpensive components. But they are not inexpensive when you cannot support them. If you can't find the original documentation, your best bet is to replace the device and make sure you save the new documentation in a safe place.

Recording Changes to Configuration Files

Adding REMark or comment lines within the configuration files to highlight and explain the changes is a positive and highly recommended step of configuration management. You will find that many programs that make modifications to your setup files also add their own unique comments for your possible inspection.

Since all of these files are ASCII text files, any basic *text editor* (one that reads, creates, and saves files in plain ASCII text, without regard for type style or size, justification, etc.) can be used to create, edit, and add comments to them. Under DOS (from version 5.0 on), you can use the DOS **EDIT.COM** program. Under Windows, you can use the Notepad program, usually found in the Accessories program group.

WARNING

Unless you are familiar with them, do not attempt to use programs or tools, or to change files or commands—especially without a backup of a working file. You should be familiar with (or refer to DOS- and Windows-specific documentation) for the finer points of text editors, DOS commands, batch files, and command-line structures that are illustrated in this section.

Don't be concerned right now about how the specific command lines used in this section would affect your configuration, they're only examples used to illustrate the process of commenting on changes. Make new backup copies of at least the setup and configuration files on your system, if not your entire hard drive system, before making changes.

KEYBOARD

To make a backup of your **CONFIG.SYS** file, for example, use the DOS **COPY** command to copy your working **CONFIG.SYS** file to a similar filename. Pick a filename that is easy to remember, and one that would likely not be overwritten, deleted, or used for another purpose. Using the original filename and a unique extension, such as your initials, usually suffices. For this example, you must be in the *root directory* (the highest level directory) of your *boot drive*, assuming that your boot drive is C:. If in doubt, at the DOS prompt, type **C: [Enter]**, then type **CD \[Enter]**, and then type **COPY CONFIG.SYS CONFIG.JA [Enter]**.

The method for adding comments to your configuration files is very simple. You must provide some form of mark or delimiter at the start of each comment line so that the program reading these files does not confuse comments with actual commands. Typically this is a REM phrase for CONFIG.SYS and AUTOEXEC.BAT files and a semi-colon (;)for INI files.

NOTE

You will see that we have used lowercase characters to set off the remarks and comments from the typically upper case contents of most DOS and Windows files. In this instance the case is insignificant to the processing of these files, but you should keep program commands and options in their original case when you edit any of these files. Many programs are case sensitive in their interpretation of command lines.

Comments in the CONFIG.SYS File

Prior to DOS version 5.0, there was no provision for comment lines in the **CONFIG.SYS** file. Every line of **CONFIG.SYS** was read and taken to be a command line. DOS would try to interpret all of the information and make use of the items it found. Any text that was not a legitimate command caused an error message to appear on the screen as the file was processed at boot-up.

With version 5.0 and above, it is possible to use the text **rem** or **REM**, followed by a blank space. This stands for and is interpreted as a *remark* or *comment* rather than a command, as a marker or separator for comment lines in the **CONFIG.SYS** file. You may also use the **rem** or **REM** marker to disable a command line, to change some way in which your system performs, or while testing the process of making changes to your **CONFIG.SYS** file. Either of these uses for the **rem** statement are commonly called *REMming out* or *commenting out* an active line, or *adding a comment* to a file. A **CONFIG.SYS** file with a "remark" separator and a comment would appear as follows:

```
DEVICE=C:\DOS\HIMEM.SYS
DEVICE=C:\DOS\EMM386.SYS
DOS=HIGH
rem the following line is used for fancy screen attributes
DEVICE=C:\DOS\ANSI.SYS
BREAK=ON
```

If we want to disable the loading of the ANSI.SYS device driver in this **CONFIG.SYS** file, we simply add **rem** as the first characters on the line specifying the device driver, as follows:

```
DEVICE=C:\DOS\HIMEM.SYS
DEVICE=C:\DOS\EMM386.SYS
DOS=HIGH
rem the following line is used for fancy screen attributes
rem DEVICE=C:\DOS\ANSI.SYS
rem above line REMmed out for testing
BREAK=ON
```

Notice that we also added a comment line indicating that the ANSI.SYS line was disabled (or "REMmed out") intentionally, and why. Removing the entire line for ANSI.SYS would accomplish the same thing, but it would create more work for us if we wanted to reinstall the device driver later.

Comments in the AUTOEXEC.BAT File

The process for the **AUTOEXEC.BAT** file is quite similar to that for the **CONFIG.SYS** file. The **rem** statement simply disables an active command line or prefaces a comment, as shown below:

```
ECHO OFF
CLS
PROMPT $p$g
SET PATH=C:\;C:\DOS;C:\WINDOWS;C:\BAT
CALL C:\BAT\NET.BAT
rem CALL C:\BAT\LOGIN.BAT
MENU
```

In this example, CALL C:\BAT\LOGIN.BAT is disabled by the **rem** placed in front of it. Do you notice anything missing from this file? The comments, perhaps? Yes! Let's fix that:

```
ECHO OFF
CLS
PROMPT $p$g
SET PATH=C:\;C:\DOS;C:\WINDOWS;C:\BAT
CALL C:\BAT\NET.BAT
rem disabling the LOGIN since we are taking this system to
rem another office with different network setups.  Manually
rem login instead.
rem CALL C:\BAT\LOGIN.BAT
MENU
```

By substituting a pair of colons (::) for the **rem** characters, you can take advantage of a recently popular shortcut used for comments in BATch (**.BAT**) files. This shortcut can speed up BATch file processing and avoid the possible misinterpretation of the contents of **rem** lines as commands.

As documented in DOS BATch file documentation, BATch files are read, interpreted, and acted upon in sequential, line-by-line order. There are only three types of entries that can appear in the lines of BATch files: **REMark** lines, DOS commands, and labels. *Labels* are short lines of text preceded by a single colon used to identify a grouping of BATch file commands. The colon or double-colon is valid only in BATch files, since labels are indicated by different symbols in CONFIG.SYS files. The CONFIG.SYS labels do not work for BATch files.

DOS must spend time interpreting each line looking for DOS commands to be executed, including those preceded with the **rem** statement, unless that line is only a label. Label lines are skipped over, so no time is spent interpreting them. Since label lines are not interpreted they can be used instead of **rem** lines to save time.

To use a label line instead of a **rem** statement, create the label line as an entirely meaningless one using a pair of colons followed by a blank space. The blank space tends to be a matter of style; it makes it easier to recognize the line as a comment or disabled command line.

This technique also avoids having the line confused as a legitimate working label, and since the colon symbol itself is not a valid label for DOS it is ignored.

Our example from above can therefore be changed for faster processing and greater clarity to the following:

```
ECHO OFF
CLS
PROMPT $p$g
CALL C:\BAT\NET.BAT
:: disabling the LOGIN since we are taking this system
to
:: another office with different network setups.
Manually
:: login instead.
:: CALL C:\BAT\LOGIN.BAT
MENU
```

All of your batch files can and should benefit from these techniques in order to properly manage your system configuration.

Comments in Windows Files

Microsoft Windows makes the processes of commenting and of disabling lines in its configuration files a bit easier. All of the typical INI files (such as WIN.INI and SYSTEM.INI) used by Windows programs regard the semicolon (;) as a useless character and skip over lines that begin with it.

A partial **WIN.INI** file with a comment and a command that has been disabled with a comment is shown below:

```
[windows]
spooler=yes
load=C:\WINDOWS\SYSTEM\POINTER.EXE
c:\netscape\tcpman.exe
; COMMENT: I won't be using these features this week...
; nwpopup.exe c:\sndsys\audcntrl.exe
C:\DVX\dvwinmon.exe
run=
Beep=yes
NullPort=None
BorderWidth=5
CursorBlinkRate=530
```

In this example, one line is disabled—the one loading NWPOPUP.EXE, AUDCNTRL.EXE, and DVWINMON.EXE. We made the comment obvious above our disabled items, leaving the disabled items intact for replacement later.

WARNING

You should be aware that Windows is limited to reading only the first 32k of your **WIN.INI** and **SYSTEM.INI** files. If these files become too large by the addition of fonts, features, or your comments, some features may not be available within Windows, or you may not be able to run the Windows **SETUP** program to reconfigure Windows. The solution to this potential problem is to reduce the number of fonts and text and graphics converters, and keep your comments and unneeded lines to a minimum.

Making Changes To The Windows 95 Registry

There are several ways to effect changes in the Registry files used by Windows 95:

- Using Window's **REGEDIT** program
- Working in any number of different dialogs from the Taskbar's Start//Settings//Taskbar... options
- Within the Control Panel
- Changing Properties for Folders, program shortcuts, etc.

Unfortunately there is no way to temporarily earmark, comment out, or disable entries within the Windows Registry files for later recovery. If you make a change, it is permanent until you manually change it back again. Sometimes Windows 95 will be smart and change something back for you by itself.

Your best preventive medicine and eventual recourse in case you make mistakes with the Registry is to make separate backup copies of both Registry files, use the Windows **REGBACK** program, or a Registry change tracking utility like Norton Registry Tracker supplied with the Norton Utilities for Windows 95.

Making System Changes

By undertaking the discipline of good configuration management, you're in a position to address the questions you need to ask before installing new devices or software:

- Are changes necessary?
- Are the changes going to improve performance or functionality?
- Do you have enough memory or disk space?
- Do you have the right CPU?
- Do you have enough plug-in slots of the right type?
- Do you have enough disk drive mounting slots?
- Will the changes affect other programs or devices?
- Do you need a CD-ROM drive? Sound card? New video card?
- Are enough I/O addresses and IRQ and DMA assignments available?

With your complete system inventory, outside and in, you'll have these questions answered already or at least have the information to answer them; you will be familiar with these items as you find them mentioned on the side panels of most software and hardware packaging.

This is almost enough information for you to decide that your system can accommodate that new graphics or multimedia program you've been wanting to try. But what if you need to get set up for multimedia before you use that program? Few product packages tell you the configuration information you need to know without opening the box and reading the manual, which most stores frown upon before you buy the product.

Often, knowing what that information means seems just as elusive.

Find a store that has the software or hardware you are interested in already set up and on display for you to try out. Check that system's configuration to give you better ideas for your system.

TIP

Visit the vendor's Web site to check product specifications, FAQ (frequently asked questions), and support information before you buy. You may find that all-important setup tip *before* you run into installation problems.

TIP

These issues of actually preparing for and making changes to your system are where we get to the nuts and bolts or—more appropriately—the switches and jumpers of our system configuration. We will cover these items and what they mean for various devices in the chapters ahead.

Summary

This chapter has been a condensed view of configuration management and the basic procedures that set the groundwork for safe and conflict-free changes. We've discussed some of the simple steps you can take toward positive configuration management: back up the files critical to running your system, document what's in your system, and keep track of how it changes over time. By doing so, you leave yourself a way to restore the configuration to its previous condition if a change should go wrong, and you get the information necessary for planning future improvements.

Configuration management provides the resolution of any existing conflicts, plus a smooth transition into system software and hardware upgrades with fewer (we hope no) conflicts. As you progress through this book, many more design and implementation details will become evident that indicate the need for the basic steps and tools indicated here. We'll cover the use of these tools and the information they can provide us in a subsequent chapter.

CHAPTER 2

THE LEGACY LIVES ON: The Early Standards We Live With

Topics covered in this chapter:

- Legacy devices
- Logical devices
- What has to be configured?
  - Addresses are in hexadecimal numbers
  - I/O addresses
  - Upper memory information
  - IRQ
  - DMA
- Plug and Play implications

Part of Webster's definition of *legacy* is "something transmitted by or received from an ancestor or predecessor or from the past." We might add the synonymous term *of historical significance.*

As much as we want our PCs eventually to "just know" how to set themselves up and take care of any problems by themselves, we have to face the fact that we are dealing with a distinctly technical situation. The PC was designed by, and possibly for, engineers—people who were comfortable dealing with haywire prototypes, bare wires, hot soldering irons, and wire clippings all over the floor. That was the state of the technology when the first PC was introduced in 1981. The engineers have based the PC's foundation on the goals, technology, and experience available then. And although we as users no longer have to deal with bare wires and soldering irons, that foundation is the legacy we've been given.

When working with a PC, you are involved with a piece of history. Unless your system is a very early original IBM model PC5150 or one of similar vintage, you probably don't have to worry too much about it weighing 50 pounds, 5 of which are dust bunnies, 10 of which are the disk drive, another 10 in add-in devices, and the rest comprising sheet metal and plastic or ceramic-encased chips.

But if you can't wax nostalgic about the good old days, don't fret. You're not missing much; most of it still exists intact, as designed, right there in that sleek 15-pound mini-desktop with the 2.5 gigabyte hard disk, 32 megabytes of RAM, and more computing power than was used to put astronauts on the moon. So the box got smaller, lighter, better suited to existing in the family den, and it displays a world of color. It's still a PC and it always will be. Today's PC still starts up looking for the same devices, running the same or similar internal self-checks, trying to boot up its operating system off the same kinds of storage devices, and using memory the same way the original PC did. It just does it faster, and with a few more external complications. Even though we've already put out $3,000 to buy a system and software, we still have to go through certain rites of passage to print out our resumes, Christmas letters, and tax forms.

The PC as it exists may not be playing by *our* idea of fair rules as we would write them if we could start from scratch and design a new machine today, but we have to play by the rules it presents to us. The design team at IBM did impose some good rules, which give some order to the world of PCs. Fortunately, many ingenious people in and out of IBM found some ways to work with, work around, or bend the rules, in our favor.

Unfortunately, a few other equipment designers have broken the rules or tried to make them up as they went along when inventing new PC devices. This can cause us endless days and sleepless nights, until we dismiss the renegade devices to the trash can after we couldn't resolve the conflicts they created for us.

After all is said and done, though, 99% of the problems we encounter can be fixed with a little shoulder shrugging, rolling up our sleeves, and counting to ten with all fingers crossed as we boot up with a new attempt at correcting system conflicts.

Our adventure begins with explaining the bare rules as they have existed for many years. This sets the foundation for any and all developments, problems, improvements, and solutions we benefit from today as we go along. The premise here is to become aware of the rules, whether we like them or not, and take advantage of the structure and opportunity they provide us.

Ideally we would address, by example, every possible system conflict that ever existed. Since there are millions of PCs, thousands of devices, and hundreds of revisions of BIOS, neither you nor I have the time nor space for the immense volumes of cases that have been encountered—surely we'd miss one or two in the process. Instead, as the rules become known in this and the following chapters, they will become clearer, and the pieces will fit into place. We will not be able to work around all of the existing rules—we can't always get what we want—but we can get nearly any PC to live up to the reputation and performance appropriate to the resources at hand.

Thus we enter the legacy of IBM-compatible computing. Our first encounter begins at the beginning (with the original IBM PC, PC/XT, and PC/AT) if only because you've already had enough surprises jumping into the middle of this world.

Legacy Devices

Legacy devices, if not preset or fixed in their configuration as built into the *motherboard* or *system board*, require us to manually set jumpers (tiny connections between two protruding connector pins on system boards or I/O cards) and switches, usually in accordance with a table of possibly dozens of variations of settings, and in comparison to or contrast with other devices in our PCs. Legacy devices typically do not lend themselves to automatic or software-driven reconfiguration.

Among the legacy devices we have no configuration control over are:

- CPU and Numeric Processor (IRQ 13)
- Clock and timer resources (IRQ 0 and 8)
- Memory and device addressing chips (DMA 0 and 2)
- Keyboard (IRQ 1)
- Diskette Interrupt (IRQ 6)

These listed devices are part of the system board or BIOS programming and, as with other devices we'll see, must remain as-is for a PC to function as a PC.

Almost all PC devices prior to implementation of the Plug and Play standard are considered legacy devices. These include add-in cards and other accessories, and to some extent, the basic PC system itself. Some recent devices may be configured through software settings rather than hardware jumpers, but they may not necessarily adhere to the new Plug and Play standard. Even MicroChannel, EISA (Enhanced Industry Standard Architecture), and VESA (the Video Electronics Standard Association) Local Bus devices, which provide enhanced configuration and performance features, may fall under the category of legacy devices. PCI (Peripheral Component Interconnect) devices have been designed with Plug and Play in mind, and most if not all of them will meet the PnP standard. PCI devices can also be used in some non-PC systems that support the PCI bus, such as the new PowerPC systems, as these require automatic recognition and configurability of hardware devices.

It will become evident and almost tedious to notice how many of the PC devices we have used for years, and still buy and use today, have been influenced by IBM's original design. In 1981 when the PC was designed, it had 1% or less of the power and expandability it has now, and many fewer options and devices to attach to it. In fact, except for some critical low-level hardware and software constraints and basic functions, today's PC only vaguely resembles the original PC.

Perhaps no other invention has seen so much advancement, proliferation, and acceptance since its introduction as the IBM-compatible PC. Yes, personal computers in general have evolved from a half dozen or so attempts to provide small computers to the average person, yet only two of the original contenders in this market thrive on: the products of Apple Computer, followed by the growth of the IBM PC and its descendants. If you consider (or have) a Silicon Graphics or Sun workstation a personal computer, I'll certainly accept that and envy you.

For the past several years, while Apple Macintosh users claim to have merely plugged in new disk drives, keyboards, networking features, and document scanners (with multimedia features built into the basic Macintosh system), users of IBM-compatible PCs have struggled with dozens of different hardware and software configurations. Our struggle will probably continue for a few more years.

We fight minuscule hardware jumpers, illegible labels and switches, interpreting 'SIO01' and 'PRT02', converting ones and zeros to On and Off or Off and On, and deciphering not just device addresses or identifiers, but IRQ and DMA settings. All because a system designed by and for engineering uses found fame and fortune in the hands of unsuspecting users.

For all the progress we've seen in computer system development, we must still at some point deal with the technical issues of PC system configuration. Even if we invest in a new Plug and Play-compatible PC system, we will probably still use many of our "old" non-PnP devices. Such will be the case for the next two to three years (the typical life span of a new piece of hardware) as we come to replace some or all of our systems and devices with 100% PnP devices.

For those of you still supporting even a small number of older-style PC, XT, and AT systems, legacy is our only option. It may seem easy for some to say that these systems should be replaced. However, several thousand of them abound in businesses, schools, churches, and homes that simply don't need or can't afford newer systems.

In any case, legacy devices present the bulk of the configuration and conflict issues we face in dealing with PCs. The next section addresses the most common types of add-in devices with which you could encounter configuration problems.

Logical Devices

The concept and application of logical devices seems to confuse and befuddle many PC users. We expect computers to be logical, but admittedly this is not an easy topic to cover. Unlike the name, it is not always logical, or the logic seems to change between device types and their assignments. Maybe there should have been an accommodation for literal versus figurative or representative devices, but we have to deal with it in terms of physical versus logical when we discuss PCs.

Your PC system consists of a lot of physical hardware devices with lots of technical names, numbers and functions associated with them. This does not seem to make computers very personal does it? Well, it didn't make anyone using DEC VAX, IBM mainframe, UNIX or other systems very comfortable either. Because of this, somewhere along the line the technical folks gave aliases or more easily recognized names to commonly used devices in a computer system.

Names like LE0, DD1:, CON:, and PRT: don't seem much more intuitive or logical, but it would have taken too long to write programs if you had to specify "Printer in Jack's Office" every time you wanted to send program output to a printer interface. ("Ah-ha" you say, you can do that now under Windows 95...patience, we're getting there, and we're just talking about raw hardware in your PC for now!)

We're spared from a lot of the details of getting data from the CPU to a printer port, or taking data off the Internet into a serial port and onto a disk or screen. However, we still have to know that these devices exist, where they are, and what they are called or named, while leaving the lower level details to the system BIOS, the operating system, and programmers.

Since we just want to get our letters and reports out to a printer, not to some obscure technical system address like 3BCh, a PC system offers us many named devices to interact with, whether we're writing or installing software, or configuring hardware.

Partially for our convenience, to eliminate the complexity of dealing directly with the cold technical details of physical addresses, IBM provides logical or "plain-English" translations of the technical complexities of addresses. So we have at our disposal a means to gain access to devices by thinking of their function, rather than having to rewrite or configure each application for the hexadecimal addresses that an individual computer system uses. (Initially, IBM's "logical" translation from the technical nitty-gritty to more digestible terms also facilitated programming in the BASIC language.)

IBM provided for a handful of devices its developers believed we might have use for. These include:

- COM (serial) and LPT (parallel) I/O ports (which are probably the ones we're concerned with the most often)

- Disk drives (A:, B:, C:, etc.)

- Keyboard and Video output (combined as the CON: or system console)

This is a good list for the most part. Unfortunately, this list of common logical devices has not been expanded on, except to add LPT2:, LPT3:, COM3:, COM4:, and the occasional special hardware and software interfaces that give us other unique COM and LPT devices.

NOTE

In actual use with programs and DOS, these devices must be expressed with their numerical designation followed by a colon (LPT1:, for example, and COM2:), while generically, it's LPT and COM. Specifying only LPT or COM in DOS commands will result in an error message, and the desired command or operation will not occur. For the console and devices of which there is only one of that type, there is no number. You may see CON but the computer must use CON:.

It might be advantageous if we could invent some new devices for the system. It would be much easier if we could also refer to and use devices such as a sound card by calling it a new logical device SND:, or perhaps spell it all the way out as

SOUND:, use MIC: or MIKE: for a microphone input, MSE: or MOUSE: for the mouse, MDM: or MODEM: and perhaps even PHONE: for a telephone interface, and so on.

The use of logical device names simplifies things for us in some ways, but ultimately, these plain-English devices, services, and resources are still just labels for those physical memory addresses and their attendant internal signals. However, the internal rules used to determine where and what these devices are become confusing and seemingly contradictory between the hardware and BIOS in the system, and the applications we use.

NOTE

The logical assignment of parallel I/O (LPT) ports to specific hardware addresses is not as critical for most applications as is the assignment of serial I/O (COM) ports. Most software that uses the COM ports works directly with the hardware, bypassing the features built into the system BIOS (because doing so is much faster than using the BIOS features). Because most communications applications access the hardware directly, but make their own assumptions about logical names and physical addresses, the physical and logical device matching (in the order shown in Table 2.12) is expected and critical.

Communications applications also require specific matching IRQ assignments to function properly.

Applications that use printers historically haven't dealt with the system BIOS services to access a printer, and may not make use of hardware addresses or interrupts. The more recent development of bi-directional parallel I/O ports, however, makes matching the physical and logical assignments of parallel ports with IRQ assignments essential for inter-system file transfers and obtaining information from new, "smarter" printers.

The new operating systems and environments—Microsoft Windows, Windows NT, Windows 95, and IBM OS/2—which strive to fill in where the BIOS and DOS could not, by making the hardware easier for us to use, must work on top of the same, limited, complex, conflict-threatening foundation we are all dealing with: a PC, its BIOS, and thousands of add-in devices.

Consider Table 2.1, a listing of the most common physical and logical devices encountered in a PC system, to be a foundation set of rules for your system configuration.

Table 2.1 Logical Versus Specific Physical Translations for Common PC Devices

Logical Device Name	Physical Addresses	Associated IRQ	Function
COM 1	3F8-3FFh ('h' indicates a hexadecimal number)	IRQ 4	1st Serial I/O Port
COM 2	2F8-2FFh	IRQ 3	2rd Serial I/O Port
COM 3	3E8-3EFh	IRQ 4	3rd Serial I/O Port
COM 4	2E8-2EFh	IRQ 3	4th Serial I/O Port
LPT 1	3BC-3BFh	IRQ 7	1st Parallel I/O Port (on monochrome systems)
	378-37Fh		(on color systems)
LPT 2	378-37Fh if (LPT1: is at 3BCh	IRQ 7 (change to 5)	2nd Parallel I/O Port (on monochrome systems) (278h is the
	278-27Fh (if LPT1: is at 378h)	IRQ 5	accepted LPT2 device on color systems)
LPT 3	278-27Fh	IRQ 5	2nd or 3rd Parallel I/O Port

NOTE

The issue of logical versus physical devices in a PC is not always an easy one to understand, much less explain. Yet this issue is one of the most significant rule-creating and binding aspects of a PC system, and the root of many conflicts.

The easiest way to deal with this issue is to simply follow the original rules that IBM defined for all of the devices in your system. In fact, that's what is advocated throughout this book: knowing the rules and complying with them.

During the Power-On Self-Test (POST) when you boot up your system, the system BIOS performs an equipment check, looking for specific devices at specific physical addresses in a specific order. As these devices are found, they are assigned sequential, logical port numbers. BIOS uses this information to control the I/O ports for any application that relies on the system BIOS to provide access to these ports. Thus, when you are working directly with DOS or its applications, such as PRINT, and you send a file to be printed to LPT1:, DOS passes some control over the printing to the system BIOS, and the BIOS "finds" or sends the file to the physical device associated with the "name" of LPT1:.

Where problems originate is in the fact that POST bases its naming strictly on a first-come, first-served basis. Although the logical and physical addresses are matched as shown in the table, and those addresses are what your system and devices will be looking for during operation, the actual order in which these logical devices are assigned are may differ. Here's an oversimplified look at the programming logic for finding and assigning COM port labels to serial ports:

- POST will look for a communications port first at address 3F8h.

- The first serial device that POST finds becomes COM1:. If no serial device is found at 3F8 to assign as COM1:, POST continues the search at address 2F8h.

- The ports are assigned in the preprogrammed order of 3F8h, 2F8h, 3E8h, and then 2E8h.

- A port assignment is not permanent—if a device addressed "earlier" in this order (before 2F8h, 3E8h, or 2E8h, depending on what already exists) is added, the assignment shifts in order to have COM1: assigned to the first available device in this prescribed order after subsequent bootups.

It does not matter to POST or the system BIOS services if the first serial device POST finds is at 3F8h, 2F8h, 3E8h, or 2E8h. But it matters a lot to your serial communications, since COM ports require properly matching IRQs. It is easier and proper to create a configuration by the given assignments and BIOS rules.

Subsequent logical port assignments are made as devices are found in the search process. If you have physical devices only at addresses 2F8 and 3E8, they become—to your system BIOS, and thus to DOS—logical ports COM1: and COM2:. This is contrary to the rules set forth in Table 2.1 in two ways. First, the hardware address is wrong, and second, the resulting IRQ assignment is wrong, according to what BIOS and our applications expect. To make matters worse, many serial port cards associate both the address and the IRQ together with each other, such that you may not be able to change the IRQ assignment.

For parallel (LPT) ports, the logic is a little more straightforward, as follows:

- If there is a parallel I/O port device at 3BCh it becomes LPT1:.

- If there is no parallel I/O port device at 3BCh, but there is one at 378h, it becomes LPT1:.

- If there is no parallel I/O port device at 3BCh or 378h, but there is one at 278h, it becomes LPT1:.

- If you subsequently add a parallel I/O port device at 3BCh or 378h, it becomes LPT1: and the device at 278h becomes LPT2:.

- If the device you added above was at 378h, and you then add a parallel I/O port device at 3BCh, it then becomes LPT1:, the device at 378h becomes LPT2:, and the device at 278h becomes LPT3:.

The apparent confusion and variable assignments for LPT ports (as noted in Table 2.1) begins with IBM providing a parallel port at 3BCh using IRQ7 on monochrome display adapters. Any parallel port added to a system had to be at either 378h or 278h. When IBM introduced color systems, any parallel port provided with or added to these was addressed as 378h. Quite possibly this is because you could have both a monochrome display adapter and a color display adapter in the same system, working at the same time. Subsequently, for a color system with an add-in parallel port at 378h, a second port was provided for at 278h.

All three ports can coexist, though the port at 3BCh and the one at 378h will be forced to share IRQ7. Since IRQs are not normally used for printing, this did not usually create a problem, but it is in fact a conflict that is tolerated.

NOTE

If you need a second non-conflicting parallel port, use 3BCh or 378h only as the first port, using IRQ7, and add a port at 278h using IRQ5 for the second port.

NOTE

Windows 95 does not assign a port at 3BCh as a logical/LPT device at all. It merely indicates the presence of Printer Port in the Control Panel//System//Device Manager table. Thus, it is not possible to use this port to assign printers to for printing under Windows 95. DOS programs that use logical/LPT designators will also not be able to use this port through Windows 95. DOS programs that address physical ports by direct addressing may gain access to this port under Windows 95.

Logical Order Please

Always keep in mind is that the numeric designation indicates a logical ordering of devices. In order to have a No. 2 or a second of something, you must have a No. 1 or first something. You simply cannot reserve, save, or leave gaps in the logical numbering of the devices, as some people have wanted to do.

For example, we cannot leave the logical LPT2: assignment open or save it for a possible later expansion of the system by trying to force just an LPT1: (3BCh) and an LPT3: (278h) existence with the intent of filling in the gap later with an LPT2: (378h) device. BIOS and DOS simply will not allow this gap to happen. If there are two LPT port devices, they *will* become LPT1 and LPT2. Similarly, you can't have COM1: (3F8h), COM2: (2F8h) and (try to) have COM4: (2E8h) leaving a gap at COM3:— BIOS will simply make the port at 2E8h into COM3:, which is technically a misconfigured system. If you later install a port addressed at 3E8h, the assignments will change such that it will become (properly) COM3: and the 2E8h device that was COM3: will (properly) become COM4. The configuration will be complete and correct.

I know that many have tried to save device assignments, for some reason of configuration planning or anticipating expansion of the system later, with questionable or disastrous results, but this is a case where BIOS is too smart for us. It would be all right if all of our operating systems and programs referred to the physical device addresses (which would alienate about 95% of the PC user population from ever using PCs easily) so the techies could play as they wanted, but reality and standards dictate that it's easier to use the logical assignments as they were intended.

The same logical assignment process is used for detecting disk drives, video displays, and so on—but the system BIOS is designed to give us error messages only if there is a problem detecting the memory, keyboard, video display, or if the disk drives aren't properly set up. Since all applications need the console (keyboard and display) and some means of loading the operating system, applications, and stored data (the disk drives), these critical items warrant configuration warning messages about missing the operating system or having no bootable devices.

Since communications and printing are supposed to be handled by the system's BIOS and DOS services rather than having the applications circumvent these services, IBM didn't think it significant enough to provide error messages if the serial or parallel ports are not properly detected or configured.

For all of the more or less invisible help provided by the BIOS and DOS, neither one of them will tell you what your configuration should be, what conflicts exist, or how to fix them. Windows 95 and OS/2 lack significant detection or help tools in this regard. Windows 95 can tell you what resources are used, but may not clearly indicate which device another conflicts with, and nothing short of opening the case and referring to the equipment manuals will actually tell you what the proper IRQ, DMA, or I/O address should be, much less what to do to fix the problem.

How Windows 95 Allows Device Naming

Earlier I mentioned that it would be nice if we could simply tell a program to "send my report to the Printer in Jack's Office," and off it would go. Indeed, Windows 95 and Windows NT let us do that, by hiding the printer address, port and even printer type information behind fancy screen names and selection dialogs. These aliases or shortcuts are merely another layer of icing on a rather bulky and complex cake. In actual use, Windows does not know if what we called the "Printer in Jack's Office" is really in Jack's office or if it's a FAX modem in the janitor's workshop—it's just a name someone called something that shows up in the printer list. If the printer really is in Jack's office, then if Jack quits and Sally moves in, someone has to rename it to be the "Printer in Sally's Office."

In some ways Windows 95 can actually complicate things, at least during setup, because the naming can mean anything or nothing. What is actually being named is a reference to a specific printer device driver, perhaps a Hewlett-Packard LaserJet 4P, that is associated with the LPT1: port (which could be addressed as either 378h or 278h) on some computer on a network that allowed sharing of that device. The good news is that once you get beyond the complicated setup process, and if Jack stays there and keeps using that office and computer and printer, printing to the "Printer in Jack's Office" is really a lot easier. Otherwise, at the lowest level, you would have to remember that you're sending HPPCL code from Microsoft Word running on your computer that is networked and addressed as 10.1.1.1 through TCP/IP on an NE2000 network card to a suitable H–P printer on that other machine, whose NE2000 card is IP numbered 10.1.1.2 and its port 378h address. Thus, in Windows 95 we not only have physical and logical devices, but we have device drivers and device names to contend with.

Logical Disk Drives

Where disk drives are concerned—since there can be diskette, AT, IDE, or SCSI interfaced drives in a system—further device numbering is used internal to the BIOS to identify these and assign logical drive letters. Drive letters A: and B: are *always* reserved for diskette drives. Drive letter C: is reserved for the first, if any, hard drive; otherwise it is assigned to the third diskette drive, or, with the appropriate drivers installed, a CD-ROM drive.

The first hard disk drive media found is termed Device 80h. Second and subsequent drives found are numbered from

81h on. If a Device 80h exists on your system it will be assigned logical drive letter C:, and so on for subsequent devices. Logical drive letters are assigned in the order of devices found, then in the order of DOS partitions found. If you have two hard drives, and the first hard drive has two partitions on it and the second hard drive has only one partition:

- The first partition on the first hard drive is called Drive C:

- The first partition on the second hard drive becomes Drive D:

- The second partition on the first hard drive becomes Drive E:

NOTE Exceptions may exist to these assignments if you've loaded and forced (with MSCDEX) the assignment of a CD-ROM drive to be Drive D:, then subsequent partitions can become drives E: and F:, *or* you could lose one of the hard drive assignments and access to it if you have a LASTDRIVE= parameter in **CONFIG.SYS** to allow for fewer drive letter assignments than you actually have or need.

NOTE There is actually little or no need for a LASTDRIVE statement (such as LASTDRIVE=N) in **CONFIG.SYS,** unless you have a specific network requirement (for Novell Netware, Artisoft Lantastic, or other). Then, your network administrator will specify what this should be.

What Has to Be Configured?

We usually can't and probably wouldn't want to alter the extremely low-level internal configurations of our PC system boards (listed above). But there are numerous devices we can, and often must, deal with throughout the life of any PC system.

Among the frequently added, changed, or removed devices anticipated in the original IBM PC, and subsequently the PC/AT, we typically encounter configurations issues with:

- Serial I/O ports, including internal modems (COM)
- Parallel I/O ports (LPT)
- Video display adapters (MDA, CGA, EGA, VGA)
- Disk drives and adapters (AT, IDE, SCSI)
- Network interface cards

Subsequent developments provided us with at least five new device types to account for:

- SCSI host adapters
- Multimedia/sound cards, with and without CD-ROM interfaces
- Video capture boards
- Document scanner interfaces
- Internal ISDN adapters

All of the devices in our systems require system resources. We can take for granted that each device consumes power and creates heat, and must be cooled by one or two meager fans. In addition, all devices in our PC system consume computer-specific resources other than power and space.

The system resources of concern here may not at first appear to be resources. But I/O addresses, IRQ settings, and DMA channel assignments are indeed computer system resources. They are limited to what is available with your system type, and cannot be expanded by adding more of them. The only upgrade step for these resources would be to change from an 8-bit (PC- or XT-class) system to a 16-bit (AT- and higher-class) system, or to go from an ISA (8 or 16-bit) system to one with ISA and PCI interfaces to gain access to more IRQ and DMA assignments.

Because of the way they handle these resources, the legacy devices require the most user or technician attention or intervention during both hardware and software setup processes. In all PC systems, there are a finite number of each of these resources with which we must try to support myriad system options.

If all of the possible combinations of IRQ and DMA signals and I/O addresses could be used in any way we wanted them to be, we would have approximately 2,000 possible configurations to deal with.

As we will see in the next chapter, the number of possibilities is significantly reduced by design and by industry-accepted standards. The most limiting factor is, of course, the least available resource: the number of IRQ signals available to us. This limits us to having only 6–8 I/O devices (see list below) active at any one time, even though we may have 10 or 12 devices in our system. But more about this later.

Of the devices we can have active simultaneously, not counting the internal system board resources, these are typically:

- Mouse (IRQ 12)
- COM1 (IRQ 4)
- COM2 (IRQ 3)
- LPT1, 2 and/or 3 (usually NOT using IRQ 5 or 7)
- Hard drives (IRQ 14, 15)
- Diskette drive (IRQ 6, DMA 2)
- Sound card (IRQ 5, 7 and DMA 1, 3 or 5)
- CD-ROM (w/disk drives, sound, or SCSI - IRQ 11, DMA 1 or 3)
- Network interface (likely IRQ 5, 7, or 10)

This list makes for a pretty full, typical system nowadays. Though I know folks who try to add scanner interfaces, infrared I/O ports, extra COM ports, etc. and simply fail to realize that something else must be sacrificed to gain any satisfaction with any one or more of these.

The installation of any new device, or any changes to a device, must be done with the limited availability of these resources in mind, and a knowledge (through the inventory described in Chapter 1) of which resources are being used by other devices.

Addresses Are in Hexadecimal Numbers

Before we tackle the details of IRQ, DMA, and I/O, a few words about the numbers and letters used in computer memory addresses are in order. You will often see the notation and numbering for I/O and memory addresses expressed in hexadecimal notation, (base 16 numbering). The design and organization of computers, in 8, 16, and 32-bit (and larger increments), dictates the use of a non-decimal numbering system. Since computer information is represented in bits and bytes (8-bits) as 1s and 0s, the numbering used more easily accommodates this. Using a hexadecimal numbering scheme also saves space in memory and on disks.

Using this numbering scheme throughout also saves us from having to convert between systems. Comparing the numbering systems simply gives us an idea of scale. Hexadecimal numbers range from 0 (zero) to F, for a total of 16 numerals (0 through 9, followed by A through F). F represents the quantity that's expressed as "15" in the decimal, or base 10, numbering that we're accustomed to using in everyday life; in hexadecimal, if you have "F" of something, you have 15 of them. If you have 10h of something in hexadecimal, you have 16 of them in decimal.

Table 2.2 Decimal to Hexadecimal Conversions

Decimal Number	Hexadecimal Number
0	0h
1	1h
2	2h
3	3h
4	4h
5	5h
6	6h
7	7h
8	8h
9	9h
10	Ah
11	Bh
12	Ch
13	Dh
14	Eh
15	Fh
16	10h
17	11h
18	12h
19	13h
20	14h
21	15h
22	16h
23	17h
24	18h
25	19h
26	1Ah
27	1Bh
28	1Ch
29	1Dh
30	1Eh
31	1Fh
32	20h

Hex numbers may be indicated by a lowercase letter *h* following simple numbers, or by *0x* preceding more complex numbers, as in 0x3FCD, or rarely, a redundant mix of the two as in 0x3FCDh. If you see a reference to IRQ 14, it's a decimal number and is equal to IRQ Eh. All tables and charts pertaining to IRQ, DMA, and I/O addresses will be in, or can be translated to, hexadecimal. Hexadecimal numbers also take up less space (fewer byte locations) in memory than their decimal equivalents.

I/O Addresses

Every hardware device plugged into the I/O slot connectors inside our PCs requires a unique hardware address. During program execution, data and commands are written to or read from these locations.

A PC or XT system affords up to 1 million locations of 8-bit (one-byte) wide data storage. This one megabyte of space is shared by BIOS and DOS information, hardware I/O addresses, DOS itself, your programs and data. AT systems by original specification provide up to 16 million 16-bit wide (one-word) locations. Current systems can provide up to 256 million or more such locations. Not all of these locations are available for hardware devices. In most systems, fewer than 800 address locations are available for I/O devices.

IBM originally defined that specific devices occupy very specific addresses. Some of these devices are internal to the system board or specific to IBM products and uses. Among these, some addresses are reserved, or are to be avoided, because of other system or IBM-specific uses, leaving approximately 25 possible addresses for all of the possible devices, features, and options we may want to put into our PCs—this in a situation where some devices require 4, 8, or even 32 locations each.

The addresses that are defined but not specifically reserved are used for the common I/O devices that IBM planned for and anticipated in its original system developments. These are the devices we are most familiar with—COM ports, disk drives, and so on. In the progression from the original PC to the PC AT, a few new devices were added, or the primary address of a major functional device (the hard drive adapter, for example) was changed to accommodate the growth from 8-bit to 16-bit systems and more options.

Tables 2.3 and 2.4 list the specific I/O addressing for PC-, PC/XT-, and AT-class systems. Many of the technical terms in the tables are beyond our need to define and understand in the context of configuration management, but we do need to know that something is assigned at a given address. This list is compiled from the dozens of I/O devices, specifications and, commonly available PC reference material.

Table 2.3 The Original IBM PC and PC/XT Device Addresses

I/O Address	System Use or Device
000-01Fh	DMA Controller—Channels 0–3
020h, 021h	Interrupt Controllers
040-043h	System Timers
060h	Keyboard, Aux.
070h, 071h	Real Time Clock/CMOS, NMI Mask
081-083h and 087h	DMA Page Register (0–3)
0F0-0FFh	Math Coprocessor
108-12Fh	Not Assigned; Reserved by/for IBM use
130-13Fh	Not Assigned
140-14Fh	Not Assigned
150-1Efh	Not Assigned; Reserved by/for IBM use
200-207h	Game Port

I/O Address	System Use or Device
208-20Bh	Not Assigned
20C-20Dh	Reserved
20E-21Eh	Not Assigned
21Fh	Reserved
220-22xh	Not Assigned
230-23xh	Not Assigned
240-247h	Not Assigned
250-277h	Not Assigned
278-27Fh	LPT 2 or LPT 3—3rd Parallel I/O Port
280-2Afh	Not Assigned
2B0-2DFh	Alternative EGA Port
2E1h	GPIB 0
2E2h, 2E3h	Data Acq 0
2E4-2E7h	Not Assigned
2E8-2Efh	COM 4—4th Serial I/O Port
2F8-2FFh	COM 2—2rd Serial I/O Port
300-31Fh	IBM Prototype Card
320-323h	Primary PC/XT Hard Disk Adapter
324-327h	Secondary PC/XT Hard Disk Adapter
328-32Fh	Not Assigned
330-33Fh	Not Assigned
340-34Fh	Not Assigned
350-35Fh	Not Assigned
360-363h	PC Network Card— low I/O port
364-367h	Reserved
368-36Ah	PC Network Card—high I/O port
36C-36Fh	Reserved
370-377h	Secondary Diskette Drive Adapter
378-37Fh	LPT 2 or LPT 1—1st or 2nd Parallel I/O Port
380-389h	Not Assigned

I/O Address	System Use or Device
380-38Ch	BISYNC_1 or SDLC_2
390-393h	Cluster Adapter\
394-3A9h	Not Assigned
3A0-3ACh	BISYNC_2 or SDLC_1
3B0-3BFh	Monochrome Video Adapter
3BC-3BFh	1st Parallel I/O Port—part of monochrome video card
3C0-3CFh	EGA Video
3D0-3DFh	CGA Video
3E0-3E7h	Not Assigned
3E8-3EFh	COM3—3rd Serial I/O Port
3F0-3F7h	Primary Diskette Drive Adapter
3F8-3FFh	COM 1—1st Serial I/O Port

Table 2.4 The Original IBM PC/AT Device Addresses

I/O Address	System Use or Device
000-01Fh	DMA Controller—Channels 0-3
020h, 021h	Interrupt Controllers
040-043h	System Timers
060h	Keyboard, Aux.
070h, 071h	Real Time Clock/CMOS, NMI Mask
081h, 082h, 083h, and 087h	DMA Page Register (0–3)
089h, 08Ah, 08Bh, and 08Fh	DMA Page Register (4–7)
0A0-0A1h	Interrupt Controller 2
0C0-0DEh	DMA Controller Chs. 4–7
0F0-0FFh	Math Coprocessor
108-12Fh	Not Assigned or Reserved
130-13Fh	Not Assigned

I/O Address	System Use or Device
140-14Fh	Not Assigned
150-1EFh	Not Assigned or Reserved
170-177h	Secondary PC/AT+ Hard Disk Adapter
1F0-1F7h	Primary PC/AT+ Hard Disk Adapter
200-207h	Game Port
208-20Bh	Not Assigned
20C-20Dh	Reserved
20E-21Eh	Not Assigned
21Fh	Reserved
220-2FFh	Not Assigned
230-23Fh	Not Assigned
240-247h	Not Assigned
250-277h	Not Assigned
278-27Fh	LPT 2 or LPT 3 —3rd Parallel I/O Port
280-2AFh	Not Assigned
2B0-2DFh	Alt. EGA
2E1h	GPIB 0
2E2h & 2E3h	Data Acq 0
2E4-2E7h	Not Assigned
2E8-2EFh	COM 4—4th Serial I/O Port
2F8-2FFh	COM 2—2nd Serial I/O Port
300-31Fh	IBM Prototype Card
320-323h	Not Assigned
324-327h	Not Assigned
328-32Fh	Not Assigned
330-33Fh	Not Assigned
340-34Fh	Not Assigned
350-35Fh	Not Assigned
360-363h	PC Network Card—low I/O Port
364-367h	Reserved
368-36Ah	PC Network Card—high I/O port

I/O Address	System Use or Device
36C-36Fh	Reserved
370-377h	Secondary Diskette Drive Adapter
378-37Fh	LPT 2 or LPT 1—1st or 2nd Parallel I/O Port
380-389h	Not Assigned
380-38Ch	BISYNC_1 or SDLC_2
390-393h	Cluster Adapter
394-3A9h	Not Assigned
3A0-3ACh	BISYNC_2 or SDLC_1
3B0-3BFh	Monochrome Video Adapter
3BC-3BFh	1st Parallel I/O Port—part of monochrome video card
3C0-3CFh	EGA Video
3D0-3DFh	CGA Video
3E0-3E7h	Not Assigned
3E8-3EFh	COM3—3rd Serial I/O Port
3F0-3F7h	Primary Diskette Drive Adapter
3F8-3FFh	COM 1—1st Serial I/O Port

When IBM invented its PS/2-series of PC systems, it added a number of internal devices and control ports, which are shown in Table 2.5 for reference only.

Table 2.5 PS/2-Specific I/O Addresses

I/O Address	System Use or Device
061-06F	System Control Port B (PS/2)
090	Central Arbitration Control Port (PS/2)
091	Card Select Feedback (PS/2)
092	System Control Port A (PS/2)
094	System Board Enable/Setup Register (PS/2)

I/O Address	System Use or Device
096	Adapter Enable/Setup Register
100-107	PS/2 Programmable Option Select
3220-3227	COM 2—3rd MicroChannel Serial Port *
3228-322F	COM 3—4th MicroChannel Serial Port *
4220-3227	COM 4—5th MicroChannel Serial Port *
4228-322F	COM 5—6th MicroChannel Serial Port *
5220-3227	COM 6—7th MicroChannel Serial Port *
5228-322F	COM 7—8th MicroChannel Serial Port *

MicroChannel systems provide an additional I/O data-bus addressing scheme that is separate from the ISA I/O bus and addressing. The last six addresses in the table do not apply or compare to non-MicroChannel systems. See Chapter 3 for more about both MicroChannel and ISA.

The addresses that were not planned for or assigned by IBM make up the only address locations that are available to be exploited by new devices. IBM did not and could not anticipate the existence of these devices before they existed. New devices not defined by IBM had to squeeze into the few address spaces left. The addresses shown in Table 2.6 are typical of non-IBM add-on devices.

Table 2.6 Common Aftermarket or non-IBM Devices Listed by Addresses Used

I/O Address	System Use or Device
130-14F	SCSI Host Adapter
140-15F .	SCSI Host Adapter (as may be found on a sound card)
220-22E	SoundBlaster (SB), SoundBlaster emulation
-or-	
220-23F	SCSI Host Adapter
-or-	

I/O Address	System Use or Device
228, 289	AdLib enable/disable decode (port is active if Sound Blaster emulation is available and active)
238, 239	AdLib enable/disable decode (port is active if Sound Blaster emulation is available and active)
240-24E	SoundBlaster; sound cards emulating SoundBlaster
280-283	Network Interface Card
-or-	
280-288	Aria Synthesizer
-or-	
280-2FF	NE1000/NE2000 network adapter
290-298	Aria Synthesizer
2A0-2A8	Aria Synthesizer
2B0-2B8	Aria Synthesizer
300-303	Network Interface Card
-or-	
300-31F	NE1000/NE2000 network adapter
320-321	MIDI Port
-or-	
320-33F	NE1000/NE2000 network adapter
330-331	MIDI Port
-or-	
330-34F	SCSI Host Adapter
340-35F	SCSI Host Adapter
-or-	
340-35F	NE1000/NE2000 network adapter
360-363	Network Interface Card (non-NE-type)
-or-	

I/O Address	System Use or Device
360-37F	NE1000/NE2000 network adapter
388, 389	AdLib sound device (if no SoundBlaster emulation active)

The addresses listed above may or may not be available on all particular I/O devices of the types listed. For example, not all SCSI host adapters give you the option of selecting either 130h, 140h, 220h, 230h, or 330h. Similarly, these adapters do not use *all* of these addresses, but may offer them as alternatives.

You'll also want to be able to look up the addresses used by specific types of devices as you add the devices in. Table 2.7 organizes the information that way.

Table 2.7 Aftermarket Devices by Type

I/O Devices	Possible I/O Addresses Used
SCSI Host Adapters	130-14F
	140-15F
	220-23F
	330-34F
	340-35F
Sound Cards	220-22E
	240-24E
Aria Synthesizers	280-288
	290-298
	2A0-2A8
	2B0-2B8
AdLib sound device	228, 289
	238, 239
	388, 389

I/O Devices	Possible I/O Addresses Used
MIDI Ports	320-321
	330-331
Network Interface	280-283 or 280-2FF
Cards	2A0-2A3 or 2A0-2BF
	300-303 or 300-31F
	320-323 or 320-33F
	340-343 or 340-35F
	360-363 or 360-37F

Note: Novell/Eagle (NE) -1000 and -2000-compatible cards consume 20h addresses, which can easily use up or possibly overlap other resources.

As you can see, there are at least six aftermarket device types (I/O devices) we will frequently encounter. To accommodate these, there are 14 address locations (possible addresses) available (14 is the number of unique addresses in the table, once repetition is accounted for and eliminated.) Since all devices cannot be configured to work in just any or all of the 14 available addresses, there may still be overlap and conflicts despite the fact that there are more addresses than there are device types. Industry acceptance has limited the addresses that certain devices may use to only a few addresses per device type—such as four pre-determined COM port addresses, three pre-determined LPT port addresses, etc. Thus, our configuration issues begin.

Why Not Use Any Available Address?

So far we've indicated I/O addressing by either IBM standards, or those accepted for use by later developments, and not considered that perhaps we should be able to use *any* available address for any device we want. Yes, we could address a SCSI host adapter using an unused COM4 address, for example, but this might confuse the BIOS or lock up the system as the POST tries to check that address for a serial port. The SCSI adapter may not understand the serial port checks, or will accept some data erroneously and respond in some unpredictable manner. Since we have no control over the BIOS and boot-up processes, we're risking unpredictable problems.

Conversely, if a SCSI-specific program went snooping around to see if a SCSI adapter is at the COM4 address, and a real serial port was there instead, we could encounter the same risks of locking up our system.

Similarly, as we get to Plug and Play (and specifically PCI and PCMCIA/PC Card devices) to maintain overall compatibility, avoid conflicts and confusion between devices, some of these new devices will also use older legacy-style device addresses.

NOTE

As we discuss devices and ports, and when we discuss system information-gathering software, you may wonder why no one makes a program that simply goes through and checks all port addresses and detects what things are connected there, rather than following these pre-assigned address rules. Actually such software has been tried, with varying degrees of success, but no one has been able to do it reliably or safely enough to avoid the kinds of lockups that inevitably occur when you send the wrong kinds of commands or data to the wrong device. Instead, as we'll see with Plug and Play, PCI and PCMCIA/PC Card devices, better ways have been established to ask devices what exists where in the system. However, these devices still use the legacy addresses for most common devices to maintain backward compatibility with our old hardware, operating systems, and programs.

Upper Memory Information

Not only do we have to consider the few specific low-memory locations available for any and all hardware devices, but some features and devices require portions of the 384 Kbytes of memory address space that is the upper-memory area between the DOS 640K limit and the beginning of extended memory at the 1 Mbyte address location. This area provides space for the video BIOS, access to video memory, hard disk BIOS, and system BIOS. Not all of this 384K is used by every system configuration. The upper-memory assignments used in the original IBM PC, XT, and AT are listed in Table 2.8.

Table 2.8 Upper-Memory Locations for Video, Disk, and System BIOS

Memory Range	System Use or Device
A000-AFFF	Graphics Video Memory (64K)
B000-B7FF	Monochrome and Text Video Memory (32K)
B800-BFFF	Not Assigned *
C000-C7FF	VGA Video BIOS Location (32K)
C800-CFFF	Hard Disk Controller BIOS Location (32K) *
C800-CFFF	Not Assigned *
D000-D7FF	Not Assigned *
D800-DFFF	Not Assigned *
E000-EFFF	IBM ROM BASIC (IBM systems only) *
F000-FFFF	System BIOS (64K)

*Those areas not occupied by a device and not assigned for working video memory (indicated by * in Table 2.8) are often configurable for use as upper-memory blocks (UMBs) by using memory manager software such as Microsoft's EMM386 or Quarterdeck's QEMM. This reuse of memory can provide up to 128K of RAM for the loading of device drivers and memory-resident programs (such as MSCDEX, DOSKEY, and SMARTDRV), instead of consuming precious lower or DOS RAM. If this memory is not otherwise configured or excluded from use by specifically configuring the memory management software or Windows, Windows will try to use any free memory it can find during its operation.*

Letting Windows have free reign of your system's memory is not always a great idea. Often as not, the memory range of B800-BFFF is used by many newer video cards and their device drivers for enhanced features of the video card. This is usually undocumented or not obvious when you set up your system, and may not be discovered until later, after the system locks up, and various attempts at reconfiguration reveal the need to specifically exclude this address range from access by Windows. The symptoms of a problem here appear as lockups or improper video displays in Windows programs or attempting to load game software. The cure, as confirmed by the many systems I've tried it on, and many e-mail exchanges, is to add a specific **Exclude** command to your memory manager. For EMM386, which is loaded in **CONFIG.SYS**, the additional parameter must be applied to the command-line (minus other commands you may also have there) so it reads:

```
device=c:\windows\emm386.exe X=B000-BFFF
```

Part of the system boot-up process is to search upper memory for add-in device BIOS code (the addresses in Table 2.9). Any BIOS code found and executed then becomes part of the normal system operation. Video adapter, hard-drive and SCSI adapter cards are the most common devices with their own BIOS on-board, which compliments or replaces the functions that would otherwise come only from the system BIOS. Table 2.9 lists the commonly available upper memory locations and the types of devices you can or may find configured to use them.

Table 2.9 Upper-Memory Locations that May Be Used by the BIOS in Common I/O and Add-In Devices

BIOS Address	Use
C000-C7FF	Color video adapters (32k)
C800-CFFF	Hard disk controller or SCSI (32K)
C800-CFFF	SCSI Host Adapter BIOS (32K)
D000-D7FF	SCSI Host Adapter BIOS (32K)

BIOS Address	Use
D800-DFFF	SCSI Host Adapter BIOS (32K)
E000-E7FF	SCSI Host Adapter BIOS (32K)
E800-EFFF	SCSI Host Adapter BIOS (32K)
E000-EFFF	LIMS EMS Memory Page Frame (64K)

NOTE

The PC system BIOS expects any hard disk controller BIOS (for ST506/412-MFM, RLL, ESDI, or IDE-type disk drive adapters) to be at C800h. IDE and SCSI interfaces cannot occupy the same location. If you have both IDE (Integrated Drive Electronics) and SCSI (Small Computer System Interface) interfaces in your system, the IDE interface will be fixed at C800h as its default address, and it will always be the primary interface for the hard drives and boot drive (while the SCSI interface will supply only additional hard drives, CD-ROM drives, and so on). Since SCSI host adapters usually have the flexibility to be configured for any one of six upper memory locations, the addressing shouldn't be a problem.

If SCSI is the only interface in the system, it can be assigned to any of the even 32K-increment address ranges from C800h to E800h. In later systems with built-in IDE interfaces, the IDE drive BIOS routines are included as part of the system BIOS, and do not create this conflict.

TIP

Many times the system BIOS offers the feature to cache or shadow certain upper memory BIOS addresses into a 384 Kbyte section of memory reserved in Extended Memory for this purpose. What this does is copy and redirect the program code from a device's BIOS ROM chip into faster RAM chips, which makes using any special BIOS code for these devices run faster. This is typically acceptable for video and system BIOS ROM chips, but many SCSI adapters will not function properly, or your system will crash when a SCSI device is used, if you allow the SCSI adapter BIOS to be cached or shadowed.

Given the option, or if you find the symptom of unusual problems with SCSI devices, go to your system CMOS setup program and be sure that the memory range for your SCSI host adapter BIOS is *not* cached or shadowed.

Also, do *not* cache or shadow any of the memory ranges that are not assigned to or used by a device's ROM BIOS. Attempting to cache or shadow the video memory ranges from A000-BFFFh, or the EMS page frame range (typically E000-EFFFh) can cause unpredictable results.

Some memory managers offer the feature of automatically optimizing upper memory configuration and the process of selecting drivers and resident programs to squeeze into upper memory blocks. For EMM386, this is feature is invoked by a program called **MEMMAKER**. For QEMM, it's the **OPTIMIZE** feature.

These are amazingly powerful utilities than try to detect upper memory uses and conflicts, and can provide you with a little more free DOS RAM when they are all done with their automatic processes. Unfortunately, they leave a cryptic trail of configuration parameters in the command lines for each driver or program you load, and if you change your configuration you have to rerun the automatic processes to be sure things are set up right again. You cannot manually change these cryptic parameters unless you become an expert in memory management, which doesn't sound like a lot of fun.

The automated processes may not consider all of the programs or hardware device features that may be encountered during games or Windows use, and you can end up with many more conflicts and problems than you started with.

Instead of using the automated processes, consider using different configuration menus or fewer devices and resident programs if you really need more free DOS RAM.

My advice here: keep it simple! Simply use the **DEVICEHIGH**, **LOADHIGH**, **LOADHI.SYS** and **LOADHI** commands manually and sparingly. Configure your system to load the largest drivers and resident programs first, then load the smaller ones later, as a manually operated best-fit technique. Do not try to force-fit a driver or program into the smallest possible spaces, because you can't always account for extra memory needs for data, or the elusive special features of Windows or game software that may crash the system later on.

IRQ

IRQ (Interrupt Request) lines are used by hardware devices to signal the CPU that they need immediate attention and software handling from the CPU. Not all of the devices in your system require an IRQ line, which is good news, because we have only 16 of them in an AT or higher class system. Of those 16, three are dedicated to internal system board functions (the system timer, the keyboard, and a memory parity error signal). The use of the other signals depends on the devices installed in your system and how they should be or are configured.

For ISA or non-EISA, non-Micro Channel systems, it is the general rule that IRQ lines cannot be shared by multiple devices, though with some care and well-written software, they can be shared. But since there is no easy way to know which devices and software can share IRQ lines with other devices, this is something we will avoid doing. Table 2.10 shows the predefined interrupts that the PC needs.

Table 2.10 IRQ Assignments

IRQ	PC, PC/XT	AT, 386, 486, Pentium
0	System Timer	System Timer
1	Keyboard Controller	Keyboard Controller
2	Not Assigned	Tied to IRQs 8-15
3	COM2: 2F8h-2FFh	COM2: 2F8h-2FFh
4	COM1: 3F8h-3FFh	COM1: 3F8h-3FFh
5	XT HD Controller	LPT2: 378h or 278h
6	Diskette Controller	Diskette Controller
7	LPT1: 3BCh or 378h	LPT1: 3BCh or 378h
8	Not Available on PC or XT	Real Time Clock

IRQ	PC, PC/XT	AT, 386, 486, Pentium
9	Not Available on PC or XT	Substitutes for IRQ 2
10	Not Available on PC or XT	Not Assigned
11	Not Available on PC or XT	Not Assigned
12	Not Available on PC or XT	PS/2 Mouse port
13	Not Available on PC or XT	NPU (numerical processing unit)
14	Not Available on PC or XT	Hard Disk
15	Not Available on PC or XT	2nd Hard Disk Adapter (later systems)

Add-in devices usually provide a number of options for IRQ assignments to avoid conflicting with other devices when installing and configuring them. Some typical IRQ assignment options for add-in devices are shown in Table 2.11.

Table 2.11 Add-In Device IRQ Options

Add-In Device Type	IRQ Choices
SCSI Host Adapter	10, 11, 14, or 15
Sound Cards	5, 7, 10, or 11
Network Card	2, 3, 4, 5, 7, 9, 10, 11 or 12

DMA

DMA (Direct Memory Access) enables a program or device to initiate data transfers between two devices, or between a device and memory, without the intervention of the entire CPU system. It's typically used for high-speed disk operations, multimedia applications, and diskette (and tape drives attached to a diskette adapter) operations.

DMA provides for faster data transfers, since transferring data with the CPU involved takes more time. However, while DMA operations are being performed, all CPU operations are put on hold until the DMA operation completes. (A properly designed DMA application will allow the CPU's operations to execute periodically so that the entire system is not "dead" or at the sole discretion of the DMA process.)

The defined DMA channel assignments are shown in Tables 2.12.

Table 2.12 PC, PC/XT, and AT DMA Channel Assignments

DMA Channel	PC and PC/XT Use	AT, 386, 486, Pentium Use
0	DRAM Refresh	DRAM Refresh
1	Available/Not Assigned	Available/Not Assigned
2	Diskette Controller	Diskette Controller
3	PC/XT HD Controller	Available/Not Assigned
4	Not Available on PC or XT5-7	Used Internally to link DMA to first DMA controller
5	Not Available on PC or XT	Available/Not Assigned
6	Not Available on PC or XT	Available/Not Assigned
7	Not Available on PC or XT	Available/Not Assigned

There are four DMA channels on PC and XT systems and eight DMA channels on AT- and higher-class systems. Of these, one channel, DMA 0, is dedicated to memory refresh operations on all systems. DMA 2 is dedicated to the diskette drive system if one is present, but this line is usually not available for connection within non-diskette I/O cards.

NOTE

The fact that DMA Channel 1 is the only one available on a PC or XT system explains why most sound cards use this channel as their initial default setting.

Once again, we see that PC and PC/XT systems provide little room for expansion. The AT and higher systems provide five DMA channels for expansion use, and in a full system with SCSI and multimedia operations, most of these are needed.

The typical DMA channel assignments for add-in devices are shown in Table 2.13.

Table 2.13 Add-In Device DMA Options

Add-In Device Types	DMA Choices
SCSI	3 or 5
Sound Card	1, 5, or 7
Network Cards	1, 3, 5, or 7

Plug and Play Implications

Having come to this point you may be ready to jump in and say, "but, Plug and Play doesn't set my devices the way your book indicates things should be set..." BINGO!

I won't delve too far into Plug and Play just yet, but this observation is certainly true, and equally or more troublesome if you're trying to maintain a stable configuration. When we cover Plug and Play and how it works, or sometimes seems not to, we'll also cover how to trick PnP into working the way we want it to so we can establish a by-the-book configuration. I'll leave it stated that you must endeavor to get all of your legacy devices into a proper IBM-standard configuration, including all of the subsequent after-market items such as SCSI, sound and network cards, before considering Plug and Play issues. This approach will reduce the variables you'll have to deal with, and make the entire configuration process easier.

Summary

Our emphasis in this section has been to illustrate the basic principles of some common system configuration items. These will be addressed again as we discuss more devices, configurations, and conflicts.

Some of the strongest tools we have to learn from and base solutions on are found in examples of what is, what works, and what doesn't. We have begun our foundation here by outlining the rules of the original PC designs and BIOS. In the next chapter, we'll discuss subsequent innovations toward better performance and configurability. Once our foundation is established, we'll look at a variety of typical system configurations. These configurations must work with and around the original PC designs, the new architectures, and the issues of physical and logical devices.

CHAPTER 3

FROM MICROCHANNEL TO PCI: Intermediate Standards and Solutions For PC Configurations

Topics covered in this chapter:

- IBM's MicroChannel: system board and add-ins

- Enhanced Industry Standard Architecture (EISA): system board and add-ins

- Personal Computer Memory Card Industry Association (PCMCIA)/PC Card: additional data bus for portables

- Video Electronics Standards Association's Local Bus (VESA VL-Bus) and Video BIOS extensions: video I/O performance

- Generic no-standards, no-jumpers, software-configured devices: mostly modems and network cards

- Hard drive detection and support

- Intel's Peripheral Component Interconnect (PCI): I/O performance

As the PC has grown up over time, so have many of its capabilities and complexities. The popularity of PC, XT, and AT systems revealed to the PC industry that higher performance and easier configurability were needed to accommodate the ever-increasing numbers of users, the resource demands of new applications, and the amount of data being used and generated.

A number of design enhancements have come along to increase performance, configurability, and expandability. We will discuss these items in terms of their contribution toward configuration management and conflict resolution, and in reference to Plug and Play as our current hope for no-hassle configurations.

IBM's MicroChannel, COMPAQ and HP's EISA, PC Card, VESA's Local Bus, and now Intel's PCI are all more or less successful attempts at making PCs more manageable for the average user, and to some extent, less expensive for manufacturers and support people. Each attempt to refine or replace the PC's bus and configuration technology, for better performance or ease of use, brings on more complexity at some point.

In the course of working with PCs, PC users, and PC technical people, I have not run across very many who can say they were pleased with the outcome of MicroChannel, EISA, the DOS-based PC Card (PCMCIA), or the VESA Local Bus. MicroChannel meant new and more expensive cards and slightly more involved configuration times. EISA was faster, but time consuming and perhaps a bit daunting in using it's configuration utilities. PCMCIA (under DOS) was a nightmare of driver and memory incompatibilities. At least the VESA Local Bus didn't involve configuration worries, and it did deliver faster video and disk interfaces.

Even though they are not PC bus standards, I've tossed in a few tidbits about soft-configured I/O cards, and the addition of secondary hard drive interfaces because they don't really have an identifiable home anywhere else in this book's context.

The talk of the town today is PCI. The speed of the PCI bus and peripherals, combined with a fast Pentium system board, a Plug and Play BIOS and operating system, and little or no configuration worries—what more could you ask for? Oh, yes, doing away with legacy/ISA conflict issues. Well, three out of four isn't all bad, is it?!

First, a brief look at a few interim PC standards. Then we'll uncover a few things about local buses and PCI specifically.

MicroChannel: System Board and Add-Ins

When IBM introduced their new MicroChannel bus and add-in card design with their PS/2-series systems, they hoped to improve and reshape the way developers and users dealt with add-in devices. The system board, add-in devices, and methods of configuration changed to a completely different style and format from ISA (Industry Standard Architecture) systems. Because of the changes in the physical connections and slots that made up MicroChannel, add-in devices designed for PC and AT systems do not fit into MicroChannel systems, and MicroChannel devices cannot be used in ISA systems.

In some ways, this change provides some configuration and performance benefits. In late-model MicroChannel systems, the data or I/O bus expanded from 8 or 16 bits wide to 32 bits wide and operated at faster speeds. The devices contain information within them that can be queried by special configuration software. System configuration can still involve the setting of some jumpers and switches, but it is otherwise aided (or limited) through the use of a system-specific reference disk. This includes a special setup program and resource files that describe the devices in the system.

IBM also required that developers would license or register their new designs with them for inclusion on IBM's reference diskettes. This proved to impede development cycles and gave the impression that IBM wanted to control the market for these systems.

Seeing that this was not a way to gain popularity in the market, IBM removed many of these restrictions from the development of MicroChannel add-in devices. However, this bus architecture did not become very popular or competitive against EISA or the later developments of Local Bus and PCI systems.

Because there aren't any non-MicroChannel devices in the system, the configuration program doesn't need to work around the limitations of such devices. It simply finds and guides you to configure MicroChannel devices into a set of configuration rules for the available system resources. The configuration software will provide the user with "pictures" of the devices it knows about and shows the preferred locations for any jumpers and switches on the installed devices and those to be added. This technology was ingenious and somewhat self-helping, but still too expensive and restrictive at the time.

Although the configuration and conflict issues of IRQ, DMA, and I/O addressing still exist, the configuration software does point these conflicts out and indicates the proper, expected settings for certain devices. The configuration or reference disk software is very helpful in some ways, but the methods are limited to MicroChannel systems only. It did begin to set a target for future configurations and designs.

Enhanced Industry Standard Architecture: *System Board and Add-Ins*

EISA is the result of cooperative design efforts between Hewlett-Packard, COMPAQ, and other system manufacturers. (Noted for its absence from this venture is IBM.) The cooperating vendors recognized the need to make configuration simpler and provide higher-performance systems.

Higher performance is provided in EISA, with a full 32-bit data bus and higher bus speeds. EISA devices extend the number and type of bus connections specific to EISA system boards: they will not plug into ISA systems. To our benefit, though, EISA does provide compatibility with ISA add-in cards in the same board and socket layout as the new EISA design.

EISA provides several configuration benefits and greater resources through a redesign of how IRQ signals are treated, and by providing extended addressing for add-in devices. These features remove some of the restrictions on the sharing of a small number of IRQ lines and fitting devices into a limited range of I/O addresses. But configuring an EISA system still requires handling jumpers and switches on both EISA and ISA devices installed in the system.

EISA systems use a system-specific EISA Configuration Utility (ECU) program. This program works with special device-specific information files provided by device manufacturers. When you use the configuration program, you can view "pictures" of add-in devices that show you how to set the jumpers and switches.

Once you've gone through the configuration process, the information is saved to the system's internal memory and on disk. When you start up the system, the configuration of your system is rechecked against the prior setup, and you are alerted to any changes detected. If you must reconfigure your system, the ECU program only lets you select resources that are available, rather than allowing a potential conflict between devices.

Though a slow and tedious process requiring special disks, a lot of device configuration files, and navigation of a complex set of menus, EISA configuration is tremendously powerful. It is not automatic, and does not in itself solve the classic configuration problems we encounter.

PC Cards/Personal Computer Memory Card Industry Association (PCMCIA): *An Additional Data Bus for Portables*

PCMCIA provides an additional data-bus scheme for any of the existing data buses we may encounter. It is designed to provide quick, temporary, interchangeable expansion for portable PC systems. Desktop systems may also use PCMCIA devices by installing a PCMCIA adapter. PCMCIA, or more simply, PC Card devices, may be *hot-plugged* or *hot-swapped* (able to be inserted or removed with the power left on!) and automatically detected as they are introduced into or removed from the system. PCMCIA consists of one or more credit-card-sized external data bus sockets for the interconnection of additional memory, software program cartridges, modems, network adapters, and ultra-small hard disk drives.

For DOS and Windows 3.x use, access to PCMCIA devices first requires the use of device drivers that establish the presence of the PCMCIA data bus and sockets to the PC system and, subsequently, device drivers for the device that is connected to the PCMCIA socket.

The use of PCMCIA and the changing of devices can require rebooting your system between uses. It can also require making device choices so that the proper driver software is loaded and does not conflict with other device drivers.

As implemented in most portable systems, PCMCIA should not present any configuration problems to the user—unless two of these devices conflict, which should be rare because the designers of PCMCIA devices work closely together to establish and follow specific configuration rules. There are no hardware switches or jumpers to be set, only device driver software options to set at the time of installation. The device driver software for different PCMCIA devices can conflict with each other, but this is usually resolved by changing the order in which these drivers are specified in the **CONFIG.SYS** file, which determines in what order the drivers take effect at bootup.

Windows 95 has PC Card support built in as part of Plug and Play, and does not require a system restart for a newly inserted device to be immediately functional. Windows 95 may require installation of additional drivers to support a particular PC Card device, and these drivers may still impose conflicts within the operating system. These occurrences are rare compared to stumbling through jumper settings, editing **CONFIG.SYS** files, and rebooting to avoid hardware conflicts. If you have a current model laptop with PC Card sockets and have ever swapped cards in and out of the slots, you've seen Windows 95 in action supporting these devices. Unfortunately, this technology is not as easily implemented for plug-in cards within the main chassis of desktop and tower systems. There is too much risk of damaging I/O cards or the system board as boards are plugged in and removed.

WARNING

The advice for non–hot-swappable devices is to *always* turn **off** the power to your system (1/0 switch to the 0 mode!) before adding or removing these devices (ISA, EISA, Local Bus, PCI, or similar bus cards).

Video Electronics Standards Association's Local Bus (VESA VL-Bus): *Video I/O Performance*

Seeking to expand the display capabilities of PC systems, the Video Electronics Standards Association defined several enhanced video display modes as extensions to the existing VGA display modes. In defining these new modes, which include better color definition and higher screen resolutions, it was obvious that systems would have to transfer more display information from programs to the display adapter.

PC system performance had to improve, at least the CPU–to–video-display portions of the system. As fast and capable as EISA is, it did not catch on as a bus suitable for video display adapters. Out of this need came the VESA Local Bus design, providing a 32-bit-wide data path directly from the CPU to I/O devices, and at (then) CPU data speeds; hence the name *local bus*. This new data bus serves to enhance video display speeds as well as providing a faster interface for other devices, most commonly disk drive adapters. (PCI cards are also local bus cards, but do not use VESA Local Bus style hardware or configuration methods.)

The existence of the VESA Local Bus itself is somewhat invisible to the user as far as device configuration is concerned; the interface chip between the CPU and the bus sockets is aware of whether or not a device occupies a socket, and it handles data and addressing internally. There are typically one to three Local Bus sockets in a Local Bus system. Although Local Bus devices require some interconnection to the ISA bus to gain access to some signals, they do not work when plugged into ISA-only sockets.

The Local Bus in itself does not involve any new (or solve any old) configuration issues. A Local Bus video card or disk adapter must still present itself to the ISA bus for proper recognition and access, using the same I/O address and IRQ and DMA lines as an ISA device. When the high-speed Local Bus data transfer features are used, the transfer is done on the Local Bus to improve performance. The system BIOS and Local Bus controller automatically recognize and handle the shifting of data I/O from the ISA bus to the Local Bus.

Generic No Standards, No-Jumpers, Software-Configured Devices: *Mostly Modem and Network Cards*

In trying to eliminate the hassles of switches and jumpers from I/O cards, thus eliminating the need to open up the system box to reconfigure a device, many manufacturers believed they could cheat the PC system configuration and develop hardware configurable with a software program. While this may begin to sound like Plug and Play, and some of these devices may use all sorts of similar phrasing ("easy plug and play ready," "just plug in and play," etc.), it's not. A manufacturer might try to exploit by chance some unused or reserved I/O address as the access point into their particular piece of hardware and its configuration circuits. Through this hidden address port, their specific software program would tell the device what I/O address, IRQ, and DMA lines to use.

This technique has been applied primarily to some advanced internal modems, many network interface cards, and some sound and scanner interface cards. Intel provides devices in each category. National Semiconductor and various off-shore, white box, or no-name manufacturers have all provided software-configurable network interface cards at some time or another.

As a typical example, card maker Not Quite Acme, Ltd. produces a fax/modem I/O card that it wants to market as a "Plug and Play"-type device with easy no-jumpers software configuration. The engineers poke around at a few PCs and decide that address 110h might be a good place to put its configuration circuits, and proceed to build in "secret stuff" that only their software program can find and use. As a safeguard just in case, they also let the card's secret stuff detect if address 110h is already used by something else (a competitor's "secret stuff") and allows the card to automatically select address 120h as an alternative place to live. So far this sounds pretty cool. No other standard device uses 110h or 120h normally, so who cares? (OK, the competitor might, if they knew about it, or they might if they knew about the competitor...but neither does...)

Let's spice this up a bit and make the competitor's (Sunny Flowers, Ltd.) device not really a competing product, but a very different one, a special caching hard disk controller with secret programmable stuff of its own inside so the user can select cache parameters and maybe even a few disk format and partitioning utilities using a special diskette they provide.

Not Quite and Sunny test their products, demo them at Fall COMDEX in Las Vegas, get a warm reception and lots of interest, and decide to build and ship 10,000 units each to your local computer retailers. You have no idea who or where Not Quite and Sunny are, but the idea of a no-jumpers 14.4 fax/modem for $89 and a new fast caching super-duper hard disk adapter for $49 is too much to resist. Off the shelf, into the basket, through the register, and on towards home to upgrade your PC go these two marvelous advances in technology.

Overcome with joy and promise of a system that retrieves email even faster now, you've torn open the boxes, tossed aside all but the setup diskettes and the I/O cards, ripped open the computer case, extracted the old modem and disk adapter cards, inserted the new ones and turned on the power. Perhaps the third or fourth screen message you're greeted with after the memory test and setup prompt indicates that you have the new whiz-bang drive adapter installed but it needs to be set up. You grab the setup disk, press **Ctrl+S** to load the setup program off the diskette, go through a few barely understandable menu selections, and finally get a screen that says "ready to reboot your system now, press enter…" (No, we didn't trash your hard drive…).

After rebooting, a few screen messages, and a nice greeting from Sunny, the system starts to boot up. Good news and congratulations! Getting a DOS prompt and then loading Windows 3.x takes 10-15 seconds less than it did before you went to the computer store because of the new disk adapter. Now, it's time to try the new modem.

When you start ProComm or your favorite fax program, it says it can't open a COM port or find a fax modem. Oh yeah, probably have to set that up too.

Pop the modem setup diskette into drive A:, go to the menu bar, select **File//Run//A:\Setup <Enter>**, click, whir, flash, system locked up - YIKES! Gee, probably not a Windows program, sure hope nothing's damaged, take the diskette out of the drive….

Ctrl-Alt-Delete, boot up messages, greeting from Sunny (the disk adapter), and stop at the DOS prompt. Type **A:\SETUP <ENTER>**…click, whir, screen flash, new message…,

"Welcome to Not Quite's Modem Setup Program…press enter to automatically detect and configure your new plug-play device…" **<ENTER>**…click, whir, diskette and hard drive lights come on…"Unable to detect modem. Possible conflict device or no modem present. Remove disk and press any key to reboot." **<ENTER>**

Screen flash, video then system BIOS messages, greeting from Sunny, greeting from DOS: "No boot device available." System is locked up.

Nuts!!! Power off, power on… screen flash, video, then system BIOS messages, greeting from Sunny, greeting from DOS: "No boot device available." System is locked up.

Now your hard drive *is* trashed. What happened here? Let's examine it.

Not Quite, not knowing about Sunny, their addresses, or their command structure, executed its innocent little detection program just fine. The problem is that the "secret stuff" that Not Quite used to find and communicate with its modem card, and the code that Sunny uses to start a data-destroying destructive hard drive format routine are "by accident" the same code.

If only Sunny and Not Quite had communicated with each other, or even considered that someone else might be just about as innovative as they were, they might have avoided designing similar non-standard hardware or allowing or writing possibly destructive utilities. Of course, you have no idea how to get in touch with either of these companies to discuss the matter. You might take one or more products back to the store—likely the hard disk adapter—complain and not know that the store folks have no idea who these two companies are. They just return the goods to the distributor (or worse, repackage the stuff and put it back on the shelf to sell again).

Thus, a hard lesson could be learned if anyone was paying attention. Simply put: if you've never heard of them, if it doesn't claim a real traceable standard, and especially if you don't have a backup—don't play with it!!

This is a harsh lesson some may actually have learned. Similar things have happened even between vendors complying with one standard or another. There is a lot of "secret stuff" going around and sometimes folks just outsmart themselves, or us, by being too tricky. Outsmart them by using recognizable and properly labeled products from reputable firms.

That's enough bad news for now. Fortunately, many reputable firms have been careful, checked themselves many times and many ways, and brought us successful, new and yet non-standard products.

So far, the Intel products have successfully provided compatibility with prior devices and techniques, and the setup software automatically checks the existing system resources and configuration before indicating possible configuration options for the new device you're installing. This software applies only to the specific device of interest, not to any other device in the system. Plugging in the new card and running the software leaves you with a clear set of safe options for the configuration of that device.

If you wish to use a specific configuration, you may have to manually change other parts of your system until the resources you want to use for this new device are available. While this is no help to the rest of your system, it is a very good way to handle the installation of a new device, since it does detect the available resources it can use and helps you set up for this.

Experience with some of the products available from National Semiconductor and a few from 3Com indicate a similar regard for the existing configuration before allowing configuration for the new device.

Some no-name products work in a similarly friendly and successful fashion, while others seem to be designed and implemented without any regard for other possibilities or the existing configuration. The resulting problem can be that they will allow you to create a device conflict during setup without telling you. There is also the potential for these devices to mistakenly reconfigure themselves internally because of poor design, or to get in the way of other device detection schemes, as we saw earlier. These problems can result in system lock-ups or the device becoming configured to some unknown address or IRQ. Thus, it will not be available for use as previously expected.

All in all, the basic ISA configuration concerns remain the same whether or not it's done by software configuration, automatically or manually. You have to be aware of what resources are in use and which can be used in your system for various devices.

Hard Drive Detection and Support

As systems have progressed, so have hard drives, both in performance and complexity. Most of today's systems also include one or two IDE drive interfaces on the system board. With two IDE interface connections, the system can support more than two physical drives attached to the system; these drives may be a mix of hard drives and CD-ROM drives.

To provide these two disk drive interfaces requires two sets of hard drive addresses, the primary (1F0h) and secondary (170h) AT hard disk interface addresses, and two IRQ lines—IRQ 14 for the primary and IRQ 15 for the secondary. These are fixed resources that usually cannot be altered in system setup, BIOS or Windows 95. This means that IRQ 15 is usually not an option for use by add-in devices or within Plug and Play's automatic configurations.

Additionally, while not an address, IRQ, I/O bus, or Plug and Play issue, new system BIOS is now able to automatically detect and configure hard drive type parameters in system setup. This feature better accommodates large hard drives or those with more than 512 megabytes of space. Hard drives were previously limited to this 512 megabyte restriction because BIOS and DOS together could not address more than 1024 physical cylinders, 63 physical sectors per track, or 16 physical heads. By supporting Logical Block Addressing, or LBA mode, the BIOS removes the physical numbering restrictions from drive configurations, allowing DOS and Windows 95 to actually handle their current limit of single drive volumes up to 2 gigabytes in size.

However, because they still use a 16-bit File Allocation Table (FAT-16), DOS and Windows 95 still maintain a 2 gigabyte per partition/volume limit, requiring you to configure multiple partitions (with **FDISK** or similar partitioning software) if your disk drive is larger than 2,048 megabytes in size. Microsoft released a special OEM version of Windows 95 (for system manufacturers only to distribute) that uses a 32-bit File Allocation Table numbering scheme, increasing the single-volume parition size limit to 2 terabytes in size, using smaller data cluster sizes of 4k bytes. Since FAT32 is not compatible with many disk utilities and is not supported by Windows NT, you may not see it or want it in use on your system until there is much more support for it.

You can tell if your system has or supports multiple IDE drive interfaces by getting into its CMOS setup program and looking at the main/basic setup screen where disk drive types are listed. If the listing indicates space for details for more than two hard drives, it's likely that somewhere in the advanced parts of your system setup are configuration details to enable or configure the second(ary) IDE interface and drives. Also within the main/basic setup screen or where you configure hard drives for each interface, one of your options may allow you to select **Auto** or **Auto-Config** for the drive type, indicating that the boot-up portion of the system BIOS is able to detect and configure hard drives automatically.

The configuration details screen for the drive interfaces or the PCI configuration screen may also let you change the address and/or IRQ for these interfaces, but these should be left at 1F0h and IRQ14 for the only/first or primary interface, and 170h and IRQ15 for the second interface, to maintain a standard configuration.

Intel's Peripheral Component Interconnect (PCI): I/O Performance and Plug and Play

In yet another effort to provide higher I/O performance in PC systems, and to match it closely with the original CPU designs, Intel and others designed the PCI bus. PCI exists essentially for the same reasons and performs much the same service as VESA Local Bus and then some. It performs much the same service as Local Bus, though it uses different techniques. Video display, disk drive, and network interface adapters are the most common items to benefit from PCI's high performance.

These techniques are such that they can be and have been applied to non-Intel, non-PC systems, such as the Power PC. PCI is completely different from VESA Local Bus in connections and configuration. PCI devices physically appear to be backwards from ISA devices, and they use a smaller socket that fits between and apart from ISA sockets. Typically there are three or four PCI sockets on a PCI system board, along with three or four other ISA bus connections.

PCI devices maintain compatibility with their ISA counterparts as standard devices as well as being PCI devices—a PCI video card functions just like an ISA video card, only faster. The addressing and IRQ issues do not equate to most of the ISA concerns we have here, because the I/O bus and IRQ lines are routed and handled quite a bit differently.

Interesting Facts About PCI

To appreciate PCI and why it may be the closest thing in hardware we can come up with to preclude having device conflicts, we have to look inside it a bit. Reading about ISA, MicroChannel, EISA, and Local Bus is a bit boring, and I found nothing impressive or worthwhile to include or update about them in this book. PCMCIA comes close to interesting, but not in the context of common PC conflicts. If it were economical, fast, and easily applicable to today's desktop and server PC problems, it would be so noted.

A study of PCI reveals not only examples about and solutions for our need for speed, but also the limitations all PC designs have left us with to date—device identification, configuration, upgrades, more add-ins, etc. PCI was and is a big technical issue to fund, design, implement, and manage, but we don't have to do much but buy it, plug it in, and enjoy it—really!! Couple PCI with Plug and Play, and we've really got something—not everything yet—but something significant.

Local Bus

While the first impression here is that this may have something to do with the VESA Local Bus, we're close, but only in terms of name and theoretical application. I didn't really define this before in this chapter because VESA Local Bus is all but a legacy technology in itself. It seems more important to cover it here because we are trying to configure our systems for optimal performance, and the best way to get that performance at this time is with the kind of technical benefits PCI gives us.

A *local bus* is a generic term referring to the data and address lines connected directly to the CPU, and typically to memory. The local bus operates at nearly CPU operating speeds—33 to 66MHz, depending on the vintage of system board and chip set. It's an excellent place to get at raw data fast. Normal I/O bus devices, those legacy/ISA things we're really worried about, do not connect directly to the CPU bus. They connect instead through a set of buffering and interface chips that slow the CPU data down to something more suitable for the older devices we have, and the way they are connected to the system board.

By the original IBM PC/AT-standards, the speed for legacy/ISA bus slots and devices is a mere 8 megahertz, translating to 8 megabytes/second data transfer rates, even though many systems do run faster (12 or 16 MHz). Since we wouldn't gain much benefit out of serial, parallel, or game ports running any faster than they do already, it's okay to leave these devices working at legacy speeds. It's when we begin to run video and audio conferencing, network servers, or otherwise need to move lots of data very fast that a faster local bus really helps us out.

It may be easy to be fooled into thinking that any device built onto the system board—a serial port, network, disk or SCSI adapter—is using a local bus connection. In fact, most systems offering these built-in features are not using a local bus for I/O, except for the specific VESA Local Bus or PCI slots on the board. You may notice that some built-in IDE interface plugs indicate "IDE Interface" and "PCI Interface" separately. Indeed the PCI-labeled plug is a PCI/local bus interface, and can be faster, while the other is using a separate legacy interface scheme and will be slower. It is also possible to have both IDE interfaces connected to the PCI system. The system setup program should also indicate a distinction between the two interfaces.

Speed

There are two important reasons for the flexibility and success of PCI. First, the bus can be very fast. Because of its method of processing data signals on the bus wires, PCI can achieve a maximum data throughput of 528 megabytes per second (64-bit data transfers on a 66MHz PCI bus).

Second, the bus can be as slow as it needs to be—down to 0 megahertz, or turned off if need be. This allows PCI to serve us for a longer useful life since initially our PCI add-in devices may be slower than the maximum performance, yet we may want to use much faster devices as we upgrade our systems. Typically, we may experience 132 megabytes per second transfers, which is just about fast enough to keep pace with high speed networking, an application program or two, and maintaining a full-motion video conference. We really are speed demons when it comes to computing these days!

Addressing

The PCI bus, being separate from the ISA I/O bus, does not present us with typical addressing conflicts. PCI addresses are simply not shared with the legacy devices. Since PCI is a standard and all PCI manufacturers must adhere to the standard (we'll see if this holds true for our friends Not Quite and Sunny), addressing ranges are worked out ahead of time before a product is released. The PCI standards organization keeps track of and openly shares information about all developers' devices.

To maintain compatibility with legacy BIOS and operating systems, the PCI chip system reserves and simulates the same device address presence that would be used by legacy/ISA devices. Thus, a PCI VGA video adapter still uses and presents a video adapter address presence at 3B0 and 3C0h, reserves data transfer areas at A000-BFFFh, and uses the video BIOS range of

C000-C7FFh. Fortunately these ranges, as well as those for many network cards and disk adapters, are at lower risk for conflicts than serial, parallel, sound, and other legacy adapters.

Interrupts and DMA

Unlike PCI's addressing, IRQs are *not* handled entirely different from legacy/ISA IRQs. On Intel-based CPUs there is only one processor interrupt line. This line must be used by all hardware interrupt drive devices. Thus, the PCI interrupts must pass through the same circuitry as the legacy/ISA interrupt signals. Using a special PCI chipset and interrupt routing scheme, having a higher priority status on the legacy/ISA interrupt chips than legacy/ISA devices, and running off the local bus at higher speeds, PCI presents little interrupt overhead or performance problems compared to our issues with legacy devices. Those devices must be carefully configured for their priority and conflict avoidance.

Using an EISA-like interrupt signal detection system and the PCI interrupt routing scheme, three interrupt lines are actually shared between all (up to 32) physical PCI cards or connections. Each PCI card or connection may contain multiple devices, allowing up to 256 total PCI interfaced items in one system. Sounds like plenty of room for expansion!

Nevertheless, the PCI interrupts will never collide with legacy interrupts, unless you can and do change this configuration in your system setup program to assign a legacy/ISA IRQ line to a PCI device. Not all systems allow you to do this, so you're again protected from the misconfiguration gremlins.

Universal Device Drivers: Fcode

Complex devices such as video and disk drive adapters usually have their own ROM BIOS code that loads at boot-up to provide enhanced features beyond the simpler ones in the system BIOS. Since PCI devices can be applied equally well to Power PC and other PCI-equipped platforms, this ROM BIOS code must be useable by all system types encountered. Just any program code cannot simply run on Intel-based, Power PC, RISC and Sun systems—there must either be a common language, or different machine-specific versions of code, to accommodate all platform types.

Rather than stuff a card with all sorts of different CPU program code types, having to figure out what processor the system is running, and having to allow for new CPU types later on, the PCI folks decided to provide code in a relatively little-known, small, fast language known as *Forth*. In turn, each PCI-based computer system must be able to process Forth code in real time. So, while you might have thought that all low-level hardware code is done in a CPU's native machine code, assembler code, or derived from C, we now have another control language with which to consider opportunities.

This Forth or *Fcode* is only run at system boot-up, as devices are detected, identified, and configured for operation. If the card is designed to accommodate it, a card vendor can supply you with BIOS updates to load into the card, and if you look at those updates closely, you might actually be able to make out snippets of the Forth language as it's stored in the card's memory.

Since there is special Forth code for every PCI device, there must also be special PCI BIOS accommodations made in the system board or chip set to run and use this code. PCI system BIOS handles this and lets us gather and control a lot of information and configuration elements for PCI devices. Each PCI device is uniquely identified by its type, vendor, model, and version which can be read out of the system with PCI-aware diagnostic or information tools. This information is very important for auditing systems and knowing what's inside.

All of this is not a major configuration issue for us in the legacy world, but it does illustrate how far we've come toward solving some of the problems of the PC world. With that, we begin to see how PCI works so well with Plug and Play.

Plug and Play

PCI devices are by their nature designed to be Plug and Play compatible. PCI device configuration is handled internally through the system BIOS and setup, where addressing and interrupts are assigned by physical socket position. The BIOS does not allow you to configure the system with conflicts at the PCI level. It intervenes and precludes an improper selection if another device or socket already uses the parameters you try to set manually.

Summary

This overview of enhancements to the original PC designs should indicate to you how much things have changed in a few short years, and how much they can and will change toward making PC systems easier for us to set up and use.

Now that we have an initial set of rules to go by—and this recent overview—we can proceed to create our own "plug and play" PC systems. Armed with our new skills and all of this information, we are better able to deal with conflict resolution. This, in turn, allows for easier system upgrades.

CHAPTER 4

PLUGGING AND PLAYING TO PC97

Topics covered in this chapter:

- Plug and Play: the PC configuration crap shoot
- The significance of Plug and Play
- The Plug and Play standard
- How Plug and Play *really* works
- PC95: today's PC defined
  - What Microsoft said a PC should have been
- PC97: PC95 advances
  - What Microsoft now says that a standard PC should be

We've seen more than our share of technical details by now, and you may be hoping that this chapter is the one that makes it all go away, makes it all better, lets us all sleep at night, wake up refreshed and enjoy better days ahead. I wish it were so. For the most part, Plug and Play is a wonderful concept. Some day it may even become reality. If it does, this book will be obsolete except for its historical value.

It will take a complete redesign of most of the PC I/O system as we know it to make Plug and Play a reality. This means that there can be no more jumper- or switch-set *legacy* devices, at all, anywhere in the system, period—*yeah!*

It will take all of the hardware vendors who make add-in serial ports, parallel ports, IDE interfaces, sound cards, scanner interfaces, SCSI adapters, modems, ISDN adapters, video capture cards, video display adapters, GPIB (General Purpose Interface Bus) and specialty instrument control cards, game and mouse ports, network adapters—you name it, *all* of them—to redesign and replace all of the devices with PnP-compliant ones. It also means that the system board will have to lose any and all of its 8- and 16-bit ISA slots in favor of PCI slots. Furthermore, it means that any and all software that addresses hardware devices directly will have to work through the services of an updated PnP-compliant operating system. That operating system will have to be aware of or have drivers for *every* imaginable PC interface device in existence (except, of course, the legacy devices, which would no longer be a part of new systems).

Obviously this is no small task. Hundreds of manufacturers, thousands of products and programmers, and millions of users will be affected in one way or another. Still, the effort is underway. Microsoft is looking forward to and supporting the efforts. Vendors are lining up and catching on. Supporting older, slower legacy devices is costing us all a small fortune in downtime and support.

At some point, both a complete absence of legacy devices and complete availability of all new systems and devices will have to take place. This point may not be reached by 1997 or 1998, but I suspect by the year 2000 there will not be a newly manufactured piece of legacy PC hardware or software available anywhere. If PnP doesn't fully catch on, we'll be revisiting the subject of system configurations again and again.

Don't rejoice too soon. This does not mean that we will have replaced, or that we'll *have* to or be able to afford to replace our existing, still working legacy systems. While many are happily computing away with Windows 98, 99, or 2000 on new "Octagium Pro 500" systems, having never heard of IRQ, DMA, or I/O, not having seen an add-in card jumper or CMOS setup screen, many will still be happily computing away with 1997-vintage systems, dreading the inevitable upgrade path and costs into new hardware and software.

NOTE

Octagium is purely a speculative name for fun. If someone has or does name a system of CPU as such, I'll yield claim to it.

Somewhere in between will still be many users and their legacy and PnP devices, fighting it out over who gets which resources when and why. For my nickel, I hope someone fixes Plug and Play as we know it so we can get to the rejoicing stage.

We're about to explore Plug and Play, and you may see quite simply why we still need to attend to some legacy and configuration management issues, until the Utopian glory days of trouble-free personal computing arrives.

Plug and Play (PnP): The Solution We've Been Waiting For

The no-conflict, no-hassle configuration solution we think we've been waiting for is rapidly but yet uneasily headed our way. COMPAQ, Phoenix Technologies (a primary provider of BIOS for many systems), and Intel are spearheading this effort to design cooperative, integrated PC systems, system and add-in boards, and BIOS to work together intelligently. Microsoft also has a significant buy-in to PnP with support for it in or coming to their operating systems.

Plug and Play begins at the very basic and lowest level of our PC systems—the system board and BIOS. These must be designed and implemented to work together. The instant we start up a PC system with PnP, this new BIOS (or rather, enhancements to existing BIOS) goes to work detecting devices toward automatic configuration of the system. A full and PnP-only system, without legacy devices, will configure and verify itself and make the expected devices and services available to us without much, if any, thought or effort. But today there is no such thing as a Plug and Play-only system. Legacy devices (COM and LPT ports, for example) still exist, even if they are built into the system boards—though they may be configured by software.

Plug and Play is designed to work with and around existing legacy devices, whether they are ISA, EISA, MicroChannel, PCMCIA, Local Bus, or PCI. During system startup, PnP's device detection begins to detect any and all system devices and resources that are in use. It also determines whether the devices it finds are PnP devices; if not, PnP devices will use the resources available after non-PnP devices are configured. If you add a new non-PnP device that conflicts in any way with an existing PnP device, the existing PnP device will be reconfigured at startup to keep your system working.

Plug and Play devices and BIOS can't do the intelligent configuration work entirely by themselves. The BIOS and hardware only make provisions for detection and configuration; they do not act directly on their capabilities. The amount of time and memory space allowed or acceptable for BIOS to do its job is just not enough. For this, we depend on the strengths and capabilities of a Plug and Play operating system. We don't seem to mind how long it takes to boot up and configure the system, nor how big the programs actually are that must do the work.

Windows 95 has PnP technology built in to allow automatic configurability during installations, upgrades, system changes, and to alert you to any changes in your system. Windows 95 may then give you the option of having it reconfigure itself or any PnP hardware, so the system will have access to all of the expected devices and services.

PnP can be *the* answer to configuration and conflict concerns if your system contains *only* PnP-compatible devices. If any legacy devices exist, as they certainly will for quite some time, you must still follow the existing standard configuration rules. PnP will not do anything different with or for standard PC port devices, such as the addressing of COM ports, LPT ports, their IRQs, and so on. PnP devices, for the most part, are still expected to use the originally designed and defined PC configuration standards to work properly with software.

In the prior chapters we've discussed "the rules" and some of the traditional configurations that have developed to date to establish a known, workable PC foundation. For now, that foundation is still extremely important, and is not to be overlooked in our zeal to arrive at an ideal Plug and Play system.

From this point on PnP seems to ignore either the rules or prior significant conventions of how we've configured our systems in the past, and the software that must use the devices in the system. We are at an interim point in the transition from legacy to full automation that may be worse during this time of change than holding fast to the solid legacy foundation we've built up thus far.

Plug and Play BIOS and Operating Systems

Plug and Play depends on compliant hardware and software routines that can identify PnP hardware devices and control their configuration. PnP BIOS merely makes the few I/O devices typically built into the system board (I/O ports, disk adapters, etc.) to be PnP-compliant. This means they can be identified and configured by PnP configuration manager software. The BIOS does not actually provide the configuration services: these devices still need an external configuration manager to handle them as PnP-devices.

To date, PnP configuration management is handled only by the operating system. For many of us now this means Microsoft's Windows 95, although the current version of IBM's OS/2 is also a PnP-compliant operating system with configuration management capabilities. LINUX and other operating systems are developing PnP support as this book is being put together. Oddly enough, version 4.0 of Microsoft Windows NT ("New Technology") lags behind its little brother, Windows 95, as it does not have PnP support. By late 1997 or certainly 1998, Microsoft is supposed to have PnP support in Windows NT.

That the operating system carries the bulk of the configuration burden is not necessarily a bad thing. It is far easier to download a new configuration program file for the operating system than it is to update the system BIOS code. Also, the configuration management software is too large to fit into most system ROM chips. Also, to configure additional ROM would take up precious memory addressing space we would rather use for other things.

Whether or not your PC system contains PnP BIOS or has PnP hardware built into the system board, a PnP-compliant operating system such as Windows 95 is still able to work with add-in PnP hardware devices.

It is within this configuration management software, how it implements the Plug and Play specification and configures hardware devices, that our attention must be focused. This is where the "work" is done. This software determines the configuration of any ISA/legacy devices, sets off the PnP hardware identification process, and then allocates resources to the PnP devices before the operating system can use them.

We still have to live with how, when, or which PnP hardware wins our identification crap shoot, and thus which device gets configured first. After that, we hope that the configuration management software (our operating system) will be able to make the right configuration assignments. More on this as we go along.

Extended System Configuration Data—ESCD

Within specific PnP BIOS implementations and during its operation may come a new allocation of memory to what is called the ESCD, or *Extended System Configuration Data* area. This is an 8 Kbyte block of RAM located in the upper memory region, often found between E:A000h and E:BFFFh. It is used to store information about PCI and Plug and Play devices. You may notice references to the ESCD during system boot-up as PCI and PnP devices are discovered and their initially or previously assigned resources are listed on the screen.

We don't interact directly with this region of memory, but its existence is worthy of note when configuring memory managers, or if you ever wonder why a mysterious 8K block of upper memory is not available for loading device drivers or TSR programs into high memory.

Support for and use of the ESCD memory allocation depends on the BIOS. The configuration manager software may often read, from but may not write to or update the ESCD data directly. Instead, the configuration software typically acts on the hardware devices. The ESCD data is updated on the next system boot-up based on the configuration of the hardware it finds, saving and making this data available to further configuration manager operations.

The existence of the ESCD information may or may not save time in loading the operating system, since the BIOS has already discovered and recorded information about PnP devices. Thus, the operating system would not have to discover all of the Plug and Play devices all over again—but some PnP devices may require drivers to be loaded into the operating system first, before PnP discovery and configuration of the device could be done anyway. Certainly the ESCD could be useful where an independent configuration manager, outside of the operating system, is used to support PnP devices.

How Can You Tell If You Have Plug and Play BIOS?

This is an excellent question and one to which there is no obvious answer. During the initial part of boot-up some BIOS will report the existence of their PnP BIOS support and which version of the BIOS is in the system—but most do not. I would have expected this information to be available within most utility programs such as those from Norton (System Information), Quarterdeck (Manifest) or similar, but this is not the case. There is no standard definition for how or where PnP BIOS is indicated or detected, unless you invoke a specific PnP test or configuration program to look for PnP devices in the system. So far, the most reliable program available is **PNPBTST.EXE** from the people who should know, BIOS-maker and PnP specification partner, Phoenix Technologies. You can get this program from their Web site at **http://www.phoenix.com/techs/freeware.html**.

The Legacy and Plug and Play Dilemma

We've come to accept a certain basic configuration for most of the common devices found in a typical PC. In review, this gives us a typical PC system with items and their configuration as listed in Table 4.1 below.

Table 4.1 Typical Legacy Resource Assignments

Device	Address	IRQ	DMA	System Device
RAM Refresh		0	*	
System Timer	40h	0	*	
Keyboard	60h	1		*
Cascade for IRQ 8-15		2	*	
COM2	2F8h	3		
COM4	2E8h	3		
COM1	3F8h	4		
COM3	2F8h			
LPT2	278h	5		
Sound Card	220h	1, 3, or 5		
Diskette Adapter	3F0h	6	2	
LPT1	378h	7		
Real-Time Clock	70h	8	*	
		9		
Network Card	280h	10		
SCSI Adapter	330h	11	3 or 5	
PS/2 Mouse Port	64h	12		
Numeric Co-Processor	F0h	13	*	
Hard Disk Interface	1F0h	14		
2nd Hard Disk Interface	170h	15		
VGA card	3B0			
	3C0			

Understanding that it would be a tremendous effort to redesign the entire PC system as we know it, many of the resources assigned to common PC devices will never be suited to Plug and Play or automatic configuration. A computer simply needs

105

things like its clocks, CPU, and *very* basic low-level items to be left as and where they are, consuming the resources they do, so the computer can do its job—boot up and predictably run certain pieces of software. Those items that we cannot anticipate or expect to change regardless of legacy, PnP, or other changes in the PC platform are marked with an asterisk (*) in the System Devices column in Table 4.1.

This leaves us a few devices—mostly those troublesome I/O-things—that *could* be affected by Plug and Play. The questions then become: do we want to affect them? Should we affect them? Can we affect them and if so, how? If some of them are not PnP devices, how do we get them to work together?

Plug and Play Doesn't

First, experience and anecdotal references have shown many of us this all too familiar phrase: that Plug and Play does not play, or play well, or play as we might expect it to, with our existing systems. Next, we wonder why, after all of the hype and technology behind this supposedly marvelous solution to such basic problems, does this technology really not work?

The answers may be solid, logical, and reliable only in very specific cases where a vendor or other very technical people have researched and tested specific cases. For the rest of us—the millions of us who can't get access to all the whiz-bang technical tools and details—the answers are unfortunately more vague and troublesome.

Experience and research into what information is available is very telling, beginning with the Plug and Play specification and how it is designed to work. After the fixed resource and legacy devices are identified, Plug and Play, in a nutshell, works as follows.

The PnP device identification and resource assignment process, by design, may be thought of as a crap-shoot, or as some have expressed it, like a fast game of one-card poker played between devices and the PnP software.

A device's ability to win the crap shoot to be eligible for a spot in the configuration order is at best dependent upon the following variables:

- the speed at which a device can respond to automatic identification processes
- how each PnP BIOS vendor actually wrote their PnP BIOS code
- how each device's PnP hardware and internal programming was designed to work
- system timing considerations
- location of a PCI device in a particular slot

Once the configuration order is determined by the "crap-shoot" method, a device's resource assignment is dependent upon:

- which resources a device is designed to be able to use (vendor programming of the device)
- which resources the operating system or device driver allows a device to use (vendor, driver, and operating system variables)

The crap shoot is repeated at every boot up, and configurations *do change* and can become more complex as you add a new PnP device to the system. A device's configuration should not change with each boot up, but might if it has defective internal firmware.

If you're looking for a distinct set of rules for some priority and pre-determined resource assignments, you'll be hard pressed to find them. Apparently, neither the vendors nor the Plug and

Play specification authors wanted to tie anyone's hands and limit their ability to use whatever resources were available in any order that you could get them.

For the most part, vendors have limited themselves to using resources that only make sense, based on legacy rules, tradition, and convention for the particular device of concern. This means that we probably won't see, for example, a VGA card vendor, the device driver programmer, or the PnP operating system folks allowing a VGA card to use assignments typically used by COM or LPT ports, sound cards, or other typical devices.

In most cases you also won't see I/O addresses thrown about and assigned with wild abandon, but you may find IRQ and DMA assignments not falling into place as you might expect. The fact that the configuration can change between system boot-ups, and when a new device is added, makes PnP all the more interesting and challenging in some cases.

Since for most of us Windows 95 is our operating system, and it controls and keeps track of the actual PnP device configuration process, the odds in the crap shoot tend to even out to being a little better than playing Russian roulette with a fully loaded gun.

You will usually not (but can) find that your once-stable PnP device configurations change when a new device is added. This may become evident when you add a PnP network card and suddenly find that you can't load its new drivers from your CD-ROM drive because the PnP routine has shuffled the CD-ROM interface configuration around, temporarily or permanently disabling the CD-ROM drive.

Plug and Play can outsmart itself on numerous (and as indicated by the PnP BIOS, device driver, and operating system variables above) unpredictable occasions. This is where we enter a new phase of configuration management and have to start loading the dice so we get and retain some of our own control over the configuration again. We'll cover this topic as part of Chapter 7.

Microsoft's PC95: Defining Compatibility

PC95 was Microsoft's initial answer to, or dictate of, what a properly configured and configurable PC system should have been by the end of 1995—to work with Windows 95 and similar PnP-compliant operating systems. The PC95 standard was intended to make PCs more affordable, approachable, and easier for non-technical users. This means that there *should* be no user concerns over I/O addresses, IRQ, DMA, ports, logical devices, etc., and thus no manual configuration when buying or upgrading a PC system.

To fully meet this goal, all hardware devices would have had to become Plug and Play compatible and be able to be dynamically reconfigured as new devices were added or old ones removed. This includes all hardware, meaning that even disk drives will also have to support configuration changes (such as first, second or further drive IDs, SCSI device numbers, and so on).

But PC95 is about more than compatibility. Windows 95 and PC95 were designed cooperatively, with the features of Plug and Play, VESA (video modes and performance), automatic power management (to serve the U.S. Environmental Protection Agency's Energy Star program for energy conservation in computing devices), and other new PC device standards in mind. Since Plug and Play was designed to also be compatible with legacy devices, they are likewise covered under the minimum PC95 requirements. To encourage this, Microsoft licensed systems as being "Designed for Windows 95," complete with an identifying logo saying so, if they meet certain minimum requirements.

These requirements were tested with Microsoft's Hardware Compatibility Test for Windows 95. They include CPU type, amount of RAM, video display capabilities, CD-ROM drive performance and capabilities, and multimedia (sound and video playback) capabilities. (See Table 4.2.) To date, the Hardware Compatibility Test is not available to the general public, but we can compare its requirements to a variety of system components to see if they might comply.

Similar testing was provided for software products as well. As many developers have found, there were several issues relating to interoperability between devices and software that have probably allowed several exceptions to the originally stringent tests. For example, software "Designed for Windows 95" had to run on both Windows 95 and Windows NT according to the test criteria. Unfortunately, it is possible to create quite good software for either environment, using the unique features and benefits of a particular environment, that were not available in both operating systems. Thus, Microsoft had to start issuing exemptions to their own rules for many software products very quickly as Windows 95 came to release and acceptance. No doubt similar exemptions were granted for many hardware systems as well.

Table 4.2 PC95 System Requirements

System Components	Minimum Requirements	Recommendations
BIOS	Plug and Play BIOS Version 1.0a with resource readback	PnP with soft-set for all resources
CPU	80386 or equivalent	80486DX-33 or equivalent
RAM	4M	8M
Video Adapter	640 x 480 x 256 colors	1024 x 768 x 256 colors

System Components	Minimum Requirements	Recommendations
Video Display	640 x 480 color	VESA DDC1/2B standard and Display Power Management Signaling (DPMS) for shutdown
Pointing Device	Dedicated port or integral device	
Parallel Port	Supports compatibility (output only, to printers) and Nibble modes (bi-directional data transfer)	Full IEEE-P1284-I Enhanced Capability Port (ECP) mode compatibility
Serial Port	One; two if mouse uses COM port	16550A or compatible serial I/O chip
Hard Disk recommended	Not required if networked	80-120M min.; 500+M
Diskettes	3.5", 1.44M, providing write-protect signal if diskette not present (for disk presence test)	
Sound		22Khz, 8-bit, mono output only
Labeling	Standardized icons for device plugs for easy identification	
System Board		• Advanced Power Management BIOS interface v1.1; software-controlled power supply power-down • High-speed expansion bus (PCI or VL-bus)
General		• CD-ROM drive with soft-eject control • SCSI-2 interface • Clearly labeled switches and jumpers on all boards

System Components	Minimum Requirements	Recommendations
General (continued)		• *Plug and Play* expansion cards
		• Standardized cabling that cannot be plugged into the wrong card or device

The PC95 standard, and in essence the Plug and Play standard, was also to provide for several more configuration options than found on standard PC devices. Having more options available provides a great deal more flexibility for adding devices to our system, though most of the popular and commonly desired items may already be provided with an off-the-shelf PC system.

NOTE

Refer to Chapter 2 for the limitations imposed by legacy devices.

NOTE

If you review Table 4.2 and compare it to your existing system, you may find that except for PnP-BIOS, your system may already be close to meeting the PC95 standard and some of its additional recommendations. If you establish and manage your system's configuration adequately, in essence acting as the Plug and Play manager for your own system, you could at least be "PC94"-compliant without having to replace your system board and other devices.

Additional Features and Benefits of PC95

PnP hardware and software not only address the issues of configurations and avoiding conflicts; they open the door for several new features to be introduced into our PC systems. These new features extend themselves to both usability and environmental issues.

Energy Conservation

A few years ago, energy conservation was simply considered getting more life out of the batteries in laptop systems. On our desktops, the video monitors, the disk drives, and an otherwise idle system are power hogs. They not only use a lot of electricity to run, they also generate a lot of heat, which in most cases we eventually remove with air conditioning. The cumulative effects of several dozen PCs running in an office has overburdened the cooling systems in buildings that were designed before PC systems were in common use. Even with new building designs, PC systems can create a waste of energy overall.

Advanced Power Management in PC systems can be thought of as the ultimate "screen saver" of the '90s. Instead of displaying flying toasters or psychedelic fish, these new features dim or turn off our monitors, stop our disk drives from spinning, and even put the computer system to "sleep" if we leave our systems inactive for a certain period of time. In essence, we will be saving the batteries of the environment.

As to the question of whether it's better to leave your system on or turn it off between uses, as far as energy conservation is concerned, it is better to turn it off. In terms of wear-and-tear on cooling fans, drive motors and power supply components, leaving the system turned on is better. Basically, the choice depends on how often you need access to your system or how long a time there is between system uses. If automatic power control is designed into the system, the electronic circuits will control the power smoothly, preventing the turn-on/turn-off surges that are suspected of causing many system failures.

In reality, the PC95 system need not be completely shut off, so that it can come to life again as you need it. Those items that are shut off internally are protected by the power supply regulators, so there is no great influx of current through the AC power line as there is when you operate that big red on/off switch on the side.

On/Off Control in the Keyboard

OK, so our friends using Apple Macintoshes will laugh at us for bringing it up, but once we have software control of the power consumption of our system, it's a relatively simple matter to design the ability to monitor the keyboard periodically to see if anyone's pressed a certain key.

Windows 95 is already designed to shut down the system as part of its exit routine from Windows (although it doesn't go to DOS, like with Windows 3.x). When you elect to shut down Windows 95, you have several options; one of them is to restart the system (reboot) and the other is to perform a shutdown, which currently instructs you that it's safe to turn your system off, or in some systems actually does shut down the system.

Since there are no arms, hands, or fingers provided to toggle the big red switch, the shutdown command goes to an electronically controlled power supply. The big red switch may stay on, but the supply will be turned off inside.

To turn the system back on, we need to get access to that internal electronic control, and since the keyboard is close and used most often by users, it seems like an obvious place to put the **On** button, just like the Macintosh. OK, so there's no **On** button on your PC keyboard yet, but any key should do!

Accessibility

Windows 95 provides a set of installable options to make the use of a PC system easier for physically impaired users. Currently these options consist of "sticky" keyboard keys, many special one-key operations, large and high-contrast screen characters, and similar items.

The PC95 standard allows for the interconnection of a variety of devices, some yet to be invented, through a feature and new standard called the *ACCESS.bus*. These devices may replace or supplement keyboards and pointing devices with special articulation controls, depending on the nature of physical impairment and mobility.

This effort is to be applauded and greatly encouraged throughout the industry, for both hardware and software design. We're all aware of programs that *require* a mouse, if only because a programmer forgot to include the standard set of alternate keyboard commands for a function or designed a new control whose odd new behavior would take forever to get used to.

There are thousands if not millions in the world who would be able to get a lot more out of life, and put a lot more into it, if only they could use these wonderful PC systems. Developers of hardware and software should be encouraged to ensure accessibility for all current and potential users.

Microsoft's PC97: Compatibility, Performance and Then Some

Just when we thought our 150MHz Intel Pentium processor in a system with 16 megabytes of RAM was good enough, along comes something newer, faster, and of course, something we don't have now and that our present system may not be upgradeable to.

Microsoft believes that in order to get the full benefits of software and technology, a certain set of minimum speed, RAM, and feature criteria should be met inside the PC hardware. Of course, the software they want you to benefit from would be theirs (ActiveX, MMX-compliant applications, etc.). Intel plays no small hand in this, anticipating that if they help developers create new features and software that users will need or want bigger faster processors, so they do their part, quietly or not, to drive up the minimums as well.

Admittedly, we do get to enjoy some of the benefits of technology's advances, and anything that will keep us away from having to worry about PC resource configuration issues (and also away from bugging all those technical support people), gives us more time to enjoy or produce with our computers.

Table 4.3 below lists the basic performance and feature recommendations and requirements for various Microsoft PC97-compliant systems.

Table 4.3 Significant System Performance and Feature Requirements for Basic PC97

Attribute/Feature	Basic PC97	Workstation PC97	Entertainment PC97
Minimum CPU:	120 MHz Required	166 MHz Required	166 MHz Required
256K minimum L2 cache	Recommended	Required	Required
Minimum system memory:	16 MB	32 MB	16 MB
Advanced Configuration and Power Interface (ACPI) support	Required	Required	Required
Hardware support for OnNow	Required	Required	Required
BIOS support for OnNow (x86-based systems)	Required	Required	Required
System BIOS support for alternate boot devices, for x86-based systems	Required	Required	Required
BIOS boot support for USB keyboard, if USB is the only keyboard	Required	Required	Required
Industrial Design: All expansion slots in the system are accessible for users to insert cards	Required	Required	Require
Industrial Design: Audible noise meets PC97 standards	Recommended	Recommended	Required

Attribute/Feature	Basic PC97	Workstation PC97	Entertainment PC97
All devices and drivers meet PC97 standards	Required	Required	Required
All bus and devices to be Plug and Play compliant	Required	Required	Required
All devices support correct 16-bit decoding for I/O port addresses	Required	Required	Required
Devices and buses support hot plugging if using USB, 1394, or PC Card	Required	Required	Required
The user is protected from incorrectly connecting devices	Required	Required	Required
Minimal user interaction needed to install and configure devices	Required	Required	Required
Device driver and installation meet Windows and Windows NT standards	Required	Required	Required
Standard system board devices use ISA-compatible addresses	Required	Required	Required
Universal Serial Bus with one USB port, minimum	Required	Required	2 USB ports required
Support for other high-speed expansion capabilities (CardBus required for mobile)	Recommended	Recommended	IEEE 1394 Required
If present, PCI bus meets PCI v. 2.1 and higher, plus PC97 requirements	Required	Required	Required
ISA expansion bus	Optional	Optional	Optional

117

Attribute/Feature	Basic PC97	Workstation PC97	Entertainment PC97
Wireless capabilities in PC system	Recommended	Recommended	Required
Support for installing the operating system	Required	Required	Required
Audio support in PC system meets PC97 requirements	Recommended	Recommended	Advanced aud Required
Communications device provided with PC system	Recommended	Required	Required
Display adapter meets PC97 minimum requirement	800x600x16 bpp (640x480x8 bpp, small LCD)	1024x768x16 bpp	1024x768x16 bpp (BPP=Bits per pixel, color resolution)
Support for NTSC or PAL TV output, if no large-screen monitor	Recommended	Recommended	Required
Color monitor supports DDC 2.0 Level B, EDID, and 800x600, minimum	Required	Required	Required
System supports MPEG-1 playback	Required	Required	Required
PC97 DVD playback requirements, if PC system includes DVD-Video	Required	Required with DVD-Video	Required with DVD-Video
Support Int 13h Extensions in system and option ROMs	Required	Required	Required
Host controller for storage device meets PC97 requirements, if present	Required	Required	Required
Primary host controller supports bus mastering	Recommended	Required	Required
Hard drive meets PC97 requirements, if present	Required	Required	Required
Media status notification support for removable media	Required	Required	Required
Legacy floppy disk controller built into system	Optional	Optional	Optional

Attribute/Feature	Basic PC97	Workstation PC97	Entertainment PC97
CardBus for high-speed expansion capabilities on mobile PCs	Required	Required	Required
Mobile unit and docking station meet PC97 requirements as a pair	Required		
Docking station meets ACPI requirements	Required		
Docking station meets all Basic PC97 requirements for general devices, expansion cards, system bus, and system board	Required		
Automatic resource assignment and dynamic disable capabilities for mobile/docking station pair	Required		
Automatic resource assignment and dynamic disable capabilities for replacement devices	Required		
"Multimedia PC" PC97 minimum requirements	Required	Required	designed to meet meets MPC

Data source: Microsoft PC97 Specification

Legacy/ISA Devices Will Be Optional

Hoping to relieve us of one of our biggest headaches—the configuration of legacy devices and finding resources for them—the PC97 specification allows legacy/ISA device capability to be optional. This is in favor of system boards having built-in Plug and Play I/O ports and devices, and using only PnP/PCI add-in I/O cards. If this works out well, a lot of us techies will end up as legacy resources too!

Computer Availability On Demand

Of particular note are references in Table 4.3 to something called "OnNow," which refers to the ability to start our systems as quickly as possible, whether that means the system will be in a power-on but dormant/sleeping state, or able to boot up faster from data stored in memory rather than having to load entirely from the hard disk.

Admittedly, as power and speed hungry as we've become, being able to use your computer on demand is probably a good thing. The other advantage to an OnNow system is that there should be less worry about the configuration changing between power-down and power-up times, and the not too logical Plug and Play crap shoot of system configuration at start-up.

New I/O Connectivity

There didn't seem to be any other place to mention the next few items except in the context of Plug and Play, PC97, and beyond. Ridding ourselves of the common legacy/ISA hassles inside the box and getting more performance and fancier devices to play with can't be accomplished without addressing a few things outside of the box too.

We've probably exhausted ourselves impatiently waiting for sluggish downloads from various Web sites with 28.8 Kbps modem. Even if we've been able to enjoy the speed of ISDN (but not the costs), today's PC I/O connections have reached their limits in terms of satisfying performance.

The PC box is only so big, and when we start adding on musical instrument devices, portable storage units, and begin to dabble with virtual reality, finding the slots and wrestling with all the cabling only goes so far before we need something better.

Three new I/O interfaces, each with its own set of benefits and applications as well as costs, will be appearing on the PC horizon *very* soon. The Universal Serial Bus (USB) addresses the everyday, low-cost, multiple device attachments most of us will be using everywhere we sit with our desktops or tote our portable systems too. The IEEE-1394 *Firewire* I/O system allows us to hook-up a variety of very high speed devices out of sight or at least off of our desktops. The Fibre Channel I/O system will service (both internal and external) ultra-high speed data delivery needs.

Of course, these interfaces feature the ease of Plug and Play, and give us more I/O speed than we might have ever dreamed of. Personally, I'm really looking forward to the day that I can toss out my serial ports, cables and switch boxes and use one simple cabling system to hook up all the devices around me, and move them from system to system much more easily than we can today.

Universal Serial Bus

Also coming along in 1997 is a new breed of peripheral interconnection called the *Universal Serial Bus*, or USB. This interface will allow hot-plugging (connection or disconnection, as with PC Card devices) of up to 127 I/O devices along a single connection chain. Here again Apple Macintosh fans may laugh, because the Mac has had features like this all along (plugging the mouse into the keyboard, and the keyboard into the system box, all on 'one' connection, for example), though perhaps it is not as fast or versatile.

Each USB peripheral is by nature a hot-plugged, automatically identified, and configured device that will be detected and have drivers loaded as needed by the operating system. It is truly Plug and Play from the outside in. The system's USB port will require no legacy resources, thus avoiding all possible conflicts. The USB port works as part of the chip set with drivers intended to sense and register devices when they are attached or disconnected. Our first taste of this will come with USB drivers for Windows 95, and the feature will be native to Windows 97 and beyond.

USB is designed to be a low-cost method of providing up to 12 megabits/second data rates, serving a wide range of peripheral applications from mice, keyboards, and gaming devices at the low end of the spectrum, to phone and compressed audio, video, and data services at the upper end of its useful speed range.

The key features here, in addition to Plug and Play and speed, are both a simple and low-cost implementation. The cabling design eliminates the need for all those 9-25 pin adapters, null modems and other collective junk hanging around your PCs. Also, the USB port provides power for many low-current devices, so you can probably get rid of a few of those nagging power bricks and stubborn little black wires too. You'll find ISDN or similar low-cost, high-performance network connection devices as well as printers and virtual reality attachments using USB very soon.

IEEE-1394—Firewire

Talk about fast when it comes to new I/O interfaces and you have to be talking about *Firewire*, a 400 megabits per second serial data connection bus intended primarily for multimedia peripherals such as external/portable storage, sound devices, and fast, high-density printers. It's a little too fast for your average keyboard, mouse, printer, or modem applications, but you can expect to see this interface available for systems coming in the next year or so.

Firewire has the capability to handle 1023 networks of 63 nodes, and each node can contain 281 terabytes (that's a *lot*) of memory space. Average cabling length is limited to 4.5 meters, but 14 meter cabling is provided for, as well as repeating through each node device to extend the end-to-end distance between farthest devices out to 224 meters. It's not a network solution, but one that does provide extensibility of high-speed peripherals that are otherwise currently limited to distances of a few feet between devices (as with SCSI). No existing network cabling or fiber optic solution delivers this much performance, no matter the distance.

With this Plug and Play compliant interface, once again, legacy/ISA resources won't be a problem, but I suspect we'll face a few more software driver compatibility issues.

Fibre Channel

Briefly, Fibre Channel (it uses copper wire, as the fabric or medium linking items together, not fiber optics) is a 1 gigabit/second multi-purpose (networking, data bus, etc.) solution for high-speed data access needs. It is being implemented in high-end disk drives, network and server systems, and LAN/MAN data communications paths. You probably won't see much of this on your average desktop system, but it will be part of everyday computing connectivity somewhere in your computing life within the next year.

Summary

We've explored Plug and Play both from its theoretical and practical aspects, and peeked inside the industry's goals and dreams for ideal new PC setups. If even one-half of the configuration benefits mentioned become reality in the next year, most of us will be enjoying relatively hassle-free computing. If we begin to see even less than one-half of the I/O speed benefits offered, then gaming, Web surfing and other typical PC activities will become more approachable, pleasant and productive. Still, there are and will be for some time to come, many mysteries and new considerations for how we'll be able to transition to and use all of these technological advances with existing and new PC systems.

Having covered the rules, and now the promises of things to come, it's time to delve deeper into the realities we face right now—mixing old and new, understanding how they must be made to work together, and finding some practical examples of common pitfalls and their solutions.

CHAPTER 5

THE WINDOWS REGISTRY

Topics covered in this chapter:

- What is the Registry?
- What's in the Registry
- A practical view of Registry data
- How your configuration affects the Registry and how the Registry affects your configuration
- How you can affect changes in the Registry
- Don't neglect legacy and the PC foundation

This chapter will be short but sweet, and to the point. First, for significantly greater detail about the Registry, you should gather up John Woram's *The Windows 95 Registry* from MIS:Press, Ron Petrusha's *Inside The Windows 95 Registry* from O'Reilly & Associates, and/or Rob Tidrow's Windows 95 *Registry Troubleshooting* from New Riders. These are all very comprehensive and friendly works covering the Registry issues from stem to stern. You'll also find lots of cumulative hints about various unsupported devices at the Windows 95 Annoyances

Web site, http://www.creativelement. com/win95ann/, and many bug and patch notices at http://www.bugnet.com. Combined or separately, all of these works and several other on-line references, will either help make you an expert, or make you wish you'd never asked.

What Is the Registry?

In a nutshell (and quite over-simplified), the Registry consists of proprietary Microsoft database files, in both Windows 95 and Windows NT (with important differences between the two) to supplement and in most, but not all cases, replace the old Windows 3.x INI and CFG files. In many cases, a lot of the INI file information is duplicated in both INI and Registry files. INI files still exist in both operating systems for backward compatibility with older Windows software.

In the case of Windows 95, the Registry database exists as two files, SYSTEM.DAT and USER.DAT. Each contain both static and dynamic system- and user-specific information relating to the system hardware, software, and various environmental configuration items.

These files contain at least three data elements for each piece of information represented—a hierarchical key value (an 'HKEY'-prefixed data field) that you might otherwise refer to as the pointer or index field, a data definition value (defining what the data typeactually is within the HKEY reference), and the actual data value itself.

There are six primary or top-level keys:

- HKEY_CLASSES_ROOT
- HKEY_CURRENT_USER
- HKEY_LOCAL_MACHINE
- HKEY_USERS

- HKEY_CURRENT_CONFIG
- HKEY_DYN_DATA

These keys may be seen in Figure 5.1, or by running the **REGEDIT** program provided with Windows 95.

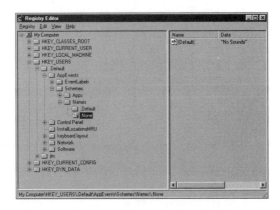

Figure 5.1 Basic Microsoft REGEDIT program dialog.

If you venture further into the Registry with the **REGEDIT** program and expand the key views available (double-click on a key or single-click on the [+] box), it will seem as though you are peeling back layers of a very large and complex onion. (Yes, some of us have shed a few tears in this process too!) What you'll find are sometimes obvious and logical (but most often cryptic and daunting) names, labels, and data values.

Interestingly enough, you'll eventually encounter what appears to be duplicated data values under two or more keys, at different layers. You may at first think that this is the reason your Registry files are so large (my **SYSTEM.DAT** file routinely tops 1 MB in file size). In fact, if you change one of the values, then recheck other duplicate entries, you'll notice that the apparently duplicate values have changed as well. What's going on here?

Not only is the Registry hierarchical in structure, it is also referential. That is, there can be and often are many different pointers or keys that refer to the exact same data points. This is one reason why, aside from the proprietary nature of the Registry, no one can describe exactly what the Registry data structures appear like. Thus, you will probably never see a database utility to convert Registry data into Microsoft Access, Excel, xBase, or other common data formats, as it simply and practically cannot be done.

Although there are duplicate references aplenty in the Registry, there are also non-duplicate entries that can contain the same or similar data. Thus, changing one value may *not* change all or more than one value. How do you know? Without significant research into every key and value, this question may remain unanswered for some time to come.

What's in the Registry

Registry data includes, but is not limited to, the following types of data:

- Basic and detailed system information
- Installed hardware devices
- Hardware configurations
- Installed software
- Software registration information
- Software configuration
- Application and file type associations
- Fonts and display information
- Desktop configuration
- Regional information

- Accessibility options
- User information including desktop profiles and preferences
- Application and file use history

Basically, you name it—if it has anything to do with your system, chances are some reference to it is in the Registry. Oddly enough, much of the information we're looking for in the context of this book is *not* in the Registry, including but not limited to what we might expect of this large configuration database—IRQ, DMA, and I/O information as Windows sees it. That's left up to Plug and Play which we can't get access to.

A Practical View of Registry Data

In actual use, each data value is referenced by or organized with at least one, and in most cases, several sub-levels of keys until the data value is accessed. Thus, a single data value, such as which port my mouse is attached to, may appear several layers down into the Registry hierarchy, as shown in Figure 5.2:

```
HKEY_LOCAL_MACHINE\SOFTWARE\Logitech\MouseWare\Cur
rentVersion\COM1
```

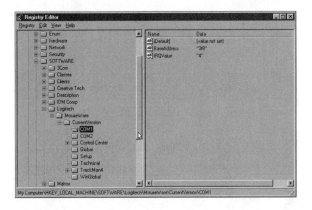

Figure 5.2 The Registry Editor dialog showing mouse port values.

Only in this key field, by the way, can I find any reference to legacy hardware port values (3F8 and IRQ4) for the COM1 I/O port. These are absolute/direct hardware values, and, as we've discussed previously, would be different if logical COM1 were assigned (by the BIOS) to a different port address or IRQ assignment.

The COM 1 port is also listed under two other system configuration keys, as shown in Figures 5.3 and 5.4, but you will notice that in neither of these listings will you see a reference to I/O addresses or IRQ assignments.

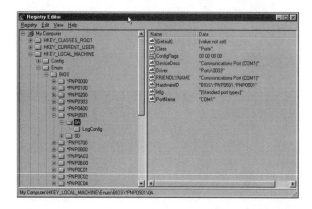

Figure 5.3 The Registry Editor dialog showing enumerated port values.

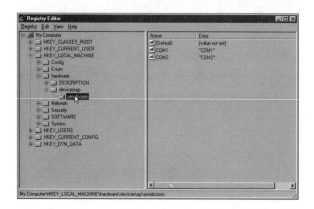

Figure 5.4 REGEDIT dialog showing 'serialcomm' values.

What we seem to be able to draw from this lack of conclusive legacy device information is that the port enumeration process (something Plug and Play and Windows 95 do internally) that associates ports with some predefined 'PnP' device label, (per Figure 5.3) would have to know or be told what 'COM1' or other devices mean or physically are in terms of addressing, IRQ and if applicable, DMA.

It also shows, as illustrated in Figure 5.4, that the 'serialcomm' device that Windows 95 knows as COM1 is indeed related to a data value of 'COM1,'and similarly for the 'serialcomm' device COM2 relates to a value of 'COM2.'

If you delve further into Plug and Play (Chapter 4) and the Registry, you will find that Plug and Play defines many device types and their hardware values during its discovery processes and provides references to them for the operating system's use. Practically and realistically, we simply install a modem via the Control Panel, and then select that modem from within our application's device list by some name or another—foregoing port assignments, etc. If you thought the logical-versus-physical device translations that BIOS does was complicated, PnP just added at least one if not two more layers of translations to the process of simply getting a piece of software to talk to a piece of hardware. What happened to the good old days when computer techies wrote their own programs in BASIC or assembly language to directly address either a simple logical device, or the actual hardware itself?

How Your Configuration Affects the Registry, and, How The Registry Affects Your Configuration

Your system configuration, as detected and set by the following items, has a tremendous effect on the Registry:

- Boot-up/BIOS

- PnP BIOS/ESCD

- Windows SETUP

- Windows Add New Hardware

- PC Card/PCMCIA

- Windows 95 PnP Configuration Manager

The Registry does *not* affect the configuration; it merely stores it and makes the info available to the software and services.

The limited changes you can make to the hardware information stored within the Registry do not activate the Configuration Manager to make changes to the hardware configuration. If you change the Registry, you are only changing the stored information, not the device itself. Microsoft's preferred access into various Registry data is to use the Control Panel and other user-level controls, such as those built into the Explorer dialogs. Further, upon a restart of the system, the information may be changed back to the prior values discovered to exist in the hardware, if you did not otherwise manually change the hardware to match the new Registry values.

How You Can Affect Changes in the Registry

We've shown a few screen shots from our use of the **REGEDIT** program, if only to display data points and illustrate the complexity (and sometimes the lack of data) in the Registry.

While there are times that **REGEDIT** is the most appropriate or only tool available to work directly with the Registry data (for example, to forcibly extract or change application data or remove lingering application references after deleting or un-installing a piece of hardware or software),

REGEDIT may be too cumbersome or risky to use on a regular basis.

WARNING

As with any major or minor configuration change, other utilities and diagnostics that work with Plug and Play and hardware devices can either affect the Registry or make changes that cause the Registry to get out-of-sync with the actual system and make the system unuseable. It can and probably will happen to you if you tinker with the system enough times.

Thus, *BACKUP* the Registry files before working with any configuration items. This means make copies of the **SYSTEM.DAT** and **USER.DAT** files to a safe place, preferably a bootable diskette. Merely exporting the Registry data *does not* make a backup suitable for full recovery purposes. Also, copy the DOS **ATTRIB.EXE** file to the diskette so that you can unlock the .DAT files in the C:\WINDOWS directory. This allows the backup files to be copied back over the corrupted ones.

TIP

If you have to boot from a rescue diskette or to the "Command Prompt," or otherwise copy Registry files because Windows 95 will not run, you need to unlock the existing **SYSTEM.DAT** and **USER.DAT** files, by removing their Read-Only file attributes. This is accomplished by using the DOS **ATTRIB** program, with the following command-lines:

```
ATTRIB -r -a -s -h C:\<windows>\SYSTEM.DAT
[Enter]
ATTRIB -r -a -s -h C:\<windows>\USER.DAT [Enter]
```

(where <windows> = your active Windows 95 location).

You may also need to remove the attributes in the same way to gain access to these files for copying to another directory or a diskette.

Easier Tools to Use for Most Registry Work

Instead of using the **REGEDIT** program to directly, and with considerable risk (since there is no means to "comment-out" or temporarily alter a Registry value for later editing), Windows provides more practical and suitable tools. Backup files of Registry data, **SYSTEM.DA0** , and **USER.DA0**, are made by Windows 95 as it starts up and discovers changed data. Otherwise, you have to backup the data with the Windows 95 **CFGBACK** program. (Available with the Windows 95 Resource Kit.)

We can also affect the Registry indirectly when we start up our system because a hardware detection process runs then, and a similar detection process occurs when new PnP devices or PC Card (PCMCIA) devices are added. We can also invoke this process with the **Add New Hardware** applet in the Control Panel.

The Control Panel is also the home to many other *applets* (little applications) that present and allow changes to Registry data in a context more appropriate to an end-user view of the system components. The standard Control Panel applets in a typical Windows 95 installation are:

- 32-Bit ODBC
- Accessibility Options
- Add New Hardware
- Add/Remove Programs
- Date/Time
- Display
- Fonts
- Joystick
- Keyboard
- Mail
- Modems
- Mouse

- Multimedia

- Network

- Passwords

- Printers

- Regional Settings

- Sounds

- System

- Telephony

Figure 5.5 The Windows 95 Control Panel with additional features.

Typically, you might find yourself interacting with **Add New Hardware**, **Date/Time**, **Display**, **Modems and Printers**, and little else.

The most powerful of the applets is **System**, which contains a Device Manager tab (see Figures 5.6 and 5.7) to access hardware settings. This is our direct access to the Plug and Play Configuration Manager that is so important to PnP devices and PnP BIOS working with Windows 95 (and beyond).

Figure 5.6 The Device Manager dialog.

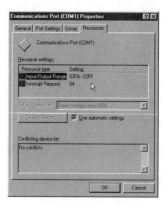

Figure 5.7 The Resources dialog for COM1.

Changing settings in a device's Resource screen may or may not actually reconfigure the device—certainly not legacy/ISA (fixed-setting or jumper or switch set devices, that you must physically change by hand) or those devices that require special device-specific configuration software. Many Plug and Play devices also cannot be either fully or partially reconfigured in the Resource dialog, especially those devices that must have their own special settings in order for the system to function (certain aspects of disk drive and video adapters for example are expected to have fixed assignments—remember the rules).

Similar to the Registry's multiple access points to the same or similar data values, the **Modems** applet also gives us access to the same COM port resource settings you might also access through the Device Manager. So, if it's easier for you to think in terms of your modem when considering COM port values rather than the COM port itself, Windows 95 gives you the option to approach the hardware from a different context.

TIP

Microsoft also provides a very powerful and practical utility called **TweakUI**, available from its Web site at http://www.microsoft. com/windows/download/tweakui.exe. TweakUI provides access to several desktop, mouse and other settings, normally resident but practically inaccessible within the Registry, that can enhance the way Windows 95 behaves. None of the features available within **TweakUI** affect hardware device configurations however.

If you have a portable/laptop system or if your desktop has a PCMCIA/PC Card interface on it, the system configuration can change when PC Cards are inserted or removed. Similarly, "Docked" and "Undocked" portable systems also affect the system configuration because a docking station may contain additional network cards, parallel, or serial ports that are not part of the original/bare portable configuration.

At this point, I won't go into detail about the different resources and values you can access for the various hardware devices in your system. As we'll see in the next section, the Registry and its access methods (**REGEDIT** or the Control Panel) do not give us access to all of the foundation elements we need to deal with to establish and maintain a proper system configuration. Also, some points are better illustrated in Chapter 7, which covers typical conflicts and their resolution.

Don't Neglect Legacy and the PC Foundation

It bears repeating here that as good as Plug and Play and Windows 95's configuration detection and setting features are, they cannot handle the settings for or resolve conflicts with legacy/ISA devices. If the basic system and its devices are not configured properly, no amount of software or fancy user interface or complex Registry data or tools are going to do any good. Also, from Chapter 4, remember that Plug and Play does not always play by the expected or desired standard configuration rules for basic PC devices.

Certainly, as your system boots up, the PnP BIOS detects devices, and as Windows 95 starts up, many devices are determined and configured for us automatically. Sometimes the devices aren't really *configured by* as much as they are *reported to* the Registry and Windows 95 for what they are, so programs can access them. What's really happening is that *Windows 95 is being configured to work with the devices found.* The devices are not being configured to suit Windows 95, since device drivers are used to match specific devices to the Windows environment and functions. Devices are identified and reported in terms of pre-defined PnP device types and attributes rather than discrete hardware devices (those with addresses, IRQ and DMA assignments). If the hardware devices are configured wrong, Windows 95 will be configured wrong; some things just may not work as we'd expect them to.

Changing devices at the Device Manager level may not always affect a change to the hardware—unless the device is a PnP device or otherwise allows the internal Configuration Manager (Resources dialog) to change the resources. Again, typically, this only reconfigures Windows, and we still have to deal with configuring the hardware. This is why Windows 95 will present a dialog telling you to shut down your system, reconfigure the device manually, and start up again, for changes made to many legacy and some PnP devices. So much for Plug and Play—you do the work, the operating system might be able to figure it out after the fact. As discussed in Chapter 4, and as we'll see in Chapter 7, we may not want Plug and Play to do some of these configuration things for us anyway.

For example, if COM1 is misconfigured and there is only one COM port in the system, and that port is (improperly, for being the only COM port) addressed as 3E8h (the COM3 address) using IRQ 4, Plug and Play and Windows 95 will simply accept this port assignment and go about their merry way. If you use the Device Manager to tell Windows 95 that COM1 should be addressed as 3F8h, suddenly the port will become unusable (and the device's dialog will indicate so), because you have not actually changed the port's settings, just those in Windows 95. More confusion. Your misconfigured system (because the COM port itself is misaddressed, mismatching physical versus logical assignments) is now doubly misconfigured because the operating system doesn't match the prior (incorrect) BIOS/logical device assignment.

Yes, Windows 95 and the device attached to the COM port may work just fine in a misconfigured system, if the misconfiguration is compensated for by misconfiguring Windows, but this only complicates future upgrade and maintenance issues you will more than likely encounter through the life of your PC system.

Use or Avoid the Registry for Configuration Management?

The PnP device discovery and configuration routines and the ESCD are responsible for providing the initial system hardware configuration information. If you're hoping to use the Registry to alter or correct a system configuration issue, such as a misassigned

COM port address or IRQ, you may have figured out that this isn't the place to do it. The Registry and the tools that can affect it inside the operating system are not as effective as providing a good configuration *before* the operating system loads up. They deal with what they are told; they do not make any attempt to inform of or perform a configuration correction. It may be obvious that Windows 95 actually allows the use of a misconfigured system, by compensating for the misconfiguration. This may help you get some work done now, but does not help you later on.

NOTE

To illustrate this point, if you *do* operate with a currently misconfigured system under Windows 95, using our example of COM1 being misaddressed (at 3E8h), and assign or change applications to use a modem on that COM1 port as-is, then later add another COM port, addressed (properly) as COM1 or COM2, thereby changing the prior COM1 assignment to become COM2 (remembering our logical rules from before), the application that used a modem on (the prior) COM1 will suddenly find no modem on COM1 and fail.

Although Windows 95 allows you to alter hardware settings, the Registry and **REGEDIT** application are obviously not the place for altering your system hardware configuration—not the least because they do not provide for it. Neither are the Device Manager or any other context-sensitive approaches (such as the **Modems** applet to access COM port settings) the appropriate place to manage your PC's configuration. For at least this reason, the whole of this book, and all of the technology from "PC Day One" and beyond must still be attended to. *We* must manage our own PCs, and as a result, the operating system and applications that use the hardware. We cannot count on the hardware, operating system, or software to do that for us.

It bears repeating that it is imperative to understand that PnP and the operating system *react* more to what is than they pro-actively *establish* or *correct* things to what should be, all legacy/ISA, customary/traditional issues considered.

Instead, the physical system configuration drives or determines how and what the operating system will find to work with. This may not be what we expected of Plug and Play, but then most of us are not, and will not be, dealing with pure Plug and Play systems just yet. When we do, we will have more information available to save us some time and point us in the right direction. By the time we do have 100% PnP systems and no legacy devices to contend with, perhaps too all of the software vendors will fall into better compliance and leave the configuration of devices up to the operating system rather than propagating the need to worry about hardware details.

Summary

Certainly Plug and Play and the Registry have a tremendous influence on our systems, but they are not the exclusive or pivotal points of reference for new PC configuration issues that we've been seeking.

Having discovered that it is rarely if ever effective to go to the Registry to resolve system configuration and conflict issues, and quite possibly detrimental to your system if you doit's probably time to consider just how we actually do address these issues in our current systems, and look ahead to enhancements and expansions.

From here we'll go on to show the configurations and some upgrade examples for a typical system so you can get more familiar with what all of this means.

CHAPTER 6

WORKING INTO THOSE BIG UPGRADES

Topics covered in this chapter:

- Working with the rules
- General configuration precautions
- What to expect from a new operating system
  - IBM's OS/2 Warp
  - Windows 95 and Windows NT
- What you can expect with hardware upgrades
- What to expect from Plug and Play
- Memory types and address ranges
  - An address assignment can consume multiple memory locations
  - Lower memory
  - Upper memory
  - Extended memory

- Virtual memory
- Address decoding
  - Incomplete information
  - Determining if a device uses addressing improperly
- Please excuse the interruption
  - Making the best use of IRQ selections
- Upgrading a typical "clean" 386/486 Pentium configuration
  - Out of the box
  - Getting ready to upgrade
- Plug and Play enters the fray
  - Upgrading to a PnP sound card
  - Upgrading to a PnP network card
  - Adding a SCSI host adaptor
  - When Plug and Play loses its mind

When you consider any upgrade project, especially one as significant for you and your system as a new operating system or a major hardware addition, you should make every effort to ensure that your system is configured properly *before* performing the upgrade. This helps ensure that the upgrade goes smoothly and quickly so you can begin to enjoy it rather than regret it. Of course, this is no different from the advantages of having your system configured properly in the first place, but if you've waited until now to deal with the issue, you may as well deal with it all the way.

The information in this chapter applies before performing any upgrade, including the following:

- Changing to Windows 95 or NT
- Adding a sound card

- Adding a video capture card
- Adding a CD-ROM drive
- Adding a local area network card
- Adding a high-speed modem or a fax/modem
- Changing from IDE (Integrated Drive Electronics) to SCSI (Small Computer System Interface) hard drives
- Mixing IDE and SCSI hard drives

Somewhere in one of these upgrade processes, some device may be found to conflict with another device; a port will be found to be improperly addressed; a logical device will not be available or it will not function as you expect it to. If you're lucky, the installation program for your new sound or network card will help you through the configuration details. Operating system upgrades are considerably more complex, because they must work with *all* devices in your system.

If you're not so lucky, you may be able to get through an upgrade process but, having finished the installation, suddenly, *nothing*. You encounter a system error message and the system is frozen.

Or you're clicking around in a fresh installation of Windows 95 trying to find your system settings, and you decide to add a new network protocol in the Add New Hardware Wizard. In checking your hardware, the Help dialog box appears, telling you, *Device conflicts with another in your system...* What will you do?

You could fight these conflicts for an hour or so and then call another expert or call technical support. Worse yet, you might simply back out of the process, uninstall the upgrade, try it again, or give up and keep using DOS and Windows "the old-fashioned way." Instead of the frustration and within a few minutes—perhaps 30 at the most—you could determine your configuration, correct any problems, and begin enjoying the new upgrade.

Working with the Rules

OTHER REFERENCE In Chapter 2, we discussed the hardware, BIOS, and DOS design rules for PCs. If you have not yet read and followed through with the system inventory and configuration records portions of these chapters, *stop now, go back,* and do some basic configuration management homework. You will be very glad that you did! Having accomplished those steps, you will find the items covered later in this chapter easier to understand and implement.

The rules or design of PC systems could not and did not anticipate the number, variety, and complexity of the devices that have been invented to plug into a PC, even though this may seem a bit odd for a system that was designed by and for engineers. It took many other engineers only a few years to work around the existing rules and fit new devices into the holes and gaps left available in the IRQ, DMA, and I/O design.

The challenges were significant. Engineers designing new hardware had to hope that IBM would not overshadow any new work and try to force major new devices into the existing PC standard. Fortunately for us and several hundred hardware and software companies, IBM—perhaps not knowing what to do with the PC after it was introduced—decided to let the market and new designs flourish on their own (for the most part).

Since the release of the IBM PC to the marketplace, we have seen dozens of innovations that have allowed us to be more productive and comfortable with the PC, and we have been able to enjoy it a lot more. Some of these innovations have come from IBM, and many have come from third-party or aftermarket sources. Not all of them were introduced for the PC initially, but made their way to the PC market as users and investors saw their potential. Among these are innovations and their originators are:

- Monochrome graphics (Hercules)
- Color graphics (IBM)
- Enhanced color graphics (IBM)
- 16-bit data and processing in the i80286 CPU (Intel)
- 32-bit data and processing in the i80386, i80486, and Pentium CPUs (Intel)
- High-resolution color display (VGA)
- Enhanced VGA display (VESA)
- Networking (Novell and others)
- Memory expansions and enhancements (Lotus-Intel-Microsoft and others)
- SCSI, the Small Computer System Interface (an ANSI standard)
- Pointing devices (Xerox)
- Graphical user interfaces (Xerox)
- High-speed modems (Hayes, USRobotics, Ven-Tel, and others)
- High-capacity/high-performance disk drives (Shugart, Seagate)
- CD-ROM drives (Sony)
- Sound and music interfaces (Creative Labs)
- High-performance I/O interfaces (COMPAQ, H-P, IBM, Intel, and others)
- EISA (COMPAQ, Hewlett-Packard)
- VESA Local Bus (Video Electronics Standards Association)
- PCI (Intel)
- Real-time video capture and playback (various)

- High-performance and multiple-processor systems (systems using Intel's Pentium-series processors)

To fit all of this into a system with relatively limited expansion options (considering the original PC design) is indeed amazing. Yet we are here, doing it and enjoying it. Combining and progressing through these features over the years has been tremendously exciting for millions of people. It has caused a great many of us to learn new things and provided untold opportunities for users, designers, programmers, content providers, and the like.

The existing rules have added to the original rules, and just when we think we've run out of room, ideas, and resources, something else comes along to extend the life of what began as essentially a "smart" data terminal.

In the process of upgrading our system's hardware and software, we are going to work with all of the rules and enhancements that IBM and others have provided for us. We will see some limitations and make some judgment calls based on available resources, the hardware we have at hand, the hardware we want to add, and our overall needs. We will also expand on I/O addressing as it relates to the memory types in your system.

NOTE

As we go along, it should not come as too much of a surprise that it may be more efficient to invest in a second PC system, dividing the type of work to be done between systems configured specifically for one type of application and hardware or the other. For instance, one system may be set up with several modems or a mix of modems and network cards to handle telecommunications, while another system could be set up for multimedia production work with scanners, CD-ROM drives, and printers. You would share data between the two systems as a small peer-to-peer network.

If an application works best under one operating system or the other, but this differs from the other applications to be used, configuring the ability to switch operating systems at bootup may also be considered. If information needs to be shared among systems, networking and the attendant configuration issues with that upgrade is another consideration. This is part of the planning and configuration management process, as well: evaluating the type of work you do, what you do it with, and what system configuration will get it done best.

General Configuration Considerations

Most of the precautions in this book apply to all system configurations, but some have special significance for new operating systems and most hardware upgrades. When setting up your system, either to establish an initial configuration or to change devices with an upgrade or replacement, there are any number of known and often unknown limitations we could face. Some of these are the obvious limitations of which I/O addresses and IRQ and DMA channels an add-in device or its software will let us use.

Add-in devices don't always allow complete freedom of choice for their configuration options. Some devices provide a list of fixed options, locking certain addresses, IRQs, and DMAs together without any flexibility. You might find this circumstance with cards that provide only a few jumpers or switches to set only a few predetermined options.

Similarly, not all software allows complete and flexible configuration of the ports, IRQs, and DMA channels it will support. Investigate carefully how configurable a software package is before buying. Many stores will let you view the software on a demo system, allowing you to check out the setup and other features of the package.

Generally speaking, operating system upgrades and use are quite possible and successful. Large companies (Microsoft and IBM) have invested a great deal of time and money in making their products succeed. To do so, the products have to be readily installable.

If you can reconfigure other devices in your system around any limitations your new hardware may present, you'll be OK. If not, consider buying a more flexible add-in device—one that lets you set any configurable item independent of the others.

SPECIFIC DEVICE

In more than one case, accepting a common default network card I/O address of 300h has been known to cause problems with installations of, or changes to, OS/2 and Windows 95. This address is specified by IBM to be for a "prototype card." Even though the address range at 300h has a full 20h locations (300-31Fh) mapped out for it, OS/2 and Windows 95 don't always like this location in some systems. The best solution appears to be to set the network card for an adequate and clear address range, such as 280h, 2A0h, 320h, or 340h. The default IRQ for many networks cards is IRQ3, which obviously conflicts with COM ports 2 and 4; thus, a re-configuration of at least the IRQ is required.

What to Expect from a New Operating System During Installation

For the past several years, software marketing departments, the press, and users have been anticipating the direction computer owners would turn for a higher-performance operating system and interface environment. The old 8-bit DOS we've been using since 1981 has been enhanced by a variety of utilities and user interfaces, from the Norton Utilities to Microsoft Windows (1.0 to 3.x) to Quarterdeck's DESQview/X, but none of these interim improvements has really been able to take full advantage of 32-bit processors, data buses, and just plain speed in getting data from one place to another.

All of the DOS add-ons to date have had to maintain a firm grasp on compatibility with the DOS file systems and other system- and software-related I/O functions so that the same software and files could be shared with older, slower 8- and 16-bit PCs. Since you can't buy a new 8- or 16-bit PC any more, and we demand higher performance in display, data transfer, and program execution speeds, the only choice is to make a full-scale transition of operating systems to make use of the power and speed available in 32-bit PC systems. With the exception of the FAT-32 (Microsoft's new file system definition to use larger drives more efficiently, distributed in later OEM releases of Windows 95), NTFS (Windows NT File System, a completely different and faster disk file tracking system available only with NT), and HPFS (the High Performance File System, available with IBM's OS/2), we still strive to maintain file-system compatibility with good old DOS, just to keep things simple for the time being.

We have also come to expect that systems be easier to set up, easier to use, and easier to fix or upgrade. As you might expect, "easier" should also apply to our pocketbooks. We should be able to enjoy greater productivity at lower cost, and now our demands are finally being met.

We've had access to the UNIX operating system for years; we still do and still will. UNIX is very powerful and works on more types of computers than any other operating system, but it is also very costly and complex to implement and use. There are many attractive and effective graphical user interfaces for UNIX, but they, too, are costly and complex. Even though UNIX is almost universal across various systems, it has never been designed, packaged, or supported for use by the general public. Yet we've wanted to be able to use something with the high-performance, multitasking, interconnection features of an operating system like UNIX.

You can buy LINUX (a UNIX-clone operating system) with a bunch of great little utilities in one or the other how-to books for about $40 in nearly any bookstore in the country. Most high-tech engineering firms have UNIX systems running ever so gracefully on expensive workstations. But, until the UNIX community at large takes us out of the 70s and into at least the 80s or early 90s with a "Joe Average"-can-run SETUP-and-go version, and are prepared to support as much hardware as Windows 95 or NT, and as much software as is currently available for Windows *without* some Windows/DOS emulation software in the middle, UNIX is *not* (yet) for the general public.

Yes, I've built a LINUX system and got it running on my network. I hope to do more with it soon. I've used Sun OS, Ultrix, and a smattering of Solaris. But my available learning curve time versus my need to be productive, as well as that of millions of others, keeps many of us bound in Microsoft-land for mainstream operations. The x86 hardware devices and their problems are here to stay awhile longer. When I can create a Word document on a UNIX-based or like system to share with my PC and Mac friends, the world will truly be a lot better off. Still, an x86-based UNIX or LINUX system requires a proper configuration, just like everything else.

At one time, Microsoft and IBM were co-developing the operating system that became IBM's release of OS/2. Due to a variety of competitive and business differences, Microsoft left OS/2 for IBM to develop by itself while Microsoft pursued a higher-performance variation of Windows, which became known as "NT," for *new technology*. Thus the user market already struggling with the differences in system performance, and the tentative shift to using Windows, had to wait a little longer for Windows NT and/or OS/2 to come on the market and be competitive. Unfortunately OS/2 lost its edge in the marketplace with insufficient stability or applications, and NT is still too expensive for most of us to use as an everyday desktop OS. There are also other concerns about backward compatibility with older DOS programs, especially graphical ones like games and scientific/engineering programs.

Windows NT gained popularity and was implemented on a large number of various platforms and user systems in very special, limited environments. Versions of NT were developed for systems other than x86-compatibles—such as the PowerPC—as a power-user's operating system. OS/2 made it to market and stuttered along mostly in IBM-supported corporate environments until version 2.0 was stable enough for power users to buy and try. Even though IBM made it to market first with a 32-bit operating system that users could afford and work with easily (OS/2), the majority of PC users have a significant investment in Windows and have decided to bet on Microsoft.

By the time Microsoft gave us our first glimpses at test versions at what we heard would be "Windows 4.0" or "DOS 7" or "Chicago" and finally became "Windows 95," IBM had put enough polish and support behind OS/2 upgrades to release version 3.0 as the first 32-bit operating system for the average user. Many of us are enjoying full-time use of OS/2 while running side-by-side comparison tests with Windows 95. There are some tremendous similarities in the two systems' improvements in ease of installation, use, and performance versus DOS and Windows 3.x. Also, these two new operating systems share certain system configuration requirements and precautions before they can be beneficial to the general user market. Indeed, this is what the next few sections are intended to cover—preparation and optimization of your system configuration for the new 32-bit operating systems and some generic upgrades.

IBM's OS/2 Warp

Not to give IBM's impressive new operating system a bad name, but in my experience, OS/2 Warp can be incredibly unforgiving if the system hardware and configuration details are not set up properly. The cryptic, numbered error messages you might receive are unfriendly, poorly documented, and generally not the least bit helpful to you in terms of correcting problems.

Warp comes with a System Information Tool, but this is not normally installed unless you specifically select it at installation time. If you forget to install this tool, when you can't get the new operating system to run you can't get to the tools that might be able to help you solve the problem.

If you have a problem with Warp, go back to DOS, check your configuration, correct any problems found so that your system has no IRQ, DMA, or address conflicts, and start over. An easy Warp installation can take up to an hour of your time if all goes well. A problem-ridden Warp installation may never succeed, consuming entire evenings or days if you let it.

Windows 95 and Windows NT

Windows 95 is impressive and almost fun to experience, even during the installation process. After over two years with this OS I'm still disappointed in one thing: while you can save many personalized configuration items here, you can't save some other critical system settings (like personal desktop preferences), apart from the entire installation, while having Windows 95 ignore bad system/hardware configuration data to do a clean re-installation if something gets confused.

On most systems the installation is remarkably smooth, trouble-free, and reliable for a long time. On still others, owing either to Plug and Play, system board chip set, memory, or peripheral issues, Windows 95 has been a virtual "dog" to install or maintain. The name brand, cost, or perceived quality of a system does not seem to matter in this regard. I have home-built clones that have been trouble-free and high-end commercial systems that have consumed too many days of my time to get working right. How can you tell before you start if you will have installation or maintenance problems with Windows 95 on your system? From the outside, or looking to the inside, you probably can't tell. My suggestion is to check out the Web sites and on-line forums for your system's manufacturer to see what the presence of various FAQ (frequently asked questions) lists, bug fixes, README and patch files can tell you.

Windows NT is admittedly more complex, and in the current release (4.0) does not fully support Plug and Play. However this support should appear in version 5. When installed and running, NT is quite stable and performs very well.

The differences between Windows 95 and NT in this and other regards might be obvious, or not. Windows NT is a much further developed and tested 32-bit operating system. Windows 95 must use DOS as a starting foundation, maintain full compatibility with most DOS and Windows 3.x applications, and support 32-bit applications at the same time, under the same boot and run conditions. This makes for considerable complexity and provides many opportunities for failure, either by hardware or memory conflict. It is often found that many graphical DOS-based programs work better under NT, as it creates better protected and emulated virtual-DOS sessions than Windows 95. Perhaps this is the answer to so many game-players' woes we frequently hear about!

As easy and forgiving as some aspects of Windows 95 are, it too will consume an hour of your time to install, or a day if things don't go well because of a bad system configuration. In any case, be prepared—you have the resources in hand to make it all work.

What You Can Expect with Hardware Upgrades

As often as it's possible to make just about any combination of PC hardware devices work together, there are cases where two devices are just not compatible in the same system. This is usually because one or both devices lack flexibility in their configuration options, or because the software for one device or the other is equally inflexible or just poorly written.

You will find more compatibility problems with older hardware and software (designed when only the PC, XT, or AT systems existed) than you will with most products designed after i80386 systems came along. The latter are faster and take into account more memory addressing and management considerations. Not only were the electronic components used in I/O devices and system boards prior to the i80386 slower than today's components, but the methods used by some manufacturers to address their I/O devices led to conflicts with 16-bit and 32-bit systems. This consideration—the use of older (and likely slower) I/O devices—applies mainly to moving older COM and LPT ports, memory cards, and non-SCSI or non-IDE disk controllers for older-style disk drives into faster 386, 486, and Pentium systems. Some of these older devices may work, but at the cost of limited performance or possible configuration conflicts.

If you have decided to upgrade several items, you should add or upgrade only one feature or component at a time. This prevents you from creating conflicts, ensures that each new device functions properly with your present system, and avoids any confusion that could be caused by trying to deal with multiple configuration issues at the same time.

You will find it beneficial to test each individual upgrade item separately to be sure each works with your system. Then, add each consecutive item back until all of them are in place and working together.

Save Plug and Play upgrade items for last in a multiple upgrade situation, and again, add only one device at a time. This will allow the PnP items to configure themselves around the non-PnP and other PnP items. This one-at-a-time method also allows you to control some of the variables of the PC and operating system's Plug and Play functions.

NOTE

This is our first big hint towards preventing and troubleshooting any device conflict, especially those with Plug and Play devices. While conflicts are not typical with PnP devices, how they become configured—to what resources they are assigned—is greatly affected by what device is installed and set up first.

Memory Types and Address Ranges

Addressing and memory present certain connotations and expectations in terms of your system configuration. There are several significant address ranges, regions, areas, or types of memory in your PC system. By "type," we are't referring to the electronic or technical details of the components involved (such as RAM, ROM, CMOS, FLASH, dynamic, or static), but instead to the typical contents and uses for the memory and its addressing in our systems relative to devices and their configuration.

Discussion of these areas and their differences is also important for operating system setup, memory management, and their use as system resources for some devices and all application programs.

The areas of memory you will encounter with your system configuration are:

- *Base* or *DOS* memory, including lower memory (Type=RAM)

- *Upper memory*, including Upper Memory Blocks (UMB), expanded (LIMS-EMS) memory and BIOS addresses (Type=RAM and ROM)

- *Extended memory*, including high memory (HMA, Type=RAM)

- *Virtual memory*, swap space, or swap file (Type=Disk file)

Memory areas can be represented or expressed without a comprehensive study of computer memory, but those that are pertinent in the context of this book are shown in Table 6.1, and somewhat graphically in table 6.2.

Of these memory types, in the context of hardware configuration management and conflict resolution, only the base memory and upper memory areas are of concern and discussed in depth here. For specifics about your system memory or memory management software, consult the documentation for your system, operating system, and software.

Table 6.1 Memory Addressing Areas

Memory Area	Address Range	Amount
Base or DOS memory	0:0000-9:FFFFh	640K
Lower memory	0:000-0:A00h	64K (within base memory)
System Internal I/O	0:000-0:100h	256 bytes (within lower memory)

Memory Area	Address Range	Amount
Hardware I/O	0:100-0:3FFh	767 bytes (within lower memory)
BIOS data area	0:400-0:4FFh	256 bytes (within lower memory)
DOS data area	0:500-0:5FFh	256 bytes (within lower memory)
DOS	0:600-0:A00h	
Program and data area	0:A00-9:FFFFh	576K
Upper memory	A:0000F:FFFFh	384K
Graphics memory	A:0000-A:FFFFh	64K (within upper memory)
Text display memory	B:0000-B:FFFFh	64K (within upper memory)
Video BIOS	C:0000-C:7FFFh	32K (within upper memory)
Hard drive BIOS	C:8000-C:FFFFh	32K (within upper memory)
LIMS-EMS expanded memory	E:0000-E:FFFFh	64K (within upper memory; see text under "Upper Memory")
System BIOS	F:0000-F:FFFFh	64K (within upper memory)
Extended memory	from 10:0000h	At least 256MBytes
High memory	10:0000-10:FFFFh	64K (within extended memory)
Virtual memory/ swap space	Depends on configuration	Limited to available free disk space

NOTE

The variety of memory addresses shown in the tables in this chapter are expressed in what is called *segment/offset* notation. This notation makes expressing and calculating a wide range of addresses much easier to organize for programmers and hardware designers, and, to some extent, easier for us as well: the numbers aren't as "big" or as hard to do arithmetic on.

Each address includes two numeric ranges; the first is the hexadecimal number for the *segment*, representing a 64K block of memory. The second is the hexadecimal number for the *offset*, the location within—and relative to the start of—the specified segment. Thus, address 0:0h is the first byte in the first 64K of memory, and C:8000h is 8000h bytes from the bottom of the 64k segment twelfth (0Ch equaling 12 in the decimal system).

Since hexadecimal numbering starts with 0, 0Ch is the thirteenth segment and it starts at 768K (12 times 64k bytes) from the first byte of memory. By convention, since the addresses for I/O devices are in the lowest or '0' segment, the segment notation is left off of these in most places, so the abbreviated 378h is really 0:0378h in segment:offset notation.

Similarly, when we are dealing within the same area of memory, such as upper memory, it has been common to combine the segment and the offset together for brevity. Thus, where you may see C800-CFFFh, the segment:offset notation is really C:8000-C:FFFFh. The abbreviated notation is how these addresses typically appear in the documentation for various devices. It is not necessarily incorrect, just seemingly less complicated.

Table 6.2 Memory Mapping from the Bottom Up

Extended memory	to 256M Bytes
System BIOS	64K Bytes
LIMS-EMS memory	64K Bytes
Hard drive BIOS	32K Bytes
Video BIOS	32K Bytes

Text display memory and special video access	64K Bytes
Graphics memory	64K Bytes
Program and data area	576K Bytes
DOS	to 64K Bytes
DOS data area	256 Bytes
BIOS data area	256 Bytes
Hardware I/O	512 Bytes
System Internal I/O	256 Bytes

RAM

RAM, or *Random Access Memory*, is the memory you usually think about when you buy or consider how 'good' a system is. In the PC, XT, AT, and early 386 days, we bought discrete chips in 16, 64, 256, or 1,024 Kbyte increments, 9 or more at a time, to fill rows of sockets on your system board or a memory add-in card. In later 386, certainly 486, and early Pentium days we bought RAM in SIMMs or *Single Inline Memory Modules*, usually 30-pin circuit-board style devices with 9 discrete RAM chips on them. For later 486 and still early Pentium systems we bought, and still can buy, 72-pin SIMMs, and have a three choices as to type of RAM we're getting (at least Fast Page Mode, EDO and now SRAM). Many current Pentium systems and likely all future will only use DIMM or *Dual Inline Memory Modules*, packing still more memory onto a small plug-in circuit board.

RAM is used for native or hardware memory covering Base or DOS RAM (0-640K Bytes) and any Extended Memory (above 1 megabyte) in our system. Upper Memory Blocks, High Memory, and LIMS-EMS memory are special segments of RAM memory created and managed through memory management software, such as EMM386 or Quarterdeck's QEMM product.

RAM is considered pretty fast, and gets incrementally faster as we have progressed from older RAM chips through SIMMs to Fast Page Mode operation to EDO (Extended Data Output) RAM, and recently to SRAM or SDRAM (Synchronous DRAM). All this refers to the electronic technology used inside the chips and how data is addressed and kept fresh inside the system. Normal RAM loses its contents when we shut our systems down, which is one of its drawbacks. CMOS RAM, the kind that holds your system setup parameters and date/time settings, is a special lower power consumption RAM chip that sustains its contents with a small battery, but is much slower than normal RAM.

ROM

ROM, or *Read-Only Memory*, is a special memory component that has data written into it with a special device, but that allows the contents to be read by the system and software we use. It is used in a PC to contain the special boot-up code and parameters for many SCSI disk drive and video adapters not supported by the BIOS and DOS programs. A special type of ROM (Flash ROM) can be written to in-place in the system by special software. It is quite popular in new designs instead of older-style ROM chips because it allows us users to download and upgrade our system and adapter's BIOS code without having to open the box and replace chips. ROMs hold their contents nearly forever without batteries or constant updates to keep the contents fresh.

Virtual Memory

Virtual memory is an allocated file space on the disk drive that is used for temporary storage of the contents of semiconductor or chip memory. It is used when the operating system or a program determines that another program or data set needs more RAM (chip-memory) to work with; then the contents of the RAM is stored to the disk space for later use. This process is called *swapping*.

All multi-tasking operating systems use some form of virtual memory as part of their normal operations. This is more evident in Windows 95, NT, and OS/2 because we seem a little more sensitive to the performance of our systems and all the noise our disk drives make as swapping occurs. Operating systems and applications depend less upon swapping when there is more actual RAM to work with—though it seems like Windows slows down and swaps more if you have more RAM, since it makes a bigger swap file and tries to use it.

In its actual implementation, virtual memory is nothing more than a single large disk file managed by the operating system that has to keep track of the swap file's various contents and how much of the swap file the contents occupy. Because it is used as memory, many system crashes and faults are likely caused by disk errors or confusion in the swap file manager, as much as they are caused by bad programming practices or flaws in the operating system itself.

An Address Assignment Can Consume Multiple Memory Locations

As you refer to the PC, XT, and AT device-addressing tables shown here and in Chapter 2, you may notice that some devices use a range of addresses starting at a given single location. I/O ports, using the serial port address for COM1: as an example, are typically known by a single address. In the case of COM1: it would be 3F8h. This is called the *base I/O address*, but the port really uses a range of addresses from 3F8h to 3FFh, or eight memory locations. Each memory location represents a different portion or function of the serial port: one for data sent to the port, one for control information, and so on. This is typical of many I/O devices.

This issue also pertains to the BIOS addresses for many I/O devices, because the BIOS occupies a wider range of address space and can usually be configured for a variety of different locations within upper memory, as we'll discuss later.

For most add-in devices and all standard devices such as COM ports, we know by design and published standards which addresses and how much address space is "mapped out" for a given device. You will see very few cases in hardware I/O address tables where a standard I/O device is designed to allow addressing overlap, but this does happen.

SPECIFIC DEVICE

One of the most common and little-known cases of potential addressing overlap can occur with a common network interface card; the NE1000- and NE2000-compatible cards. These cards use more than the standard four addresses mapped out for the IBM PC network card (360 to 363h), actually mapping out 20h, or 32 full memory locations, from 360 to 37Fh for data and control information.

You'll see that placing an NE1000- or NE2000-type network card at address 360h will cause the network interface card to overlap the default address for an LPT port at 378h. If you have trouble staying logged on to your network while printing, or you have trouble printing while connected to your network, this is a good place to start looking. Change the network card's address to something else (280h, 2A0h, 320h, or 340h are generally good alternatives).

Lower Memory

We have primarily been concerned with I/O device addressing in what is called the *lower memory* region of the PC system. This region is a 64 Kbyte section of the greater region of memory called the *system base memory* or *DOS memory*, which itself encompasses 640 Kbytes of memory addresses. Within lower memory are stored a variety of system parameters and some parts of the BIOS enhancements and the operating system that are placed there during the system bootup process.

System information software may look at the BIOS and DOS data areas to report on certain logical devices, the state of the keyboard, types of disk drives, and other tidbits critical to the system BIOS and DOS. What we do as part of system configuration affects the information that ends up in these areas.

Hardware I/O Area

In terms of system hardware addressing, we are concerned with a very small range of addresses: the hardware I/O range from 100h to 3FFh. Within this area, based on design and current uses, we have approximately 20 usable hardware addresses within which we can configure our I/O devices.

Anytime there is activity between the CPU and I/O devices, some portion of this memory area is addressed in order to gain access to the hardware, control it, and exchange data with it.

Upper Memory

Upper memory occupies 384 Kbytes of memory range between the base or lower memory area ending at 640 Kbytes and 1024 Kbytes (1 MB). There is, by design, no actual system or accessible RAM memory in this area. In terms of total system memory (base or DOS RAM plus extended memory), this area is skipped over and not used or filled in with RAM. Any system memory greater than 640 Kbytes begins at 1024 Kbytes. Except in some very rare and unusual cases which 99.9% of us will never encounter, I/O devices are not assigned addresses here either (but any BIOS ROMs they have might be). Within this area are specific blocks for specific system functions—the video display BIOS and data paths, the system BIOS, or the BIOS for some of the I/O devices.

This region has been exploited by more than a few system features. Among these are:

- *Shadowing*, or backfilling part of this area with RAM from the Extended memory region, in which system, video, and device ROM code can be placed so it runs faster.

- *Upper Memory Blocks*, or filling this region with RAM from the Extended memory region to place some program code or data in the RAM to relieve base memory use.

Shadowing is a feature that is either built into some systems' BIOS programs, or is provided by memory management software programs. Without going into a lot of technical details, the components that store the system BIOS and any hardware BIOS are many times slower than system memory. By copying or "shadowing" the contents of the BIOS chips into faster system memory chips, many system functions work more quickly. Shadowing is implemented by some system BIOS programs and may be controlled in the system setup screens. This technique may also be complemented by BIOS caching so that the ROM's data is available to the system even faster. In addition to or instead of shadowing, memory management software such as DOS's EMM386 and Quarterdeck's QEMM perform these enhancements with software loaded when you start your system.

Upper memory block (UMB) assignments in this memory region are only provided by memory management software such as EMM386 or QEMM. These software programs may make it possible to use some portions of upper memory for storing and running device drivers and other resident software, including parts of DOS. This is a feature known as *loading programs high* (placing them into UMBs). The drivers and other resident programs you can load high would otherwise consume base memory, leaving less memory for application programs and their data. By loading programs into upper memory blocks, and in some cases also redirecting some of the extended memory into empty upper memory space, EMM386 and QEMM make more base memory available. This leaves more of the full 640K of DOS memory for use by applications software.

Expanded Memory (LIMS-EMS)

Within upper memory, there may be a 64 Kbyte segment configured as the access to *expanded memory*—memory conforming to the Lotus/Intel/Microsoft–Expanded Memory Specification (LIMS-EMS). *LIMS-EMS* is a special type of memory conceived and designed to provide additional memory for a variety of applications on older PC and XT systems that did not have the capability for more than 640 Kbytes of memory. EMS or expanded memory requires special device-driver software (EMM386, QEMM, and the like) and, prior to the i80386 systems, also required special add-in memory cards.

This memory area was intended for the data created and used by large applications, such as the spreadsheet program Lotus 1-2-3. This memory type, and how it is handled, also provided more manageable and useful memory than the extended memory that became available with AT systems (IBM called this *expansion memory*). Later versions of LIMS-EMS also made the first implementations of multitasking and program swapping possible, before the i80386 systems became available. Today, EMS is still useful and available for data storage, disk caching, and loading programs high. It does not bear any special system configuration.

BIOS Addresses

The BIOS for most devices requires 32 Kbytes or 64 Kbytes of upper memory. The beginning address for the device BIOS must typically start on a 16K, 32K, or 64K address increment, although some devices may allow the beginning of the BIOS address to be set in increments as fine as 4K or 8K. A listing of typical and recommended BIOS addresses for certain devices is given in Table 6.3.

Table 6.3 Expected and Optional BIOS Addresses

Device	Expected BIOS Address	Optional BIOS Addresses
Video Card BIOS	C:0000–C:7FFFh	None
XT and AT Hard Disk BIOS	C:8000–C:FFFFh	None (unless SCSI)
SCSI Host Adapter	None	C:8000–C:FFFFh D:0000–D:7FFFh D:8000–D:FFFFh E:0000–E:7FFFh
Network Adapter Boot ROM	None	C:8000–C:FFFFh D:0000–D:7FFFh D:8000–D:FFFFh E:0000–E:7FFFh
LIMS-EMS Memory Page (see Note below)	None	D:0000–D:FFFFh E:0000–E:FFFFh
Plug and Play ESCD storage area	E:8000–E:FFFFh	
IBM ROM-BASIC	E:0000–E:FFFFh	None
System BIOS	F:0000–F:FFFFh	None

NOTE

If you use the enhanced features of memory management products such as Quarterdeck's QEMM program, the 64 Kbyte LIMS-EMS memory page frame may occupy any available and continuous 64 Kbyte address range in upper memory. This is due to special memory handling techniques unique to these products, the discussion of which is handled extremely well in their respective documentation.

The issue of address overlap can be a problem with the BIOS for certain I/O devices, just as it can be with certain hardware I/O addresses. As with hardware I/O addresses, to avoid conflicts you should find documentation pertaining to the amount of BIOS address space the device may need. Some devices may require only 32 Kbytes for the actual BIOS program, but in fact occupy a full 64 Kbytes of address space. This is a critical consideration if you have multiple devices that require BIOS address space. You must be able to configure all of the devices' BIOS to fit into the limited number of address segments without having their total required space overlap. You'll find more on this problem in the section on address decoding later in this chapter.

Extended Memory

Extended memory became available with the introduction of the 16-bit PC/AT system and its additional addressing capabilities AT-class systems based on the 80286 CPU could address up to 16M of RAM.

With the first megabyte of RAM occupied by the 640K of DOS or conventional memory and the 384K of upper memory, 15M of RAM was left for programs to store the data they worked with. This memory area can also be used for creating virtual disk drives or RAM disks, being assigned a logical disk drive designation, and able to "fool" DOS and other programs into using RAM as a very fast disk drive. Extended memory is also a common place to reserve memory for use in *disk caching* (storing frequently used data as it passes between the system and a disk drive), or *printer caching* (holding data on its way to the printer) to improve system performance.

Until MS-DOS 5.0 was released, use of extended memory was limited, because neither DOS nor other programs had a cooperative way to manage the use of extended memory. DOS

5.0 provided the **HIMEM.SYS** device driver, to be loaded at system startup through the **CONFIG.SYS** file, which provided extended memory with better control via an enhancement called *XMS*, the Extended Memory Specification. With XMS, program developers could reliably use extended memory and began to enhance their programs to use XMS instead of EMS (expanded memory). Since extended memory exists as part of the system hardware, rather than being created and managed by a device driver (as when EMM386 creates expanded memory), it can be accessed faster and provides higher performance than EMS.

High Memory

High memory is a 64K portion of extended memory, just above the upper memory area, into which DOS can load one program or set of data, instead of placing that program or data into the lower or base memory. This area is created and controlled by the **HIMEM.SYS** device driver or a similar memory management program. Typically, it is occupied by a portion of DOS itself, when you use the **DOS=HIGH** command line entry in the **CONFIG.SYS** file.

Virtual Memory

Virtual memory or *swap space* is actually a file on your disk drive. The contents of this file change as you change applications. The operating system or environment, such as Windows, shifts the contents of RAM in or out of this file so that the program you are working with has more of the faster RAM to work with. This type of memory is not included in normal memory or I/O addressing.

Address Decoding

While known to be an issue as technology progressed from the 286 days to the 386 and beyond, Plug and Play now pays a lot more attention to the issue of a device's address decoding capabilities.

In the good old days of PC and XT systems, with an addressing capability of only 1 megabyte using 20 bits of address lines, no one cared to facilitate the use of more address bits to fully and properly qualify a device, BIOS ROM, or memory address. (Remember, a PC or XT used 8 bits for data, but still had to be capable of addressing the entire 1 megabyte address range, and does so separately from the data lines.)

I/O devices typically use 12 address bits, covering a total range of 4 Kbytes, more than adequate for the I/O range of lower/base memory (100-3FFh.) I/O devices with a BIOS ROM might properly use the entire 20 bits of addressing lines, or cheat by using only the higher 8 or 12 bits of the 20 address bits.

Ignoring full addresses by not using all of the bits is like telling someone that you live in the 300-block of some street, instead of at 312, and on most streets, the person you tell this to could end up at any of 20 or so houses and consider themselves close enough. However, they may not get to exactly where you want them to be; any house number from 300-399 isn't close enough. In a computer, ignoring the last 4 Kbytes of possible addressing could cause a program to try to read or write data to or from a hardware device, instead of the section of upper memory expected.

Also, if the hardware or device driver software does manage to locate a device on the proper address boundary, they may scrimp on using the logic fully by referring only to a relative or an offset address rather than the full address. They could allow the program or operating system to lose track of the device's full address, causing serious faults in the system's operation.

Computers can deal with the full precision of their given resources. A hardware or software designer who fails to take advantage of this, in order to save money by eliminating a few logic devices on the hardware or a little extra math in the program, is cheating all of us out of what we need and expect, and leaving our systems open to failure.

Incomplete Information

Some devices specify that their BIOS code occupies only 32 Kbytes of space (say from D:0000-D:7FFFh) and don't tell you that the actual ROM that contains this code is a 64 Kbyte device—thus there is something (albeit useless) in the address space of D:8000-D:FFFFh. This can occur in any size BIOS or ROM situation, be it 8 Kbytes of code in a 16 Kbyte device, 16 Kbytes of code in a 32 Kbyte device, or 64 Kbytes of code in a 128 Kbyte device. This is an obvious waste of limited resources, somewhat the inverse of inadequate decoding logic on the device. Ignoring this possibility—or a vendor not telling users about it—can cause a lot of grief if the memory manager or your configuration program can't detect the existence of this ROM device, despite the actual, lesser length of the code in the ROM. Quarterdeck's QEMM program, and to some extent, Microsoft's EMM386 program using the HIGHSCAN option, can avoid excess ROM collisions when trying to allocate Upper Memory Blocks into the upper memory region.

Determining if a Device uses Addressing Improperly

Unfortunately, without getting into all of the details, perhaps even into the schematic diagram with the complete parts listings for a particular piece of hardware, you won't know exactly what resources the device occupies (as opposed to those it actually uses). The device documentation or packaging may yield some clues, but as yet, truth and complete and proper disclosure in advertising in this highly technical marketplace does not seem to have caught on. If hardware designers flooded their boxes with all of this technical data, it may seem a little too daunting. ("Do we really have to know all this stuff just to use a computer?"), though I contend we all have some responsibility to provide and comprehend a considerable amount of technical information. It's either that, or we pay someone else to know and deal with this stuff.

Along with the items covered thus far, Chapter 7 covers common conflicts and their solutions; this will highlight most of the things you may encounter. In Chapter 8 we'll cover software tools that give us a lot of information about what areas of memory are occupied by detectable devices.

Please Excuse the Interruption

The PC accommodates only one hardware interrupt input to let it know that something needs its attention. Because of this, the IRQ signals from I/O devices are sent first to a component on the system board known as the *interrupt controller*. This component handles up to eight possible interrupt signals, providing for IRQ 0 through 7. It also assigns a priority to the interrupt signals it receives. Priority is given to the lower-numbered IRQs. The system clock is given the highest priority, using IRQ 0, to keep the computer's "pulse" going, and the keyboard is given the second-highest priority, using IRQ 1, so you can get the computer's attention.

Only one interrupt controller is present on the 8-bit IBM PC- and XT compatible systems. It's responsible for sending all hardware interrupt information it receives to the CPU. It also sends, when the CPU "asks" for it, the identification of which IRQ line generated the interrupt activity.

AT-compatible (16- and 32-bit) systems contain two interrupt controllers, with the second one handling IRQs 8 through 15. Since the CPU provides only one connection for one interrupt controller to signal the CPU, the interrupt signal from the second component is connected to the IRQ 2 input of the first interrupt controller. Since IRQ 2 receives the next highest priority after the clock and keyboard, and it gets input from the second component's IRQs 8 through 15, these higher-numbered IRQs actually receive higher priority than the lower-numbered IRQs 3 through 7.

Add to this a PCI bus and controller with only three interrupts and feed the PCI interrupt into the second interrupt controller circuit, and you have to wonder how it can all work strung together like this. Amazingly, it all does, and though it's probably still not an ideal system, it's all we have.

Making the Best Use of IRQ Selections

High-speed communications programs, working with modems making connections between two PC systems, will perform better if they are on COM2: using IRQ 3 (or on COM4: using IRQ 3, but not at the same time that COM2: is being used) because IRQ 3 gets a relatively high priority. This is either by design or luck as far as the PC and XT systems are concerned; hard drive use (IRQ 5), printing (IRQ 5 or 7) and diskette use (IRQ 6) are not as interrupt-intense. This practice seems to fall apart when we get to higher speed AT-class systems, except that they are faster, and the devices that use higher priority interrupts 9-15 are also not as interrupt-intense.

At connection speeds of 9600 bps or higher, even with the benefits of using the popular NS16550AFN UAR/T (serial port) chip (or after-market equivalents), it is recommended that you give high-speed communications all the priority and CPU time you can to avoid loss of data as it is transmitted, received, and handled by your communications software.

WARNING

Because COM ports are logical devices, preassigned by the system BIOS to physical serial ports and IRQs, you should not try to change the IRQ settings of COM ports to an available higher-priority IRQ line (9 to 15) unless you can and want to reconfigure your software for this type of configuration. Windows and Plug and Play do allow for this reconfiguration, but it is unusual and often overlooked, and it could make support difficult later on. (See Chapter 2 for an explanation of logical devices and how they're assigned.)

NOTE

Also in the realm of high-speed communications and IRQ priorities, configuring 16-bit network cards for either IRQ 9 or 10 will ensure efficient network communications since networks operate much faster than serial ports.

Similarly, if you are doing high-quality/high-speed multimedia work, you may wish to configure your sound or video capture card for a higher priority IRQ (9-15) if the card and its software provide for this configuration.

Upgrading a Typical "Clean" 386/486/Pentium Configuration

Now we'll look at two system configurations, covering the most available and obvious aspects of system configuration: one before we add in new features and options, and another that includes everything you might find in a fully equipped, networked, multimedia PC.

Jumping right into a 386, 486, or Pentium configuration does not necessarily ignore the many PC, XT, and AT systems that are still in use. The rules applied to, and primary resources available on a PC (8088-CPU-based system) and an 80486- or Pentium-based system are fundamentally the same, except that a 286, 386, 486, or Pentium system provides more IRQ and DMA channels. Likewise, many of the problems and problem-solving processes are the same for all types of PC systems. However, because the PC and XT systems have limited resources, it's unlikely or often impossible to consider these systems as upgrade candidates for the types of software and hardware we want to run, or which we will encounter problems with today.

For our purposes, we must take for granted in our example many of the built-in items and some unusual low-level system configuration items that are in use and can't be changed. These include the system's keyboard, memory, and clock circuits, and pre-assignments made for diskette IRQ and DMA resources.

Out of the Box

Most new PC systems sold today come equipped with the basic features and software that we will need to get started in computing. These include display, data storage, some facility for a mouse or pointing device, and access to communications features. These are provided with common I/O ports and default settings that work in almost every system for most of the common applications software. If you buy a complete new system, these features are expected to exist and work properly. A typical configuration you might expect to find is listed in Table 6.4.

Table 6.4 A Typical Basic System Configuration

Device	Address	IRQ	DMA	BIOS Location
Serial port/COM1:	3F8h	4	N/A	N/A
Serial port/COM2:	2F8h	3	N/A	N/A
Parallel port/LPT1:	378h	7	N/A	N/A

Device	Address	IRQ	DMA	BIOS Location
Diskette drives	3F0h	6	N/A	N/A
Hard drive (IDE)	1F0h	14	N/A	C:8000–C:FFFFh (32K)
PS/2-Mouse port	64h	12	N/A	N/A
VGA video	3B0-3BBh and 3C0-3DFh		N/A	C:0000–C7FFFh (32K)
Internal use (BIOS)	No hardware address	0, 1	0, 2, 4	F:0000–F:FFFFh (64K)
NPU (Numeric Processing Unit) (if present)	No hardware address	13	N/A	N/A

Based on the resource allocations listed in Chapter 2, this basic configuration leaves quite a few system resources available for expansion, shown in Table 6.5.

Table 6.5 System Resources Left Available for Expansion Use

Resource Type	Resource Units
Addresses	130h, 140h, 280h, 2A0h, 300h, 320h, 330h, 340h, 360h
IRQs	2, 5, 9, 10, 11, 12, 15
DMA Channels	1, 3, 5, 6, 7

NOTE

Table 6.5 was derived by subtracting the already assigned resources in Table 6.4 from the total of all available types of resources. This process of elimination, and tracking what's used and what's not, is key in configuration management. You will probably want to keep a list of these items handy as you work with your PC's configuration, rather than doing the work in your head. Unfortunately, most system information software that you might use to detect resources will indeed only report what is in use most of the time, but not what is left available.

Getting Ready to Upgrade

The lure of virtual travel to exotic places through new e-mail pen pals, the sights and sounds of innovative World Wide Web pages, exciting multimedia CD-ROM offerings and games can be resisted no longer. We've decided to upgrade, and we're going to do it all at once, since we'll have the covers off and the wires exposed.

Hmmm, inside this system doesn't look like it's going to provide us with a scenic coastal drive; it's more like an endless, narrow, twisty mountain road, or some 14-car freeway pile-up. Still, we'll drive on and see where this search for adventure takes us.

Let's start with the configuration of some common devices as they are taken out of their boxes. The first step is to list the system resources these devices are set up to use *before* we fiddle with installation programs, switches, and jumpers. If we upgrade this system by installing as many new devices as we can think of, our initial new configuration might begin to look like Table 6.6 (minus what's already in the system).

Table 6.6 The Default Configuration for Common Upgrade Devices

Device	Address	IRQ	DMA	BIOS Location
Serial port/COM3:	3E8h	4		
Serial port/COM4:	2E8h	3		
Parallel port/LPT2:	278h	5		
SCSI adapter	330h	11	5	
				D:8000–D:FFFFh (32K)
Sound card	220h	5	1	
MIDI port	388h			
Network card	300h	3	3	

If we overlay Table 6.6 with the details of the original configuration (Table 6.4), we begin to see some conflicts already, as shown in Table 6.7 Conflicts or duplications are indicated with an asterisk (*).

Table 6.7 The Upgraded Configuration Before Resolving Conflicts

Device	Address	IRQ	DMA	BIOS Location
Serial port/COM1:	3F8h	4 *		
Serial port/COM2:	2F8h	3 *		
Serial port/COM3:	3E8h	4 *		
Serial port/COM4:	2E8h	3 *		
Parallel port/LPT1:	378h	7		
Parallel port/LPT2:	278h	5 *		
Diskette drives	3F0h	6	2	
Secondary diskette or tape drive adapters	370h	6	2	
Hard drive (IDE)	1F0h	14		C:8000–C:FFFFh (32K)
PS/2-Mouse port	64h	12		
VGA video				C:000–C:7FFFh (32K)
SCSI adapter	330h	11	5	D:8000–D:FFFFh (32K)
Sound card	220h	5 *	1	
MIDI port	388h			
Network card	300h	3 *	3	
Internal to system		0, 1	0, 2, 4	F:0000–F:FFFFh (64K)
Reserved (NPU)		13		

After a quick review, two conflicts should be quite obvious: the new network card is trying to use IRQ 3 with COM2:/COM4:; and the new sound card is trying to use IRQ 5 which LPT2: is using. Deciding which device gets to keep its assignment and which one must change is first determined by knowing what the rules are. Then, resolving these conflicts is relatively easy.

I've flagged but do not consider there to be a real conflict (yet) between COM1/COM3 and COM3/COM4, because this is a given according to the rules. As we saw earlier in this chapter, IRQ 3 is designed to be assigned to both COM2: and COM4:. While this can be a conflict in itself, we must first adhere to the original standard. This means that the COM ports retain the IRQ 3 assignment and the network card must be given a new assignment.

Our First Conflict Solved

Which IRQ we assign to the network card depends a great deal on how many different ways we can configure this card. If it is a 16-bit network card that provides the options of using IRQ 2, 3, 4, 5, 7, 9, 10, or 11, we should opt for one of the other available IRQ settings. Obviously it should not be 4, 5, 7, or 11 because the COM ports, LPT ports, sound card, and SCSI host adapter are already using these. The obvious choice for a fully configurable network card seems to be IRQ 10. If the card is an 8-bit card, usually only IRQs 2, 3, 4, or 5 would be available, so IRQ 2 would be the only choice, so far.

NOTE

Check the type of network card you have carefully. If it is an NE2000-compatible, and Windows 95 detects it and assigns an NE2000 driver to it, then you can be limited as to the resources allowed according to the NE2000 specification. This is not much of a problem if the card comes with its own driver that allows it to use the full range of available addresses and IRQs.

But there is more to consider in this choice. In a 16-bit system, IRQ 2 receives all of the interrupt activity from the second interrupt controller, and it is recommended that a device that would normally use IRQ 2 be moved instead to IRQ 9. Since you can't get access to IRQ 9 with an 8-bit card (the connection is simply not there), IRQ 2 will have to be assigned to and share any use of IRQ 9—if your applications can properly discriminate between which hardware uses IRQ 2 and which uses IRQ 9. The only way you'll know may be to set up the configuration using both IRQs, use the software for the devices that use IRQs 2 and 9, and see if any problems arise. If either of the applications does not work properly, you will have to reconfigure one of the devices to use a different IRQ. This is one case where some configurations that should be allowed are not adequately supported by application programs, and the detection and resolution of such problems is by trial and error. Of course, we're trying to prevent trial-and-error configuration processes, and can very often do so.

Our Second Conflict Solved

Going on, we'll resolve the IRQ 5 issue between the LPT2: port and the sound card. There is a little-known consideration to bring up at this point: most applications that support LPT port functions (printing) do not have any provision for or ability to use the IRQ. Those that do use IRQs during print operations would be said to provide *interrupt-driven* printer handling—for example, the remote print server application (RPRINTER) for Novell NetWare and the interrupt-driven printing option for OS/2 Warp. (Unlike earlier versions of OS/2, Warp requires an IRQ for LPT port functions only if you have added the **/IRQ** option to the **DEVICE=PRINT01.SYS** line in your OS/2 **CONFIG.SYS** file.)

Since we are probably not dealing with a NetWare server or print server here, or at least not one with a sound card, and with the rarity of interrupt-driven printing in mind, we *could* keep the sound card on IRQ 5 and move on. However, there are other uses for the parallel port to consider: applications such as Traveling Software's LapLink which provide high-speed system-to-system file transfer features can use specific interrupts; and there are parallel-port connected network adapters and external SCSI host adapters we might use sometime. Programs that use the parallel port with these options may need the IRQ signal intended for the parallel (LPT) port. You may also have to assign a DMA channel for some applications that use Enhanced Parallel Port (EPP) functions.

We'd *prefer* a really "clean" system configuration so we don't encounter problems later on, but we might not always get it. As with the network card example, if the sound card is a 16-bit device, it should allow us access to IRQ lines 2, 9, 10, and 11, and possibly others. Early cards allowed only the choice of 2, 5, or 7. Since IRQs 5 and 7 are assigned to LPT ports, we could use IRQ 2 if it doesn't have to be assigned to the network card. Under the most ideal circumstances, and if the card or the drivers for the operating system allow for it, all these choices would be great. Unfortunately, in one case or another, we may run into limitations outside of our control. While I could probably use IRQ 2 or 9, Creative Labs' Sound Blaster and compatible cards seem to prefer IRQ 5, and many Windows 95 drivers for these cards do not allow the use of any other IRQ assignment, so we'll stick with this non-standard convention. This conflict is resolved more by reason and understanding our present needs and applications than by hard-and-fast rules.

NOTE

If you're lucky enough to be able to use network/server-based printing, perhaps you only need the one LPT port (LPT1: at 378h using IRQ 7) for all of your external peripheral needs and the sound card can continue to use IRQ 5, as in our example.

We're already beginning to encounter decisions and trade-offs in what types of things we are currently or might be using our computer for. Weight the options and consider carefully.

We'll leave the sound card at IRQ 5. The resulting configuration appears in Table 6.8.

Table 6.8 The Upgraded Configuration After Resolving Conflicts

Device	Address	IRQ	DMA	BIOS Location
Serial port/COM1:	3F8h	4		
Serial port/COM2:	2F8h	3		
Serial port/COM3:	3E8h	4		
Serial port/COM4:	2E8h	3		
Parallel port/LPT1:	378h	7		
Parallel port/LPT2:	278h	5		
Diskette drives	3F0h	6	2	
Hard drive (IDE)	1F0h	14		C:8000–C:FFFFh (32K)
PS/2-Mouse port	64h	12		
VGA video				C:0000–C:7FFFh (32K)
SCSI adapter	330h	11	5	D:8000–D:FFFFh (32K)
Sound card	220h	5	1	
MIDI port	388h			
Network card	280h	10		
Internal to system		0, 1	0, 2, 4	F:0000–F:FFFFh (64K)
Reserved (NPU)		13		

Well, this new upgraded configuration looks pretty good. Everything has a workable assignment—or does it? What about the COM ports sharing IRQs 3 and 4? Is there *any* way to resolve this potential problem?

In most cases, not all of the COM ports are used at the same time. If we have, in the past, used some COM ports at the same time we were using other COM ports, we've probably encountered some lockups, slow performance, scrambled e-mail messages on screen, or loss of data. Typically, if you have a mouse or other pointing device that uses a serial port, it is connected to COM1:.

Using Multiple COM Ports

You may have a need to use COM3: or COM4: at the same time as COM1: or COM2:. This situation will normally create an IRQ conflict between COM1: and COM3: or between COM2: and COM4:, since they occupy (but do not really share) the same IRQs.

A workaround might be to take advantage of the possibility that the LPT ports may not need to use the IRQs assigned to them. (DOS and Windows don't; OS/2 and a Novell network server provide the option to do so or not.) This would give us IRQs 5 and 7 to work with. This will work only if the software to be used with COM3: and COM4: can be reconfigured to allow the use of IRQs 5 and 7 respectively, and the I/O device provides switch or jumper settings so you can set the device for either of these non-standard (for COM ports) IRQs. Many new add-in COM port boards offer more IRQs to choose from—2, 3, 4, 5, 7, 9, 10, 11, and 12—so we may not be stuck with compromising on only 5 and 7, especially if IRQ 5 is in use by your sound card, as is quite common.

If you need to use two COM ports, your mouse is on either COM1: or COM2: and if you have a PS/2-style mouse connection on your system, change your mouse to one with a PS/2-style connection to free up the COM port you are using now. Some pointing devices come with or can use a special adapter cable to convert them from a serial port connection to a PS/2-style connection.

There aren't many easy options for using multiple COM ports no matter how you look at it. Usually something in the configuration has to give, either in hardware or in software.

Plug and Play Enters the Fray

Furthering our quest for more, faster and better, we've decided to (or had to because of a failure) swap our network card for a newer model, decided to upgrade the old sound card to a fancier version, and add a CD-ROM writer to the system. To make it all even more interesting, our system board is fully Plug and Play compatible, including the built-in hard drive adapter, and everything we're adding or upgrading with is also PnP-compatible. And of course, we're using Windows 95.

This sounds great, doesn't it? All we have to do is remove the old boards, forget the address, IRQ, and DMA mess, plug in the new devices and off we go...

What happened?

First, let's not toss out everything old and toss in everything new all at once. Following this principle, a good question to ask is "exactly what *do* we want to change or add first?" Tough choice, huh?

A tactic that has been successful for me is to consider each device in the order we want resources assigned, or that we will eventually assign them, since Plug and Play will try to fit devices into available resources in somewhat as-available or perhaps even numerical order. This gives us a little more control over Plug and Play's "crap shoot" process. If we can assert and nail down a desirable configuration for each device, one at a time, the variables tend to fall by the wayside.

Upgrading to a PnP Sound Card

In this case, the sound card seems to be the first device we'd want to change. Not only does it use lower-numbered IRQs, it can also use more resources than any other single device, since it probably supports MIDI as well as WAV operation.

Having removed our old sound card before putting in the new, initially PnP may find IRQs 9, 11, 12 and maybe 15 available and try to assign one of these to the card. We may or may not get the IRQ 9 assignment we used before. Fear not; Windows 95 will let us reconfigure this if we want to, and with the other devices coming along, we probably do.

When your system boots up after installing the new sound card, you may or may not see messages appearing on screen that indicate the presence of the new card, and/or an ESCD update message with some PnP device information listed. Whether this information is displayed or not depends entirely on your system's BIOS. Systems from IBM, COMPAQ, and H-P do not display this information. Generic or clone system BIOS, such as that from Award, often will show the information. For COMPAQ systems you can access the information in the system's built-in Setup program (later model systems with diagnostic boot sections of the disk anyway.) H-P systems usually require that a special Setup program disk be used to work on the system's setup.

Once Windows 95 starts up, it will probably flash up a dialog indicating that it has detected new hardware, perhaps is even removing old hardware from the configuration, and may require you to restart the system to enable it. If all goes well, your system will start up properly and you'll have sound still/again. If not (or in any case), we probably want to see what our new configuration is.

To see what's what we need to get into the Plug and Play Configuration Manager portion of Windows 95, otherwise known as the Device Manager. To do this, find the Control Panel, either through the **My Computer** desktop icon or the **Start Menu//Start/Settings** selection, and open it. Once the Control Panel is open, double-click on **System**. You'll see four tabs across the top of the dialog, one of which is the Device Manager. Click on this tab and then you'll see a list of all the devices in your system, from a somewhat high level.

Locate the **Sound, video, and game controllers** listing and double-click on it, or click on the **+** sign next to it. This will reveal the various types of devices contained on your new sound card. Our concern here is for the WAV or perhaps Sound Blaster-compatible device in this sublisting. Double-click on it and you'll get a new General information dialog box with more tabs at the top. Select the tab labelled **Resources**. Figure 6.1 and 6.2 show, those precious resources of interest—IRQ, DMA, & I/O.

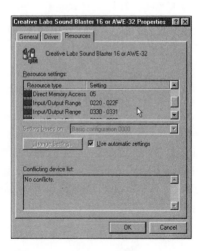

Figure 6.1 Resources display showing addresses for a typical sound card.

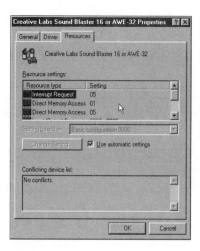

Figure 6.2 Resources display showing IRQ and DMA for a typical sound card.

In this case we got lucky; our sound card ended up configured just the way we wanted it to be, or perhaps, as much as the driver would let it be (address 220h, IRQ 5, DMA 1). Attempts to change any of these values maually (by unchecking the **Use automatic configuration** box and double-clicking on the resource name we want to change) results in a message box telling us that these values can't be changed. Plug and Play didn't help us much here. Both the device and the driver limited our ability to work on the configuration.

It's probably a good thing we chose this device first or another device may have taken the only resources that this card could use, although PnP is also supposed to check to see if a device in question can be changed, and if not, move other devices around to accomodate the unchangeable device.

Upgrading to a PnP Network Card

Moving right along, the next existing device we have to upgrade would be the network card. I'd select this device rather than the new CD-ROM device, because we also know that this type of device does work in our system and with what resources.

Beware a very important factor with this upgrade. If you are changing from a generic/NE-2000 style card to to something completely different, all of your networking parameters will have to be reentered for the new card (network number, workgroup, and IP address, DNS, gateway/router information, etc.). If changing from one style (non-PnP) to a new style (PnP) but not changing the card make/model/type, the new card *must* be configured to use the same resources as the original; then, usually, the network parameters do not have to change. Still, you should have all of this information written down, copied from the appropriate Network dialog—usually the one for the TCP/IP protocol, shown in Figure 6.3 below.

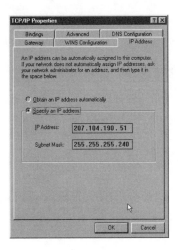

Figure 6.3 A typical Windows 95 TCP/IP Network Configuration screen.

Once you've determined and logged the network information you needed to retain for possible reentry after the network card upgrade, we can proceed.

Having shut the system down, removed the old card, and replaced it with the new, and begun to restart your system, you again may or may not see PnP and ESCD update information appearing on your screen. Windows 95 will likely indicate that it has found new hardware, and needs to restart, or not. After this we can go back to the Device Manager, locate the Network card listing and see our results, as shown in Figure 6.4 below.

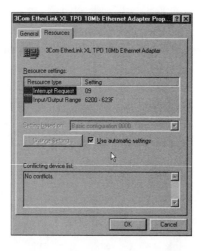

Figure 6.4 Network adapter resources.

Do you notice anything unusual about this figure? Well, yeah, the IRQ is set to 9, but we'll fix that. How about the I/O address? 6200-623Fh? This one happens to be a PCI network adapter card, and as such it uses a completely different address and data bus than our previous legacy device. We needn't worry about the address, but I really prefer that the network adapter have its own IRQ (10), rather than possibly sharing as IRQ 9 does with IRQ 2. So, can we change this, and if so, how?

In most cases you can uncheck the **Use automatic settings** box, highlight the attribute/resource to be changed, and select **Change Setting...** or double-click the resource to be changed. Then you'll be presented with a a dialog box containing the resource and controls to raise or lower the value indicated. If your system, the device driver, or device does not allow the settings to be modified, you will see a message box telling you so. In these cases, you may need to run the configuration utility specific to that device to affect a resource change.

Sometimes you have no choice, and no opportunity to intervene in the Plug and Play process. This can become a real problem if you elect to install a non-PnP device with limited resource configuration ability, or a PnP device that is stubborn about its configuration, once your existing system is all set up and working fine.

The section about Plug and Play losing its mind will give you the good news and the bad news.

Adding a SCSI Host Adapter

Finally, we'll add our SCSI host adapter, as a typical interface for many document scanners and writeable CD-ROM drives. Here again, Plug and Play has established the configuration for us, though we may wish to intervene and set the configuration manually if we have preferences and if the sytem allows us to do so. Our resulting SCSI configuration (Figure 6.5) cannot be changed, but PnP has found and set non-conflicting resources for us.

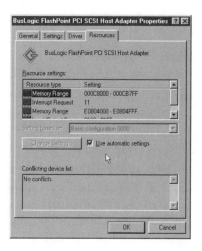

Figure 6.5 SCSI host adapter resources.

When Plug and Play Loses Its Mind

If for some reason your system crashes, or you played with some Plug and Play utility, a virus gets you, whatever, and things are really messed up, you may have to drop back a few yards and start your system configuration over again.

This would mean stripping the system of all devices not critical to booting the system up (e.g., leaving the video and disk adapters in the system and enabled), then restarting to let the BIOS, PnP, and Windows 95 reset themselves with a basic system configuration. PnP will then forget about the other devices that are no longer there. Windows 95 will probably complain about one device or the other that it knew it had but can't find anymore, but it should run.

Once this basic configuration is reestablished, you can then begin to reinstall your modem, network, sound card, CD-ROM, scanner and other adapters, in some order.

The order in which you reinstall devices may be determined by chance, by previously known behavior, or configuration limitation of the device. If you have legacy/ISA devices such as COM ports or modems that ought to be accounted for first, that's probably the place you should start.

If your COM ports are built into the system board and already configured with the new startup, then you would start installing other devices by the order in which you want IRQs assigned to them so that they get proper or desired IRQ priority handling when they run. Ultimately you may reinstall the devices in the order in which you need them to go to the next step. It might make more sense to install a CD-ROM adapter card (or your sound card if it hosts the CD-ROM interface) if you'll need the CD-ROM to be available to reinstall networking or other drivers. Otherwise, you may need to have the network interface available first if you download drivers from a local server or off the World Wide Web through your local area network.

If you're looking for logic and reason from Plug and Play here, you probably won't find any other than that which you impart on the system yourself.

If you are lucky enough to have a system and devices that allow you to use **Set Configuration Manually** through the Device Manager in Windows 95, or another similar function in another operating system, my technique for fooling Plug and Play is a little like that kid's game where you have 15 moveable little numbered square pieces in a frame with 16 holes. You have to move other pieces to make room for or navigate still more pieces to get the right openings in the right places and the right pieces in the right places. OK, so you may think of this to be a little more like the Rubik's Cube toy; it can be that mind-boggling.

Since I prefer my systems to have a predictable and known assignment for IRQs and such, I have to look into each device's **Device Manager//<device>//Resources** tab to see what is where, thus giving me an idea of what resources are unused and available. This way, I can change one or more devices to get the desired affect.

If my network card is currently on IRQ 9 and I want it on IRQ 10, but my video card has IRQ 10, I'd probably look to see if I could move the video card to IRQ 15 (if it's not in use), then move the network card to IRQ 10. Since IRQ 15 might be used later for the second IDE disk drive interface, I'd probably go back to the video card Resources tab and change the video card to use IRQ 9 instead. Windows 95 will update the PnP data and in most cases will let me continue to use the system without a restart.

Thus, I've deliberately affected my configuration to suit what I want it to be, rather than leaving it any more up to chance than necessary.

The successive process of one-device-at-a-time may look a lot like what you'd try to do for resolving conflicts with legacy/ISA devices or basic system troubleshooting. Again, we've come a long way to get to about the same place that we started at. Isn't technology wonderful?

Summary

This chapter has taken on a lot of diverse topics in an attempt to put the PC configuration rules and upgrade concerns into the integrated perspective of a typical hardware upgrade.

What we've discussed should serve as a model for the many considerations that are encountered with most systems. It is unlikely that too many systems will differ from our example.

Many systems will benefit significantly from duplicating our configuration as shown.

To take a different approach to demonstrating how to follow the rules and implement them in a typical system, Chapter 7 covers examples of resolving some of the most common conflicts.

CHAPTER 7

TOP TEN CONFLICT AREAS AND HOW TO DEAL WITH THEM

Topics covered in this chapter:

- Number 1: IRQ signals

- Number 2: DMA channels

- Number 3: I/O addresses

- Number 4: Windows 95 won't complete installation or run with a network card

- Number 5: coincident printer port and network card problems

- Number 6: coincident network card and SCSI Host adapter problems

- Number 7: there's no sound, the sound card output stutters, or voices sound like the computer took a deep breath of helium

- Number 8: Windows SETUP indicates not enough memory to run **SETUP**

- Number 9: games or windowed DOS applications appear fuzzy, or colors are changed between windows and windowed DOS sessions, or the system just plain locks up when changing programs

- Number 10: but I really need to use more than two COM ports at one time

- Bonus points

In this chapter, we will discuss some of the most common questions and conflicts encountered with PC system configurations and provide some quick solutions. Some of the items will be straightforward: "If *this,* do *that.*" Some of the items will be a little more anecdotal.

If you've rushed right into this chapter from the front cover, you may find it more beneficial to take the time to at least look over Chapters 1, 2, 4, and 5, which provide a lot of helpful introduction, background, and reference information that lead up to the direct conflict resolution we'll encounter here. If you've gone through all of the chapters, you'll recognize many of these items from the in-depth coverage already given them, but they're worth highlighting here because they are frequently-encountered conflict problems. Without further delay...

Number 1: IRQ Signals

Taking each IRQ line one at a time in a summary format, we'll break them down into the devices that might be configured on them, where the most conflicts seem to be, and what seems to work best in most cases. (See Table 2.10 for IRQ information in table format.)

TIP

The most common IRQ conflicts I hear about are between the two COM ports that are used for a mouse and a modem. A typical symptom is that an on-line session with the modem crashes whenever the mouse is moved, or the mouse fails to work whenever an on-line connection or fax call is made. If both the mouse and the modem are connected to COM1 (IRQ4), this problem is usually avoided by re-assigning the modem to use COM2 or COM4 (IRQ3). If you have two modems, you might wish to assign them to COM2 and COM4, suffering an apparent conflict between them at IRQ 3, *but simply don't use both modems at the same time!* Otherwise, a couple of my more unusual alternate IQ assignments for a COM port (5 or 7) might be better for your situation.

IRQ 0: Assigned to and used internally for system timing. The IRQ 0 signal line is never available to add-in cards; it is connected only to the internal system board circuits. If a conflict appears to arise with this IRQ, as indicated by system information software,the chances are that your system board is bad. A diagnostic program may help determine if this is the case.

IRQ 1: Assigned to and used internally for the keyboard. The IRQ 1 signal line is never available to add-in cards; it is connected only to the internal system board circuits. If a conflict appears to arise with this IRQ as indicated by system information software, the chances are that your system board is bad. A diagnostic program may help determine if this is the case.

IRQ 2: Assigned for older EGA video adapters. This IRQ line is typically available unless one of your application programs needs this line connected on your video adapter for backward compatibility with the older EGA video functions. With most of us having VGA video adapters and displays, this IRQ typically has no primary, useful assignment and can be used for other devices. If another device needs or uses IRQ 2, make sure that the jumper or switch for this IRQ is disabled on your video card. This is a good alternative IRQ option setting for sound or network card use. Because IRQ 9 uses IRQ 2 to communicate with the CPU, you should be aware that a device using IRQ2 may conflict with any device on IRQs 8-15, and especially IRQ 9, if your software for either of the devices using IRQ 2 or IRQ 9 can't determine which device caused the IRQ activity. Fortunately, most can.

IRQ 3: Primarily assigned to COM2: (at 2F8h) and COM4: (at 2E8h). Unless your system is misconfigured and you've got crossed port address assignments with COM1: or COM3:, or you are trying to use devices on COM2: and COM4: at the same time, there are few conflicts if this IRQ is used for COM2: and COM4: only. Sound cards, serial I/O (COM) ports, modems, network cards, and possibly other devices offer this IRQ configuration option. Many network cards come preset to use IRQ 3 when you buy them. Avoid IRQ 3 for the network card if you use serial port COM2: or COM4:.

IRQ 4: Primarily assigned to COM1: (at 3F8h) and COM3: (at 3E8h). Unless your system is misconfigured and you've got crossed port address assignments with COM2: or COM4:, or you are trying to use devices on COM1: and COM3: at the same time, there are few conflicts if this IRQ is used for COM1: and COM3: only. Sound cards, serial I/O (COM) ports, modems, network cards, and possibly other devices offer this IRQ configuration option and should not be put here.

IRQ 5: Primarily assigned to the second parallel port (at address 278h). Sound cards, serial I/O (COM) ports, modems, network cards, and possibly other devices offer this IRQ configuration option. Normally you would reserve this IRQ for LPT2: use, unless you need to use it for another device and you are aware that you may have to give up any interrupt-driven printing operations for a second LPT port.

IRQ 6: Assigned to the diskette drive system and is available to add-in cards through the add-in card slots. If you have diskette drives in your system, do not set any other devices for IRQ 6. Few if any I/O cards let you assign anything here anyway, so there should be no conflicts.

IRQ 7: Usually assigned to the first parallel port (at address 3BCh or 378h.) Sound cards, serial I/O (COM) ports, modems, network cards, and possibly other devices offer this IRQ configuration option, which is okay if you don't need the IRQ for printing. Normally you would reserve this IRQ for LPT1: use, unless you need to use it for another device and you are aware that you may have to give up any interrupt-driven printing operations for the first LPT port. If you need two printer ports, don't set them for 3BCh and 378h. Leave the first one at address 378h (proper for LPT1: in a color system), and configure the second printer for address 278h and IRQ5.

IRQ 8: Reserved for the internal real-time clock for AT- and higher-class systems. The IRQ 8 signal line is never available to add-in cards; it is connected only to the internal system board circuits. If a conflict with this IRQ appears in one of the system information programs, the chances are that your system board is bad.

IRQ 9: Another common IRQ option for 16-bit network cards. If you have a sound card and can't set it to IRQ 9, put the network card here. Remember, this IRQ also equates to IRQ 2, so it will get a high priority during use. If high-speed network performance is your priority, set the network for this IRQ and use another IRQ for less critical devices.

IRQ 10: A common IRQ option for 16-bit network cards. This is a safe bet unless you have other devices set for this IRQ. Check the IRQ setting of your sound card if you suspect conflicts here.

IRQ 11: A common IRQ option for many SCSI host adapters and 16-bit sound cards. Few if any conflicts exist using this option unless you have multiple SCSI host adapters, multiple network cards, a sound card, a mix of SCSI, network and sound cards, or some other device(s) set for IRQ 11. If you already have a SCSI host adapter set for IRQ 11, try using IRQ 10 for the network card.

IRQ 12: Used for the PS/2-style mouse port (also known as the internal, or on-board, mouse port) included on many system boards. If the PS/2 mouse port is enabled in your system's Setup program, and you are using a PS/2-style mouse plugged into this port on the system board, don't set any other adapters or devices for IRQ 12. IRQ 12 is commonly one of the IRQ setting options for SCSI host adapters and sound cards, which you can't use if you're using the on-board PS/2-style mouse port on IRQ 12.

IRQ 13: Reserved for the NPU (a.k.a. math chip, numeric coprocessor, or floating-point processor). The IRQ 13 signal line is never available to add-in cards. It is connected only to an NPU or CPU socket. If a conflict with this IRQ appears in one of the system information programs, chances are your system board is bad.

IRQ 14: Assigned to hard drive adapter/controllers for AT systems, and a common optional IRQ setting for the some SCSI host adapters. If you are using the hard drive interface built into your system board, or if you have an add-in–card disk drive adapter, *and* you have or are adding a SCSI host adapter or any other add-in device, do not set the SCSI host adapter or any other add-in devices for IRQ 14.

IRQ 15: Assigned to secondary hard drive interfaces, and a common IRQ option for many SCSI host adapters—few if any conflicts will exist with other devices. If you have multiple disk or SCSI host adapters, they cannot be set for the same IRQ, so IRQs 9, 10, and 11 would be likely next choices.

NOTE

Remember that Plug and Play can and will make its own decisions about many IRQ assignments. Under Windows 95 the only place to make PnP resource assignment changes may be under the specific device's **Resource** tab within the **Device Manager** under **Control Panel//System**, or use the **SETUP** program that came with the device.

Number 2: DMA Channels

As with the IRQ signals above, we'll be looking at each DMA line one at a time, in a summary format. We'll break them down into the devices that might be configured on them, where the most conflicts seem to be, and what seems to work best in most cases. Remember that DMA lines may be separated on your add-in cards into DRQ (DMA request) and DACK (DMA acknowledgment) signals, both of which must be configured to the same-numbered channel for the add-in device to work correctly.

Only in the case of a self-proprietary software-configured sound card have I ever had an obvious DMA conflict between two devices. More commonly, the device and its DOS-level driver, or Windows 95 Device Manager, are not configured to the same parameters, and the sound card may lose the ability to transfer data properly for recording or playing back sounds. If it's not a conflict, it may be simply misconfigured!

DMA 0: Assigned internally to the system board for memory refresh. You shouldn't be able to even get at it.

DMA 1: Has no predetermined assignment. It's a common choice for sound cards and SCSI host adapters.

DMA 2: Assigned to the diskette subsystem. If you have no diskette drives, you may configure anything that offers this line as an option here, but there are several others to choose from.

DMA 3: Has no predetermined assignment. It's a common choice for sound cards, network interface, or SCSI host adapter cards.

DMA 4: Has no predetermined assignment. It's available for various uses.

DMA 5: Has no predetermined assignment. It's a common choice for sound cards and SCSI host adapters.

DMA 6: Has no predetermined assignment. It's available for various uses.

DMA 7: Has no predetermined assignment. It's a common choice for sound card use.

NOTE

Remember that Plug and Play can and will make its own decisions about many DMA assignments. Under Windows 95 the only place to make PnP resource assignment changes may be under the specific device's **Resource** tab within the **Device Manager** under **Control Panel//System**.

Number 3: I/O Addresses

WARNING

You've heard about a couple of my pet peeves more than once prior to this chapter—and they would be?

• The LPT1: port at 378h and an NE1000 or NE2000 network interface card at 360h. An overlap/conflict—good example! Next?

- Network interface cards at address 300h. Excellent—where the system or operating system gets confused about what kind of device is at 300h, the original prototype card address assignment.

Surely there are others: SCSI adapters and sound cards that can be assigned to the same address, such as 130h, 220h, 330h and so on. Beware!

Also, becoming more and more common are addressing (and IRQ) conflicts with sound cards that have built-in IDE interfaces to support CD-ROM add-ins/upgrades. These will conflict with the built-in IDE interfaces on system boards. Ditch the sound card IDE interface and use the one on your system board!

130h: A common alternative for SCSI host adapters.

140h: A common alternative for SCSI host adapters.

170h: The address for the second AT-type hard drive interface, or what we know today as the Secondary IDE Interface. Beware, the IDE interface on your sound card may want to be here too. That's if you *don't* have the secondary interface on your system board enabled.

1F0h: The address for the first AT-type hard drive interface, or what we know today as the Primary IDE Interface. Beware, the IDE interface on your sound card may want to be here too—a no-no!

220h: Typically used for Sound Blaster or Sound Blaster emulations (WAV files) on sound cards.

240h: An alternative selection for Sound Blaster or Sound Blaster emulations on sound cards.

278h: Assigned to LPT2: or LPT3: and goes with IRQ 5.

280h: One of the typical choices for your network card, or the rarer Aria Synthesizer.

2A0h: Another common choice for your network card or Aria Synthesizer.

2E8h: Assigned to COM4: and goes with IRQ 3.

2F8h: Assigned to COM2: and goes with IRQ 3.

300h: A common but not ideal choice for a network card. Avoid it for OS/2 and Windows 95/NT.

320h: A good place for a network card if you don't have a SCSI or MIDI adapter at 330h.

330h: A common place for many SCSI host adapters.

340h: A common alternative for many SCSI host adapters, or a good place for your network card if you don't have a SCSI host adapter here.

360h: If you need to put your network card here, be careful. You might want to put LPT1: at 3BCh, not 378h, or the network card may conflict with the LPT port at 378h.

378h: The assignment for LPT1: in color systems; goes with IRQ 7. Beware of an IRQ conflict if you have an LPT port at 3BCh.

3BCh: LPT1: in monochrome systems; goes with IRQ 7. Beware of an IRQ conflict if you have an LPT port at 378h. Be aware that Windows 95 does not know what LPT number to assign to a port at this address, because 3BCh is the LPT port for older monochrome systems, which the Windows folks have never heard of.

3E8h: Assigned to COM3:, which goes with IRQ 4.

3F8h: Assigned to COM1:, the first or only COM port you may have. It goes with IRQ 4.

Number 4: OS/2 Warp or Windows 95 Won't Complete Installation or Run with a Network

In OS/2, networking features are an option that has to be added to an existing OS/2 installation, even if your system was networked before you installed OS/2. The installation of networking is not a complex process, and typically it proceeds rather smoothly. Networking is not available until after the installation of the add-in software and device drivers, and a shutdown and restart of the operating system. It's during the restart of the operating system that you may encounter a system error message such as SINGLE01 or SYS3175, which will be your first indication of a possible configuration conflict between your network card and OS/2.

For Windows 95, the installation and configuration of networking are an automatic part of the installation process when a network interface card is detected. Although the process may detect the network hardware and appear to configure Windows 95 correctly, you may discover that networking simply does not work after installation. This may be indicated by the lack of a **Network Neighborhood** icon on the Windows 95 desktop or network configuration problems.

If you encounter network problems such as these, check the hardware address for your network interface card. If the card is set up at address 300h, change the address to 280h or 340h. To avoid conflicts with any present or future SCSI host adapter cards at 330h, do not use address 320h; to avoid conflicts with a present or future parallel port card at 378h, do not use address 360h.

For those upgrading from prior network sitations, reconfiguration of a network card may also require editing any and all of the **NET.CFG** files that are part of your particular network configuration. Normally the **NET.CFG** file may be found in the root directory of your boot drive. For Windows 95, you must also change the resources configuration under the Windows 95 **Network** or **System** icons within the Control Panel to reflect the new network card address.

Number 5: Coincident Printer Port and Network Problems

If you're experiencing problems staying connected or logged in to your network server when you print a document on a local printer, or if you're having problems printing locally while working with files on your network, check the addresses used by your network interface card and your printer port.

If you have an NE1000, NE2000, or compatible network interface card that's set up to use address 360h and your local printer port is set up at address 378h, you have an overlap of address space. NE1000, NE2000, and compatible network cards require a full 32 (20h) address locations, including their base address of 360h. Address 378h of the parallel I/O port card falls at the 25th address location required by the network card.

The solution is to change the address assignment of one of these devices. You have three addressing options for the parallel I/O port—3BCh, 378h, and 278h. Most network interface cards provide at least six addressing options: 280h, 2A0h, 300h, 320h, 340h, and 360h.

Since most of us have color video display systems rather than monochrome (text-only or Hercules monochrome graphics), using display cards with parallel ports included on them, and the LPT1: port for these systems is generally accepted to use address 378h, it is probably best to reconfigure the network interface card to use another address. The best alternatives are often 280h or 340h, to avoid further conflicts, since 300h may cause problems with OS/2 Warp or Windows 95, and 320h will overlap the common SCSI host adapter address of 330h.

For DOS-based network setups, reconfiguration of a network card may also require editing any and all of the **NET.CFG** files that are part of your particular network configuration. Normally the **NET.CFG** file may be found in the root directory of your boot drive. For Windows 95, you must also change the Resources configuration under the Windows 95 **Network** or **System** icons within the Control Panel icon to reflect the new network card address.

Number 6: Coincident Network Card and SCSI Host Adapter Problems

If you're experiencing problems with your SCSI-interface CD-ROM or hard disk drive when working with files on your network, or if you're having trouble staying connected or logged in to your network server when you access your disk drives, check the addresses used by your network interface card and your printer port.

If you have an NE1000, NE2000, or compatible network interface card that is set up to use address 320h and your SCSI host adapter is set up at address 330h, you have an overlap of address space. As expressed before, NE1000, NE2000, and compatible network cards require a full 32 (20h) address locations, including their base address. Address 330h of the SCSI host adapter card falls at the 17th address location required by the network card, whose base address in this case is 320h.

The solution is to change the address assignment of one of these devices. Depending on the requirements and design of your SCSI host adapter, you may not have any addressing options other than 330h. Since most network interface cards provide at least six addressing options (280h, 2A0h, 300h, 320h, 340h, and 360h), it's probably best to reconfigure the network interface card to use another address. The best alternatives are often 280h and 340h. They avoid further conflicts, since 300h may cause problems with OS/2 Warp or Windows 95, and 360h will overlap the parallel port address of 378h.

For DOS-based network setups, reconfiguration of a network card may also require editing any and all of the **NET.CFG** files that are part of your particular network configuration. Normally the **NET.CFG** file may be found in the root directory of your boot drive. For Windows 95, you must also change the resources configuration under the Windows 95 **Network** or **System** icons within the Control Panel icon to reflect the new network card address.

Number 7: There's No Sound, the Sound Card Output Stutters, or Voices Sound Like Your Computer Took a Deep Breath of Helium

Your sound card requires three distinct, non-conflicting system resources—an IRQ line, a DMA channel (for both DMA Request and DMA Acknowledgment), and a hardware I/O address. If the physical configuration of your sound card does not match the settings for the card in your Windows

SYSTEM.INI file or the device driver loaded in CONFIG.SYS, or in the Device Manager under Control Panel//System, or if there is an IRQ or DMA conflict with another device in your system, the sound card will not function properly. If you can't correct these symptoms through the methods indicated here, the sound card may be defective.

Most sound cards can be configured without conflicts to use address 220h or 240h, IRQ 5, and DMA channel 1 or 3. Common conflicts may be with a SCSI host adapter that uses address 220h or 240h. Even the SCSI adapter on your sound card may use these addresses as alternates. Begin solving these symptoms by using a system-information reporting program to determine what resources are used and, indirectly, which resources are available for your sound card configuration. Make any necessary configuration changes to the hardware to suit the available resources, and then use the sound card's installation or Setup program to view the existing sound card configuration to be sure it is correct and works with the program designed for the card. In most cases, the configuration details may also be viewed and edited directly within the Windows SYSTEM.INI file (for Windows 3.x users).

Examples of driver configuration entries in the Windows SYSTEM.INI file for five different popular sound cards are provided below. Make sure the entries in your file match the actual physical configuration of your sound card.

Creative Labs Sound Blaster, Old Driver Version

```
[sndblst.drv]
port=220 ("port" means the I/O address here, and the hex address is implied)
int=5 ("int" stands for "interrupt," or the hardware IRQ, here)
dmachannel=1
Palette=
```

```
MasterVolume=10, 10
FmVolume=8, 8
CDVolume=8, 8
LineVolume=8, 8
VoiceVolume=8, 8
```

Creative Labs Sound Blaster, New Driver Version

```
[sndblst2.drv]
port=220
int=5
dma=1
```

Aria Synthesizer

```
[aria.drv]
dspport=0x2b0   ("port" means the I/O address here)
dspirq=12
midiport=0x330
midiirq=9
savemix=1
recsource=1
extmon=0
CDmon=0
extmode=0
CDmode=0
extlevel=1
```

MediaVision ProAudio and ProAudio Spectrum

[mvproaud.drv] (the port is not specified here because there may be only one choice for this device, or because the I/O address is determined by the device driver when it loads or as it is read and assigned by the device driver in the **CONFIG.SYS** file)
dma=1
irq=5

MediaVision Jazz and Jazz16

[jazz.drv] (as above, the I/O address is self-determined or assigned in the **CONFIG.SYS** file)
dma=1
irq=5

For Windows 95 users, you'll be going into the **Control Panel//System** icon, then to the **Device Manager**, to find the sound card interface listing, and to a specific sound card type to get to its **Resources** tab. By the time you get into the Device Manager, you might see a bright yellow circle with an exclamation point that indicates a device conflict exists. Go to that device's listing and begin to explore what's what. Figure 7.1 shows the typical device address settings for a Sound Blaster sound card, and Figure 7.2 shows the card's IRQ settings.

If your device is a Plug and Play card, you may or may not be able to change the settings in the Resources dialog. If it's not a PnP device, changing settings here will only specify what you want the setting to be, not what the card is actually set for. To change the resources on the actual card you'll need to remove the card from the system, or use the card's proprietary Setup program.

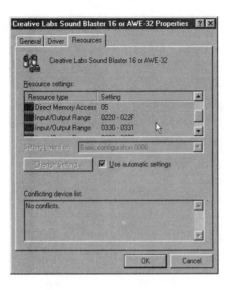

Figure 7.1 Typical address settings for a Sound Blaster card.

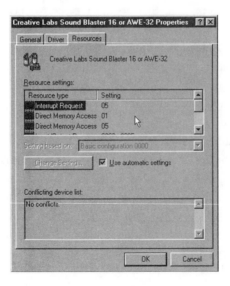

Figure 7.2 Typical IRQ and DMA settings for a Sound Blaster card.

Number 8: Windows **SETUP** Indicates Not Enough Memory to Run **SETUP**

This message reflects less of a conflict than a configuration dilemma, but it can become a common aggravation in the process of cleaning up your system configuration or performing upgrades. This message may be presented during a number of possible upgrade and configuration activities. Among them:

- using the Windows **SETUP** program to add or change video cards, driver files, or display resolutions
- using the Windows **SETUP** program to add or change network features
- using the **Fonts** feature under the Windows **Control Panel** to add display and printer fonts
- reinstalling Windows

There are two common causes and related cures for the problem:

Possibility A: The **WIN.INI** File is Too Large

The most common cause for the appearance of this error message is that your **WIN.INI** or **SYSTEM.INI** file for Windows configuration exceeds 64 Kbytes in size. These files often increase in size if you have installed a lot of printer or screen fonts, or application programs that add a lot of parameter lines to these files. The **WIN.INI** file contains more information and thus grows faster and larger than the **SYSTEM.INI** file. If Windows finds the critical elements that it needs to load and run in the first 64 Kbytes or characters of the **WIN.INI** file, you can prevent the above error message. This can apply to both Windows 3.x and Windows 95.

A quick fix is to rearrange the contents of the **WIN.INI** file. This is done with a text editor (DOS **EDIT** or Windows' **NOTEPAD** programs) to move some elements within the file to a different place in the file. You should be familiar with the Cut and Paste features of the editor of your choice.

Below are a listing of the groups of information in the **WIN.INI** file. (These are not the actual files, as they do not contain the full details that are to be found in the files.) By rearranging the sections of **WIN.INI,** at least by moving the [sounds] section to the bottom of the file, you can the file's critical setup sections within the first 32,768 characters. The [fonts] section should be near the top of the file, because fonts are critical to the appearance of Windows. Since the Windows **SETUP** program is used to change video configurations and these video configuration changes often affect the [fonts] section, **SETUP** needs to be able to find it in the file.

NOTE

When you rearrange the groups of information in the following listings, move the detailed information that follows each bracketed group heading (in the actual file, but not shown here) with the heading; the heading will be the first line of the entire group.

Primary Windows Environment Details at the Top

```
[windows]
[Desktop]
[intl]
[MS User Info]
[colors]
[ports]
```

Screen and Printer Appearance Items

```
[FontSubstitutes]
[TrueType]
[fonts]
```

Printer Specifics Below

```
[PrinterPorts]
[devices]
[Canon BJ-200ex,LPT1]
[Epson FX-86e,LPT2]
[Generic/Text Only]
[PostScript,LPT1]
[PostScript,LPT3]
[PSCRIPT]
[HP LaserJet Series II,LPT1]
[spooler]
[Network]
[Extensions]
[mci extensions]
```

Windows-Applications–Specific Details

```
[Compatibility]
[embedding]
[Windows Help]
[Cardfile]
[drawdib]
```

Application-Specific Details (these have been alphabetized for clarity)

```
[CorelGraphics4]
[GenigraphicsDriver]
[Genigraphics GraphicsLink]
[Microsoft Graph 3.0]
[Microsoft Query]
[Microsoft System Info]
[Microsoft Word 2.0]
[MSAPPS]
[MS Proofing Tools]
[MS Setup (ACME) Table Files]
[MS Shareres]
[MSWrite]
[Paintbrush]
[pcdos]
[Visual CD]
[WAOL]
[WinFax]
[WinComm]
[WinZip]
```

Text and Graphics Conversions (these usually are large sections)

```
MSWord Text Converters]
[MS Graphic Import Filters]
[MS Spreadsheet Converters]
[MS Text Converters]
[MS Graphic Export Filters]
```

Sounds at the End

```
[sounds]
```

End of WIN.INI File

If your **WIN.INI** file is less than 64 Kbytes in size, the next possibility is probably the cause of **SETUP**'s error message.

Possibility B: There Are Too Many .INF Files in the WINDOWS\SYSTEM Directory

The second most common cause of the message saying there's not enough memory to run Windows **SETUP** comes from having too many **SETUPx.INF, OEMSETUP.INF,** or **OEMx.INF** files (where *x* represents numbers to differentiate many separate filenames) in your disk drive's **C:\WINDOWS\SYSTEM** subdirectory (assuming C: is the letter of your hard disk drive). These files are used by the Windows **SETUP** program to allow you to select from a variety of hardware options for video display adapters, sound cards, and so on. You may move the files that are named **OEMx.INF** to a spare or backup subdirectory, or delete them from your disk. If you reinstall a piece of hardware, you'll be prompted for the hardware's disk with these files on it anyway.

Number 9: Games or Windowed DOS Applications Appear Fuzzy, or Colors are Changed Between Windows and Windowed DOS Sessions, or the System Just Plain Locks Up when Changing Programs

TIP

Roughly 30% of the "help me" e-mail I get concerns the bizarre symptoms that we'll see if we have memory conflicts. While everyone else is scrambling around looking for bad hardware, reinstalling applications or Windows itself, most folks find a lot of relief in changing or adding a couple of simple lines in their **CONFIG.SYS** file and restarting the system. This is true for almost any system, Windows 3.x or Windows 95.

If you click on the **MSDOS** icon under Windows, it usually opens a full-screen DOS session within Windows (no frame, dialog boxes, Windows wallpaper, and so on); but you do have the option of running DOS applications in a window instead. This is controlled by a selection for each DOS application by its **.PIF** file. For Windows 95, the **shortcut** icon represents the old PIF or Program Information File and contains many of the same DOS-compatibility details and then some.

Fuzzy-windowed DOS applications and changing colors are caused by the Windows drivers for your video adapter, or how your video adapter uses portions of upper memory, and the possibility that your memory manager or Windows is using a portion of upper memory that the video driver needs to use. This problem may be quite common with games. To solve the problem, one or two memory management changes are necessary.

The first possible solution is to add command-line modifiers to *exclude* the B000-B7FF or B000-BFFF upper memory range in the configuration of your memory manager (EMM386.EXE, QEMM386.SYS or similar) in the **CONFIG.SYS** file. These ranges are used for placing DOS text on your video screen, and, in many cases now, for accessing advanced features of the new whiz-bang VGA cards. Usually Windows and memory managers avoid this area because of this, but a Windows device driver for some video cards may conflict with the memory manager and cause display problems for DOS text applications running in Windows. If this region is left available and used by Windows as upper memory for loading programs or data, conflicts can also occur. Using the text editor of your choice, open the **CONFIG.SYS** file for editing, and if your EMM386 or QEMM command lines look like the first lines in the groups below, change (or add) them to appear as the lines that follow them.

For EMM386, change from:

```
DEVICE=C:\DOS\EMM386.EXE RAM
```

to:

```
DEVICE=C:\DOS\EMM386.EXE RAM X=B000-B7FF
```

or:

```
DEVICE=C:\DOS\EMM386.EXE RAM X=B000-BFFF
```

For QEMM, change from:

```
DEVICE=C:\QEMM\QEMM386.SYS RAM ROM ST:M
```

to:

```
DEVICE=C:\QEMM\QEMM386.SYS RAM ROM ST:M X=B000-B7FF
```

or:

```
DEVICE=C:\QEMM\QEMM386.SYS RAM ROM ST:M X=B000-BFFF
```

Save the **CONFIG.SYS** file and exit the editor. Then reboot your system for these changes to take effect. Then run Windows, open a DOS Window session, do what you did before to cause the problem to happen, and see if your problem has gone away.

If not, try the next step.

Older versions of DOS, and Windows 3.x include a file named **MONOUMB.386** or **MONOUMB2.386.** This is a special device driver file to be used within Windows to keep it from conflicting with the video memory range in the upper memory blocks (UMBs). Locate this file on your DOS diskettes or on your hard disk. If it is not in the **C:\WINDOWS\ SYSTEM** subdirectory, copy it from where you find it to that subdirectory. If you find a file named **MONOUMB.38_** or **MONOUMB2.38_** instead, you will have to be at a DOS prompt and invoke the **EXPAND** program that comes with Windows to decompress the file. The command line to use for this is:

```
EXPAND MONOUMB.38_ MONOUMB.386[Enter]
```

or

```
EXPAND MONOUMB2.38_ MONOUMB2.386[Enter]
```

When this file is properly in place in your **C:\WINDOWS\ SYSTEM** subdirectory, the **SYSTEM.INI** file in the **C:\WINDOWS** subdirectory needs this device added under the [386Enh] section, to appear as follows:

```
[386Enh]
device=monoumb.386
```

or

```
[386Enh]
device=monoumb2.386
```

Save and close the **SYSTEM.INI** file and restart Windows, repeating the steps that previously caused the display problem. If the problem has not gone away after both of these changes have been made, you should check with your system or video card vendor to obtain technical support or new video driver files. In the meantime, if you want to keep on working but with reduced resolution and colors, you can use the Windows **SETUP** program to reconfigure Windows to use a plain old VGA video driver and avoid the special video drivers entirely until the problem can be fixed properly through contact with vendor technical support or the help of a more experienced user.

NOTE

Since there are so many new devices being produced very quickly for Windows 95 (and soon to be Windows 97), it pays to check the Web site, BBS, or on-line forum of *all* of your hardware vendors to see if there are updated driver files for one or more devices. You may even find drivers that should have shipped with your device, but did not, that could be crucial to the setup of your video card or system board. This is also a perfect time to check the BugNet database at www.bugnet.com for analysis of commonly reported and verified conflicts between different software and hardware products.

Number 10: But I Really Need to Use More than Two COM Ports at One Time

Using two COM ports at the same time is fairly common, as many systems are configured with a serial port mouse on COM1: and a modem on COM2:, and these two ports do not have the same IRQ assignment. If the use of a third port is required, it would *logically* have to be COM3:, but this port would normally be assigned to use IRQ 4, which conflicts with COM1:.

The examples in this section may be used as guidelines for editing your **SYSTEM.INI** file if the options presented in Windows' **Control Panel/Ports/Settings/Advanced...** dialogs are not sufficient to define your special configuration circumstances. Each of the three examples provides command lines to be entered under the [386Enh] bracketed heading in **SYSTEM.INI**; there will be lots of other configuration lines starting at the [386Enh] brackets before getting to any COM... lines).

If you have a system and add-in card that uses the Micro Channel data bus, you can simply add a third COM port and share IRQs between COM ports 1 and 3 or 2 and 4, which must be specified in the Windows **SYSTEM.INI** file by adding the following line under the [386Enh] section:, as indicated in Example A:

Example A:

```
COMIrqSharing=1
```

This option applies *only* to MicroChannel and EISA systems. For ISA or non-MicroChannel, non-EISA systems, this line must be left set to 0 (zero) or NO, or not be present.

For non–MicroChannel, non-EISA systems, one solution may be to find an unused IRQ line that can also be configured on the COM3: port. Unfortunately, most add-in COM ports were designed with the original PC design and configuration rules in mind and provide switches or jumpers for the conventional IRQ settings for COM ports—IRQ 3 or 4. If your add-in COM port board allows you to assign an IRQ other than 3 or 4 to one of your new COM ports, and one of those IRQs is not in use by another device, do so, and then use Windows' Control Panel to indicate the new IRQ for the COM port of interest. If you *can* assign a unique IRQ to each COM port, you need to tell Windows which IRQ goes with a specific port. (IRQs 5 and 7 are simply examples here.) Example B is representative of this new configuration:

Example B:

```
COM3Irq=7
COM4Irq=5
```

An electronics technician may be able to make an electrical modification to the add-in card IRQ connections to allow you to select IRQs other than 3 or 4.

TIP

The remaining option is to seek out and purchase one of many special COM port add-in cards that provide non-standard COM port addressing (COM port addresses other than 3F8h, 2F8h, 3E8h, or 2E8h) and additional IRQ options. These cards are typically used by people who operate electronic bulletin board systems (BBSs) under Windows or other operating systems. Inquire of your local computer dealer, a local BBS, or one of the popular on-line service forums (CompuServe, America Online, etc.) for specific information in locating one of these boards.

If you put one of these special-purpose COM port options in your system, you may need to tell Windows exactly where these ports are addressed and which IRQ goes with a specific port. Addresses 130h and 138h and IRQs 5 and 7 in Example C aren't necessarily accurate for any particular card:

Example C:

```
COM3Base=0130
COM3Irq=7
COM4Base=0138
COM4Irq=5
```

Windows 3.x Bonus Points

Though not conflict resolutions, two more sets of command lines will be helpful here.

The following four lines really help the performance of communications programs running under Windows 3.X. These lines would be added at the end of the [386Enh] section of your **SYSTEM.INI** file.

COMBoostTime=100 (this line gives comm programs more of Windows' time for high- speed data transfer)

COM2FIFO=1 (include a line like this for all of the COM ports that have a 16550A UAR/T chip)

COM2Buffer=12 (this line augments the "FIFO" specifier for high-speed data transfer)

COMIRQSharing=

Add the following lines to [NonWindowsApp], which is below the [386Enh] section:

CommandEnvSize=1560 (should match the /E:#### setting in the **SHELL=** line of **CONFIG.SYS.** ("####" indicates a numeric variable value)

FontChangeEnable=1 (allows you to scale fonts in a Windowed DOS dialog screen)

`MouseInDOSBox=1` (requires that a DOS mouse driver is loaded before running Windows, which allows you to use a mouse for DOS programs running under Windows)

Windows 95 should not need any of these lines since it already provides support for mouse functionality in DOS sessions, and handles higher speed COM ports (typically to 57,600 or 115,200 bytes per second).

Summary

With the background information about the design of PC systems, a set of rules and examples, and these quick hints, you should have eliminated the most common system conflicts and have a really clean and functional system configuration. Our final chapter will walk through examples of using some of the commonly available system-information and diagnostic software to determine the system configuration and confirm that it functions properly.

CHAPTER 8

SYSTEM CONFIGURATION TOOLS AND UTILITIES

Topics covered in this chapter:

- The things system information tools can show you
- Why system information tools can't show you some things
- Using system information tools
- Managing a Windows configuration
- Some helpful Windows utilities
- Getting better technical support

So far we've covered a lot of technical details about a PC's resources, which devices consume which resources, how those devices are configured, and why.

This chapter covers using system information tools for collecting and sorting the myriad technical details you or someone else may need to know about your system. These tools will help us complete the configuration management we've been discussing all along. We'll discuss the software that shows what resources are in use in a typical system configuration. There is also information that most software and hardware companies ask for when you call technical support. We'll also cover some other handy software tools that make dealing with your computing environment a lot more pleasant.

You may already know that your system is a 486 or Pentium–something, that it has a *bunch* of memory, a *big* hard drive, a high-speed 33.6 fax modem, and that it connects to some kind of network in your office. You may even know what kind of hard drive you have, what brand of fax modem is installed, and what type of network you're connected to. However, when you call for technical support and they start playing "20 Questions" about addresses, IRQs and such, you may be hard-pressed to answer these questions as accurately. Using the tools discussed in this chapter, you'll have the answers.

What if You Don't Know what Your Configuration is?

There are numerous software tools available that detect and report tremendous amounts of information about PC systems. Some of these tools simply report on the items found in the low memory area, ports, video modes, disk drives, etc., without actually testing for the presence of these devices. There is a difference. The low memory shows what the system BIOS finds during Power-On Self-Test. POST only knows about the few basic PC devices, and can identify newer devices that look like legacy devices (SCSI adapters and drives that behave as standard hard drives, through their own on-card BIOS, for instance.) POST does not know how to identify sound cards, internal modems (except that they may appear as COM ports, without Plug and Play turning them on), proprietary CD-

ROM interfaces, network cards, etc.

Advanced system information tools—the ones you really need to use—show not only the generic details about PC ports and devices (including what their IRQ and DMA assignments are or should be) but also the many add-in devices and new features (such as identifying the PCI bus, PC Card/PCMCIA devices, advanced video cards and their features, sound cards, network cards, etc).

Of the many software tools available, only a few are aware of a significant number of specific hardware items by generic type and specific brand and model. These tools can accurately identify addresses, IRQs, and DMA assignments. One of these tools, Watergate Software's PC-Doctor program, is provided in an evaluation version on the diskette included with this book.

As good as any software program may be—and many are very good and can save you a *lot* of work—there are some cases in which it is necessary to physically inspect the hardware itself to determine specific jumper or switch settings. Table 8.1 lists the general types of information we can get and the information we cannot get from system information software.

Table 8.1 Configuration Information You Can and Cannot Get

Information Type	Generic Information	Vendor Specific Information	Unavailable Information
System Manufacturer	none	Usually read from the BIOS (see "Limitations" below)	
Machine Type	PC, PC/XT, PCjr, PC/AT, (generic AT, includes 80286, 80386, 80486, and Pentium)		

Information Type	Generic Information	Vendor Specific Information	Unavailable Information
System Board Data Bus Type	ISA, EISA, Local Bus or PCI		
CPU Type	i8086, i8088, NEC v20, NEC v30, i80286, i80386sx, i80386dx, i80486sx,i80486dx, i80486dx2,i80486dx2, i80486slc, Pentium; AMD andCyrix upgrade chips by model #		
CPU Manufacturer	Intel, NEC, AMD, Cyrix		AMD (see "Limitations" below)
NPU (math chip)	i8087, i80287, i80387,Cyrix and AMD (usually integrated with CPU)	Weitek; other non-Intel	
Base Memory	0-640k		
Extended Memory	Up to 16 megabytes in AT-class systems. Up to 256 megabytes in many 386, 486, and Pentium systems	Greater than 64 megabytes can be identified with specific system manufacturer support (see Limitations below)	
Expanded Memory	Amount of memory and the software device driver version	EMS board mfr.	
Shadowing/Cache	no generic info except CPU cache for Intel 486+ parts	vendor-specific chip and system board chipset information can be developed	special-case shadowing or cache functions where system manufacturer no longer exists to support this
BIOS Information		any available internal information if presentand the software knows how to read from BIOS chip	

Information Type	Generic Information	Vendor Specific Information	Unavailable Information
Keyboard	keyboard type		
Video Card	Monochrome, CGA, EGA, VGA	video card make, model, BIOS, video RAM, with vendor support or generic VESA VBE presence	monitor size, type, mode, display content
Serial Ports	Logical device assignment; hardware address; IRQ	generic UAR/T chip type as 8250, 16450, 16550 and 16550A; SMC and National Semiconductor parts	generic chip manufacturers
Parallel Ports	Logical device assignment; hardware address; IRQ	SMC or National Semiconductor parts; enhanced modes	generic chip manufacturers
Diskette Drives	presence and drive letter assignment for: 160k, 180k, 360k, 720k, 1.2m, 1.44m, 2.88m		diskette size
Hard Drives	presence, logical drive letter and capacity	Physical and logical parameters unless translated by controller; SCSI & IDE: drive geometry, firmware version and manufacturer	MFM/RLL drives: drive manufacturer
SCSI Devices	Drive presence only if assigned logical device (drive letter)	Host adapter mfr. info; Adaptec parts/ interfaces; ASPI driver; attached device type; SCSI ID#; host adapter address, IRQ, DMA	

Information Type	Generic Information	Vendor Specific Information	Unavailable Information
CD-ROM Drives	Drive presence only as DOS logical drive letter	Disk content type (all via MSCDEX driver program); specific device driver or drive ID support per vendor	
Pointing Device	presence; 2/3 button	mfr. details only if specific driver and device supported	
Game Port	port presence		joystick or device type
Network		specific vendor/ protocol support required for presence, IRQ, boot ROM, DMA, card make/ model	
Sound Cards		Creative Labs, MediaVision, Sierra Semiconductor, Aria, Roland MIDI, Microsoft Sound System	

Limitations to Obtaining System Information

This section contains a little bad news and some good news about the various technical advances we've made with PCs, and how we have to deal with them, if we can, in terms of system information.

As noted in the table above, a lot of the system information you might want or expect to find out about your system is impossible, or, at the very least, impractical to obtain. Until Plug and Play and PCI came along, there was no easy way to get consistent information about many generic and specific system components. For instance, it was hard to determine the manufacturer, make, and model of the system board, or of a diskette drive, of a hard disk drive adapter, or of the serial and parallel I/O ports.

Generic devices such as I/O ports are for the most part just that—generic. While it is possible to determine what kind of serial I/O port might be there (the original 8250, and AT's 16450, or the much touted 16550A UAR/T serial port chip), determining if the entire port card was made by Acme or Smith or Sunshine is not possible, and in most cases, not necessary.

System boards have no unique identifiers, and there is no way to provide them, unless the information is written into the BIOS chip. Even at that, the information is not always in the same place or the same format. Awareness and reporting of specific system boards is usually only possible if the board manufacturer has told the software developer what information is stored where that might uniquely identify the board as theirs. As an example, I've got a system board that was manufactured by Micronics, a well-known system board firm. That board was available as a generic board with Micronics identification written into the BIOS chip, and was used by Gateway 2000 where it had a Gateway 2000 identification string written into the BIOS. The identity of the board could be changed by merely writing a new BIOS file into the BIOS ROM on the board, though it worked exactly the same either way, and used the same parts and upgrade components.

While you won't find this type of identity crisis happening between systems from Hewlett-Packard, COMPAQ, IBM, or other big names that make their own boards, this type of cross-use but private-label identification of commonly available components happens daily in the PC business. Thus, if you think it makes much of a difference whether you bought a Pentium system that says Acme, Smith, or "Bill's Computer Emporium" on the front, where each of these manufacturers used the exact same Asus, Opti, "Sunshine," or even Intel system boards, it doesn't in most cases. The differences should be subtle, and left (hopefully) only to the BIOS.

What you really need to know about a system board has to do with CPU, chipset, cache RAM, and BIOS. Most CPUs are easily identified with software. Chip sets were not identifiable until recently when they began to identify themselves through Plug and Play. BIOS is similarly difficult to identify unless the software programmer knows what to search for, and where, in the BIOS chip, to tell the difference between AMI, Award, COMPAQ, H-P, Microid Research, Phoenix, and other BIOS sources, though some of this may be also determined by Plug and Play. Cache RAM was also difficult to identify until recently, when the newer Intel chipsets made it easier to detect and test for the amount of cache RAM installed. You may not get all of these nice features with "off-shore" BIOS and chips.

There are many, many cases where the original equipment manufacturer (OEM) or system designer has provided for certain capabilities outside of the original design standards for PC, XT, or AT systems. Also, new standards are introduced on a regular basis. This is a constant challenge for software programmers. In order to detect and report on the capabilities of newer and special devices, the system information software programmer must obtain detailed information about any and all PC systems and devices from the equipment designers. With this information, the software may then be enhanced to make use of this specific information. This is no small challenge. Advances in technology seem to happen at a faster and faster pace all the time.

Getting updated software into the hands of all users is a tremendous task, and it's not always as responsive as we might like it to be. Yet, being aware of these limitations is good information to have as you inspect your system configuration using these tools.

Things were a little easier when we had IBM PCs and *only* IBM PCs to deal with, and for a while when there were only IBM PC/AT systems and a few clones. When different hard drives, sound cards, and memory types came along, things only started to get complicated. When 386 and 486 systems rolled out, EISA, SCSI, network cards, advanced video features and then Microsoft Windows became popular, it seemed that personal computing was going to become rocket science.

This is indeed why Microsoft, a software firm, began working more and more with hardware developers to create standards for system devices and information. It is also why hardware vendors looked to each other for cooperative solutions so their products wouldn't fight one another when they got into our systems. Of course, the skyrocketing prices of technical support had no small influence on everyone seeking mutually agreeable solutions either. Cooperation between all of these commercial interests makes it easier for Microsoft to create and maintain its operating systems and featured software products, and easier for the manufacturers to design and sell newer and better I/O devices. Believe it or not, some things in this area of technology are getting easier for us.

The end result may seem a bit confusing from our aspect as users, because we find ourselves digging around on the Internet looking for the latest driver files to support our new toys. But the very existence of the Internet, and more cooperation between hardware and software vendors, creates better support of one form or another, and hopefully a reduction in the need to provide more and more costly hands-on support by phone. We no longer have to wait for a new driver diskette to be shipped to our homes or offices. We can worry less about *most* hardware and software updates creating problems for us.

Yet, we still have to keep ourselves aware of the limited resources we have available inside the PC box, and how to make the best use of them.

Keeping Some Parts a Secret

It is impossible for software to read the labels or to penetrate the depth of many chips and features inside our PCs. Some information about a feature or component may be completely unavailable, except by visual inspection of the components involved. This is due to proprietary designs, manufacturing license agreements, various legalities, or design limitations.

Some manufacturers want their devices to appear to be generic devices, or possibly even to look like someone else's device. This is the case for some microprocessors (many of AMD's chips specifically, as well as various levels of Cyrix, TI, and IBM chips). You may notice that even if your sound card is not a Creative Labs Sound Blaster, the system information you get tells you that it *is* a Sound Blaster, or perhaps that it is "Sound Blaster-compatible" —if only because it acts like a Sound Blaster card.

No Two System Setup Programs are the Same

While many users would like to have a single software tool that would let them edit or save the all of the system setup information stored in CMOS RAM, this little gem has been and probably will be unobtainable.

This information, consisting primarily of date, time, video display type, amount of memory, hard drive types, and diskette drive information, is usually accessible at the time you start up your system ("Press **ESC** to enter **SETUP**") or by a special Setup program provided with the system.

Very little of this information is common between systems, and that which is common represents a few of the basic features you could change in the IBM PC/AT system. Still fewer bits of information resemble the limited options we had with tiny switches or jumpers on PC and XT systems.

With Phoenix, Award, American Megatrends, and Microid Research publishing variants of BIOS for U.S. and foreign PC makers, and IBM, H-P, COMPAQ, and just about every major PC manufacturer creating their own BIOS and setup features, we now have to deal with highly customized system setup information. They are all very different from each other.

System designers may use the system setup program and CMOS memory to control and hold information about many things that the PC, XT, and AT systems never had, such as:

- CPU caches

- memory and I/O timing

- bus clock speed and 'turbo' mode

- daylight savings time

- enhanced disk drives

- newer I/O ports (EPP, ECP, Infrared, USB, etc.)

- PC Card/PCMCIA devices

- PCI bus configurations

- energy savings/power management

This information is not only newer and different from that of the AT-standard information; it is not stored the same way in all systems. Since systems change so frequently, with new features added or some taken away, it is nearly impossible to provide a single independent setup program for today's PC systems. I don't believe anyone has tried, since it would be a frustrating and never-ending task.

NOTE

There is nothing worse than having your system crash and not being able to access its setup information to get it going again. If your system came with a special SETUP program diskette, make backup copies of it *right now*! Some systems let you make SETUP diskettes from within the SETUP or system utilities programs—*do it now*!

All the Memory That's Fit to Use, But Not Detect

The IBM-PC/AT system established a standard for identifying system memory up to 16 megabytes. Many systems now hold and address 256 megabytes or more of memory, well beyond the original PC/AT standard. Handling larger amounts of RAM often requires non-standard customizations to the system BIOS, as well as other system design considerations. Because it is a customized situation, identifying this much memory requires utility and information program designers to work closely with the system manufacturers so they can learn how to detect and test such tremendous amounts of RAM. The same is true for various external or "level two" (L2) caches, and other memory control parameters that are not covered by existing design standards.

Device Driver Thwarts Detection

One of the most common causes for a piece of system information software to miss the identification of a piece of hardware, or its IRQ or DMA usage, is the existence of a *device driver program*. Device drivers are typically loaded and run on your system through the **CONFIG.SYS** file when the system starts up. While these drivers may be essential to the functionality of your system or a specific device for normal, workday applications programs, they can hide or intercept the hardware details necessary for a proper identification.

If your choice of system information software misses detecting a device that you know is in your system and working properly, try using the software after starting your system without device drivers. (In versions of DOS from 5.0 on, pressing the **F5** key when the screen indicates **Starting MS-DOS...** or **Loading PC-DOS...** will bypass the loading of device drivers at boot up.) Conversely, some devices require that a device driver is loaded at startup before the device becomes active and available for detection.

Similarly, if you run any of these programs under Windows or OS/2, the reported system information can change significantly, because these environments place several device drivers and their own device control programs between the hardware and application programs. Be aware that since system information programs are designed to interface with the hardware directly for proper detection, the use of such programs and their results may be unpredictable, or cause Windows or OS/2 to crash or lock up.

Keeping Up With The Joneses

As PC systems and add-in devices are developed and introduced to the market so rapidly, few if any software programmers can detect the new features and devices, and update their software fast enough so that identification of the most recent devices is always available in any program on store shelves or direct from the software producer. It's important to understand that if you have a piece of hardware that was just designed in June 1997, and you are using software that was updated even as recently as March 1997, there's a very good chance that the new hardware will not be identified by the old software. As magical as software is, it still hasn't been able to overcome the time-space continuum. (OK, so Einstein, Newton, and Murphy *do* have something to do with computers...)

Software that can identify the new data buses, and the devices connected to them, is under constant development and will appear with time. It is likely that more software will also identify Plug and Play BIOS and PnP devices and their configuration separately from the system and applications software that uses them.

These limitations do not have a tremendous impact on our configuration work. Those items we have the most trouble with still use the original IRQ, DMA, and address resources we have become familiar with; detecting activity on or the use of these resources is fairly standard as PCs go. For finding and reporting these resources, we'll see how to use and explore system information software.

Gathering Hardware Configuration Information

In this section, you'll learn about the types and variety of information you can obtain about your PC system using system information or hardware configuration reporting software. With an understanding of the limitations of this type of software, and the limitations imposed through some hardware designs, you may find yourself either overwhelmed or disappointed with the information reported to you.

Our primary concerns are the system resources of IRQ, DMA, and I/O address assignments. In most of the system information programs available, at least the I/O address assignment of many common devices is not reported, simply because it has been taken for granted that a specific device always uses a specific address, and this configuration resource cannot be changed. If some of these fixed configuration items *could* be changed, our task of configuration management would become many times more difficult. Having some known, standard, unchanging devices makes our job easier in some ways, even though it may appear to limit other configuration options.

DISK

Two very helpful programs are included on the diskette provided with this book: an evaluation copy of Watergate Software's PC-Doctor for DOS, and a full shareware copy of Doren Rosenthal's RCR, or Rosenthal Conflict Resolver.

PC-Doctor provides a wealth of information about your system, including our three critical hardware configuration resources—IRQ, DMA, and I/O—within a very simple menu-driven interface. It allows you to save the information gathered to disk, or print it out. RCR works with your system interactively as you use it to determine any and all detectable IRQ activity. It's a little more technical to use than most typical information programs, but that's where its value lies.

Using PC-Doctor

PC-Doctor contains the system information gathering part of Watergate Software's products which are used by technicians, power users, and PC system and device manufacturers. It is a powerful tool that addresses your system hardware and devices directly and specifically to obtain detailed device identification information.

PC-Doctor can *not* be run under Windows. To do so under these environments might cause your system to freeze or crash because of the low-level technical functions it performs. This is a concern when using this or any similar system information utilities. Conflicts occur with the device drivers or the memory protection used in Windows (3.x, 95, or NT).

This unpredictable behavior might not be destructive, but it is annoying. This behavior is usually caused by a poorly designed device installed in your system which mistakenly responds to program instructions for another device that the program is trying to detect.

Installing and Running PC-Doctor

PC-Doctor comes with a small handful of support files on the diskette with this book, and is ready to use. To keep the program handy and easy to use, you should make a new subdirectory for it and copy the files from the diskette to your hard drive.

PC-Doctor is designed to be run under DOS-only, *not* in a DOS box or from the MS-DOS Prompt under any version of Windows or OS/2. You can perform the installation in a DOS session, but you should reboot your system and stop at a DOS prompt to run the program.

NOTE

Nearly any plain DOS-only bootup situation will allow you to run this program and gather the necessary system information. This means you should boot up with a minimum of device drivers (preferably none) from **CONFIG.SYS** or **AUTOEXEC.BAT**. For DOS and Windows 3.x systems, this means you should press **F5** when you see the "Starting MS-DOS..." prompt on your screen. For Windows 95 systems, press **F8** when you see the "Starting Windows 95..." prompt on your screen, then select the **Safe Mode command-prompt only** menu item. These will leave you at a bare bones DOS prompt.

- If you do not have adequate free DOS RAM to load the program or its support files, you may receive a message indicating so, and the program will prompt you to exit. Do so, then reboot the system as prescribed above.

- If you require the information from SCSI, sound or network cards, you should load only the drivers needed to activate these cards and no more (eliminate SmartDrive or other caching programs, special video mode drivers, SETVER, SHARE, etc. from your **CONFIG.SYS** and **AUTOEXEC.BAT** files, and reboot).

NOTE

This version is intended for demonstration and evaluation purposes only. If you need to use this tool regularly, you must purchase a full version from Watergate Software. The price is quite reasonable for the features you receive.

1. Start at your root directory:

   cd/[Enter]

2. Create a new subdirectory for PC-Doctor on your hard disk drive. Assuming it's drive C:, type:

   md PCDR[Enter]

3. Copy the PC-Doctor files from the diskette (assuming it's drive A:, but it may be drive B: for you) to this new subdirectory by typing:

   copy a:\PCDR*.* c:\PCDR [Enter]

4. Change to the new subdirectory:

   cd \PCDR [Enter]

5. Then execute the main program file (again, *not* in a DOS-session under Windows or OS/2, but booted to DOS only or with a DOS diskette only):

   pcdr [Enter]

   The first time you run PC-Doctor, it tells you that it is initializing and checks itself for viruses. The initial screens will look like Figure 8.1:

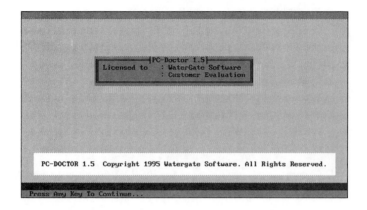

Figure 8.1 PC-Doctor opening screen.

5. Press **Enter** for the next screen, shown in Figure 8.2:

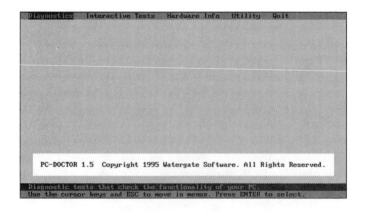

Figure 8.2 PC-Doctor title screen.

6. Press **Enter** for the next screen (Figure 8.3):

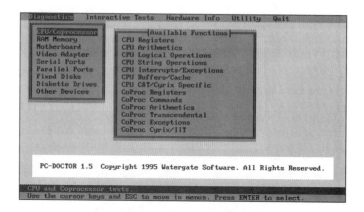

Figure 8.3 PC-Doctor Diagnostics menu.

NOTE

This version of PC-Doctor provides system information functions only. Selecting a diagnostic program will provide only a descriptive display screen.

7. Press the **Right Arrow** cursor key twice for the Hardware Information drop down menu, shown in Figure 8.4:

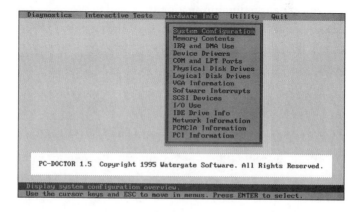

Figure 8.4 PC-Doctor Hardware Information menu.

The most critical information reports for our conflict and configuration concerns are the **System Configuration, IRQ and DMA Use, COM and LPT Ports,** and **I/O Use** selections.

What Can Go Wrong

While PC-Doctor has undergone extensive and very detailed and careful development so that it behaves well with all known hardware and system configurations, there are always a few systems, configurations, or unusual pieces of hardware that do not conform to expected and standard hardware design and operations. This can occur with all similar products. If the process of gathering information about your system becomes very frustrating you may wish to consult with a PC technician or your system vendor for assistance.

Any unpredictable behaviors or unusual results that occur when you run programs like PC-Doctor usually happen when IRQ or DMA assignment detection is performed, but may also occur when gathering any type of low-level technical information. By unusual or erratic behavior, I mean that the system locks up or reboots, or the screen blanks out. (I've never *yet* seen such a program destroy data, format a hard drive, or corrupt system setup information, though I'm sure it is possible under the wrong circumstances.)

Erratic behavior is possible because the program must actually control the specific device to get an interrupt or DMA reaction from it, or to confirm the specific identity of a device. If another device conflicts with the one you are trying to detect, or if the detected device is unusual in some way, erratic program behavior is possible.

With over 50 (100?) million different PC systems in use, it is not possible to be aware of, much less absolutely prevent, something from going wrong at *some* time—that's probably why you bought this book in the first place.

System Information

The PC-Doctor system configuration report is one of our first lines of defense in system conflict battles. Without knowing the basic contents or inventory of devices installed in your system, no configuration can be made conflict-free, except by luck or trial and error. Figures 8.5 and 8.6 illustrate a typical system hardware configuration report. Details of each line item reported (not all are shown) are given in Table 8.2.

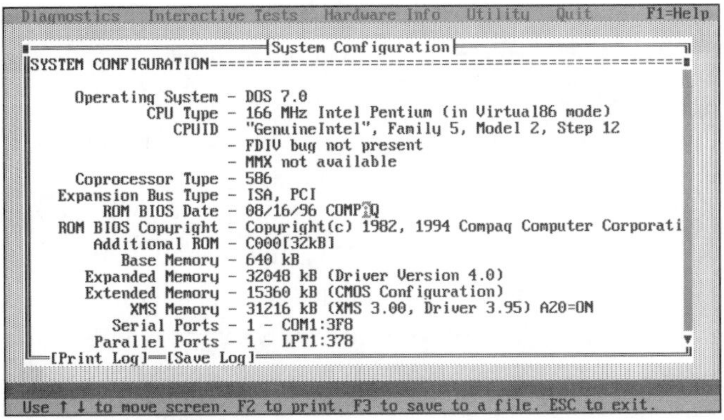

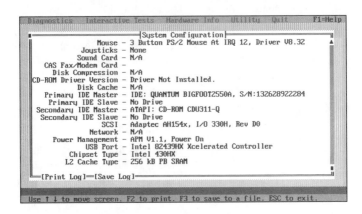

Figure 8.5 First page of PCDR System Configuration report.

Figure 8.6 Second page of PCDR System Configuration report.

Table 8.2 Description of PCDR System Configuration Report Contents

Attribute	Value
Operating System	The version of DOS the system is currently running.
CPU Type	Speed, brand, and model of the CPU chip.
CPUID	The internal CPU chip identification code (typically applicable only to Intel CPUs).
Coprocessor Type	Bran and model of the math chip.
Expansion Bus Type	Indicates all known I/O bus.
ROM BIOS Date	Date, if known, of the BIOS ROM chip/contents.
ROM BIOS Copyright	Copyright date of the ROM BIOS chip/contents.
Additional ROM	Addresses of other ROM chips (usually from video and disk adapters).
Base Memory	The amount of RAM allocated for DOS use. Typically 640 Kbytes, but may be 512 Kbytes for AT systems, or less for PC and XT systems.
Expanded Memory	The amount of LIMS-EMS memory currently managed in the system.
Extended Memory	The amount of RAM in the system beyond the 640 Kbytes for DOS (reported from the system CMOS setup RAM).
XMS Memory	The amount of memory managed by HIMEM.SYS or equivalent.
Serial Ports	Indicates number of ports, logical (COM) assignment, and physical addresses for each logical COM port.

Attribute	Value
Parallel Ports	Indicates number of ports, logical (LPT) assignment, and physical addresses for each logical LPT port.
Video Adapter	The type of adapter (Monochrome, CGA, EGA, VGA, etc.), and the video chip type if known/detected.
Fixed Disk Drives	The size of each detected hard drive.
Floppy Disk Drives	The number and type of each detected diskette drive.
Mouse	The type of mouse, if driver is present.
Joystick	Indicates presence of a game port.
Sound Card	Indicates model and address of known/detected sound cards.
CAS Fax/Modem Card	Indicates presence/type of modem card if detected.
Disk Compression	Reports type of disk compression used on current hard disk drive.
CD-ROM Driver Version	Indicates driver type/version if installed.
Disk Cache	Indicates type and size of disk cache installed and running (SmartDrive, etc.).
Primary IDE Master	Type and size of drive attached as Master on first hard drive adapter.
Primary IDE Slave	Type and size of drive attached as Slave on first hard drive adapter.
Secondary IDE Master	Type and size of drive attached as Master on second hard drive adapter.
Secondary IDE Slave	Type and size of drive attached as Slave on second hard drive adapter.
SCSI	Type of SCSI adapter, if known (usually requires ASPI or CAM driver in **CONFIG.SYS**).

Attribute	Value
Network	Indicates presence and type of network adapter (usually requires driver to be loaded and running in DOS).
Power Management	Indicates presence and status of energy saver features of the system BIOS.
USB Port	Indicates presence and type of a Universal Serial Bus adapter.
Chipset Type	Indicates the type of system board chip set.
L2 Cache Type	Size and type of External CPU cache.

Memory Contents

The Memory Contents screen indicates the amount, type, and free/available RAM, and the address and purpose of BIOS ROMs contained in the system. See Figures 8.7 and 8.8.

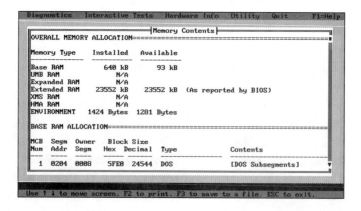

Figure 8.7 DOS Memory Contents display.

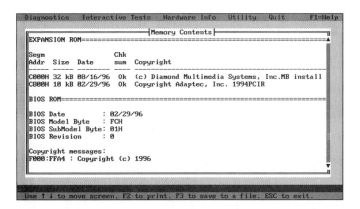

Figure 8.8 ROM Memory Contents display.

IRQ and DMA Use

Two of the most important hardware resources in your system configuration are reported in the IRQ and DMA Use screens. Two screens full of information are shown to give you an illustration of these resources. The first page is shown in Figure 8.9.

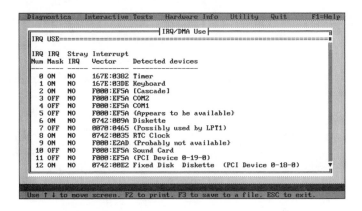

Figure 8.9 First page of the PCDR IRQ and DMA report.

- **Hardware IRQ** lines are listed in numeric order, with some additional technical information, prior to identifying the actual device known to be using the IRQ.

- The **IRQ Mask** column indicates whether or not handling of the respective IRQ is masked or filtered by another program that is monitoring it.

- The **Stray IRQ** column indicates if there was activity detected on an IRQ line from any unknown sources. This could indicate a possible conflict with another (unknown) device, or hardware failure that is falsely sending IRQ activity to the CPU.

- The **Interrupt Vector** column shows the memory address of the software program or routine that is handling the I/O for the respective device listed.

- Notice that IRQ #7 indicates "(Possibly in use by LPT1)." Possibly is because without a loopback test connector, it is normally not possible for software alone to trigger input or detectable activity on the LPT ports. (Contact Watergate Software at http://www.ws.com or 510-654-5182 for information on obtaining a full version of PC-Doctor and the loopback test plugs.) The loopback plug drawings are also included in the appendices if you wish to build your own.

- IRQs listed as "(Appears to be available)" did not have any interrupt activity from any known, standard or specially supported devices.

The second screen (Figure 8.10) indicates if there were any problems with any of the IRQ lines. In this case, there are no problems.

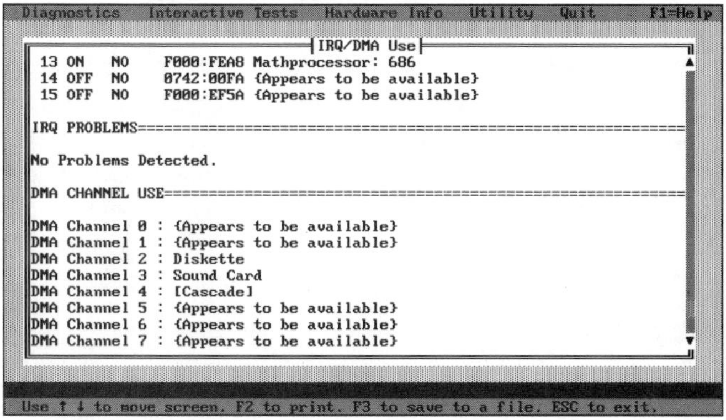

Figure 8.10 Second page of the PCDR IRQ and DMA report.

All eight DMA channels are listed in this report, indicating which device uses a specific channel, or that a channel is possibly available, as shown by the "(Appears to be available)" text next to a DMA channel. In this report, only three DMA channels are in use: 2, 3 and 4. DMA 4 is shown as [Cascade] or otherwise unavailable, because this channel is used to link the second of two DMA controllers to the first. You might also expect to see one or two functions of your sound card using DMA channels. (A sound card has been detected in this system, but its specific DMA activity cannot be determined unless the driver for the card is installed and running.)

Device Drivers

The device drivers report from PCDR provides information that is technically interesting and functional for programmers, but is perhaps too detailed for most users. The exception occurs when this information is pertinent to technical support transactions when troubleshooting a software configuration or function. The items reported are defined below (see Figure 8.11).

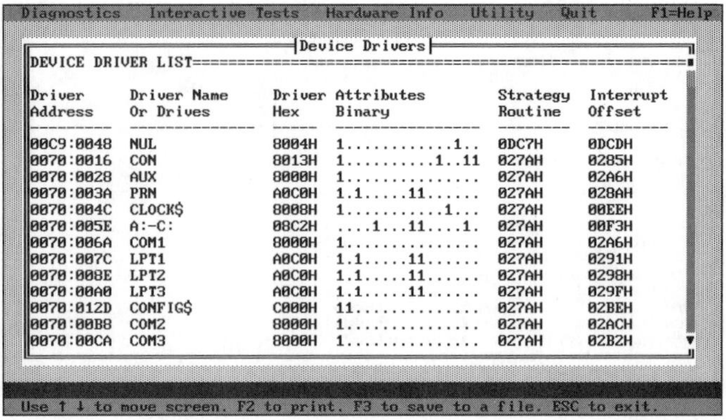

Figure 8.11 PCDR DOS Device Drivers report.

- **Driver Address:** This column indicates the actual memory address that the device driver has been loaded into and occupies as it runs.

- **Driver Name or Logical Drives**: This column indicates the internal process, device, or program name of the device driver, or the logical designation for disk drives found.

- **Driver Attributes:** These columns indicate what type the device driver is by the numerical value assigned to the type of device. A 1 in the first column indicates that the device is a character device, handing data one character at a time, and the absence of a 1 (an implied 0) if it handles data in blocks.

- **Strategy Routine:** Numeric values representing how DOS handles the device's I/O operations (not much value to us here).

- **Interrupt Offset:** The location of the software interrupt service routine that is responsible for handling I/O for this device.

COM and LPT Ports

Perhaps the most popular reason to go digging for information about your system is to figure out what the heck is going on with COM ports. This and the IRQ and DMA Use reports will be the most useful in such endeavors, and will illustrate quite clearly the relationship between physical addresses (3F8h) and logical port assignments (COM1). From the information given in previous chapters, you will be able to determine if these physical versus logical port assignments are correct. (Sorry folks, the software has not yet been written that highlights this information for you.) See Figure 8.12.

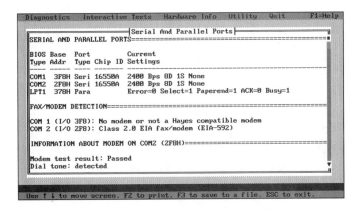

Figure 8.12 Serial and Parallel Port information.

This particular system has only two COM ports. They are addressed correctly for a proper physical versus logical association, and the associations match the proper IRQs for these two ports (see also Figure 8.9 above).

The information given in this report consists of:

- **BIOS Type:** The logical device designation given the port by the BIOS at boot-up.

- **Base Address:** The physical address, assigned to the logical device name of the detected port.

- **Port Type:** A description of the port (serial or parallel).

- **Chip ID:** The type of chip detected on the serial port(s). This is important information for high-speed COM port (modem) use. No specific chip type is associated with parallel/LPT ports.

- **Current Settings:** The initial speed and data bit settings for serial ports (this does not reflect the maximum capability of the port) and the status of signal lines of parallel ports.

NOTE

You must consult the IRQ and DMA Use report to cross-reference serial and parallel port IRQ assignments with the physical and logical COM and LPT port assignments shown here.

This screen also shows under "Fax/Modem Detection," the results of the program's attempt to detect and identify what type of modem might be present on your system, and what port it is associated with. The next screen goes on to query the modem for more specific internal information.

NOTE

Don't be surprised if your modem doesn't show up here! Some Plug and Play modems may not actually show up with a COM port or IRQ assignment until they are actually initialized and configured by a Plug and Play operating system, such as Windows 95.

Also, to specifically detect the presence of a mouse, your mouse driver must be loaded (in **CONFIG.SYS** or **AUTOEXEC.BAT**).

The serial and parallel (COM and LPT) report will also provide a summary of the information from any modems detected on the available COM ports, as seen in Figure 8.13.

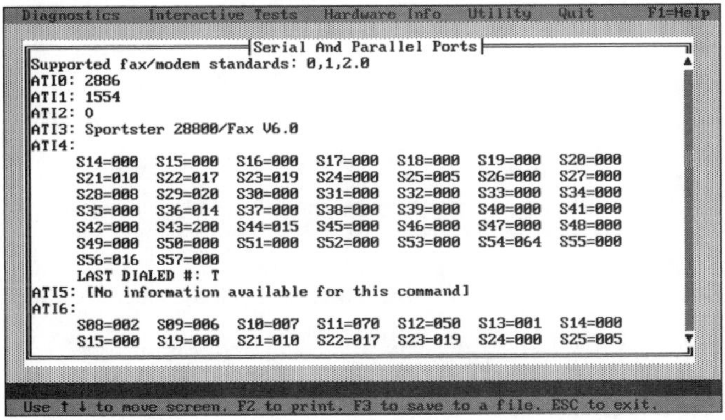

Figure 8.13 Modem information from COM2 port.

Physical Disk Drives

This report gives us details about the physical disk drives that are in the system.

The report, shown in Figure 8.14, is an example from a system with a 1 gigabyte SCSI hard drive, in which the SCSI host adapter provides a special translation for large drives. (I know it's a SCSI drive because it's my system. If we were to run and look at the IDE Drive Info report on this system, we'd also see that there are no IDE drives in this machine.)

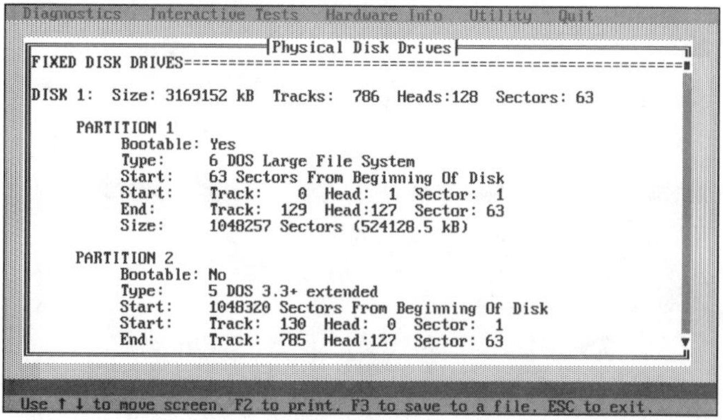

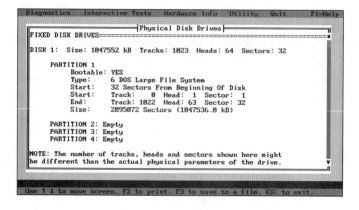

Figure 8.14 PCDR Fixed Disk Drives report (SCSI drive without ASPI driver).

The Fixed Disk report for an IDE drive in Figure 8.15 looks very similar to the report for the SCSI drive. DOS doesn't know the difference at this point, and shouldn't; physical disks are handled by the system BIOS. Logical disks, as we'll see next, are created from physical disks, and likewise display no clues as to whether or not the drive is a SCSI or IDE device. There is no indication of the CMOS setup drive type, as this now varies greatly between systems and BIOS.

Figure 8.15 PCDR Fixed Disk Drives report (IDE drive).

Logical Disk Drives

This report, shown in Figure 8.16, displays the way DOS views the disk drives in your system, by drive letter, and gives us further details.

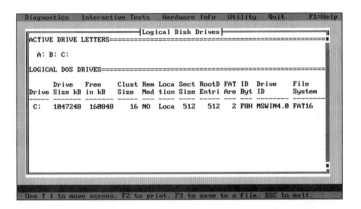

Figure 8.16 Logical Disk Drives.

In the Logical Disk Drives report we see that drive C: is the only active hard drive, with the following DOS partition parameters:

- **Drive:** The DOS drive letter. CD-ROM drives, if active through MSCDEX, and mapped network drives, are assigned DOS drive letters too.

- **Drive Size:** The actual capacity of the drive, displayed in bytes.

- **Free in kB:** The amount of the drive, in bytes, that is still free for storing more information.

- **Clust Size (Cluster Size):** The numbers of sectors per disk cluster—in this case, there are 16 (512 byte, see **Sect Size** below) sectors per cluster. A cluster is the minimum DOS file allocation size measurement unit.

- **Rem Med (Removable Media):** Does this drive support removable media? In this case, no.

- **Location:** Is this a local or network drive? In this case, local.

  Sect Size (Sector Size): The size of discrete disk sectors. Almost always 512 bytes.

- **RootD Entri (Root Directory Entries):** The maximum number of entries that can be listed in the drive's root directory, including files and subdirectory entries. (Even if you have a lot of your drive space free according to DOS, if you have 512 entries in your root directory, the drive is full and cannot hold any more data in the root directory, nor allow the creation of any more subdirectories off the root directory.)

- **Fat Are (# of FAT Areas):** Most/all DOS hard drives have 2 File Allocation Tables, as does this one.

- **ID Byt (ID Byte):** The DOS drive identifier byte information. Not a critical configuration concern.

- **Drive ID:** The volume identification type (*not* the volume *label*) assigned to this drive.

- **File System:** In this case, as with most drives partitioned and formatted with DOS versions later than 5.0, FAT-16, indicating that the maximum number of File Allocation entries is defined by a 16-bit number.

VGA Information

Just about everything you ever wanted to know about your VGA card, and then some, is listed in this report. See Figure 8.17.

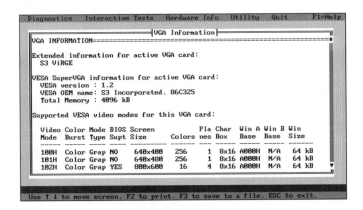

Figure 8.17 VGA Information report.

Although not reported in this case, the card is a Diamond Stealth 3D 3000, which uses the S3 ViRGE chipset, contains 4 megabytes of video memory, and supports VESA BIOS version 1.2 functions.

SCSI

The SCSI device report (Figure 8.18) requires an active ASPI (Advanced SCSI Peripheral Interface) drive, and is relatively simple at this level, telling us what the devices are in order of their SCSI unit ID numbers.

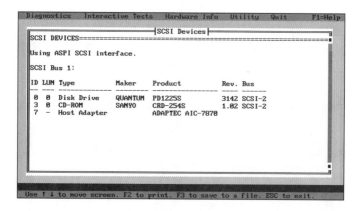

Figure 8.18 SCSI Devices report.

I/O Use

While it's normally a risky venture to have a program simply walk through a range of addresses to see if they are occupied or not, PC-Doctor is the first program I've seen to do this without regularly crashing the system. Unlike other efforts to produce a similar report, this function does not attempt to specifically identify what devices occupy what addresses; it merely reports that an address is probably occupied by *something*. It is as accurate as I can determine from knowledge of this system, and other system information.

Figure 8.19 shows the legend to the various contents of the I/O address range, and the beginning I/O address range contents. Figures 8.20 and 8.21 show the I/O address range with occupied addresses.

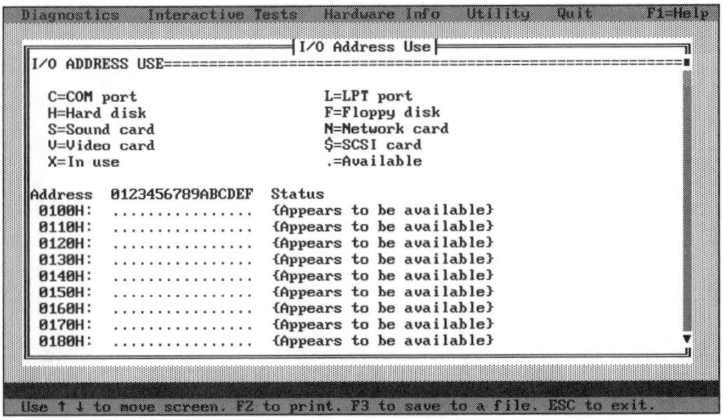

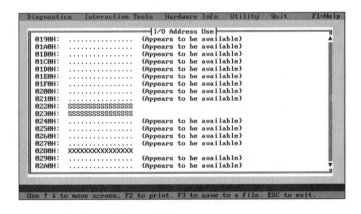

Figure 8.19 I/O Use Map, first page.

Figure 8.20 I/O Use Map, second page.

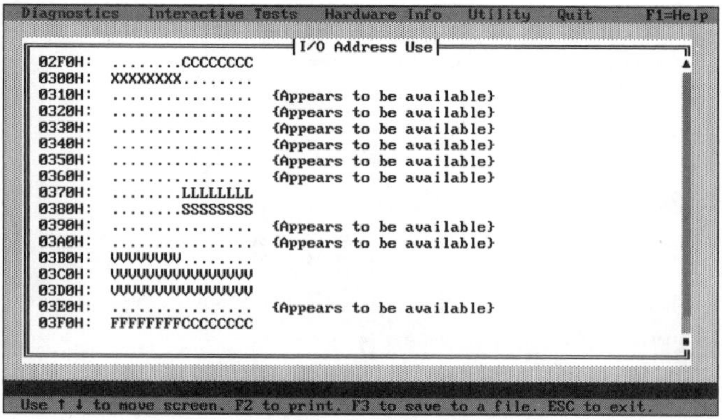

Figure 8.21 I/O Use Map, third page.

The pages of this report list memory addresses in order from 0000h to 03Ffh. This is the range where I/O devices are to be found. If a type of device (though not a specific device) is known to occupy an address, this is referenced by letters shown in the header of the first page of the report. Unknown but in-use addresses are flagged with the letter "X".

You may assume from this list that addresses without any flags (see the "(Appears to be available)" Status listing) may be available for your use to configure new I/O devices. However, you must be aware of the full address range a device uses, and of the I/O addresses that have been pre-defined for other known devices. (Yes, we're back to all those rules again.)

IDE Drive Info

The next two report screens (Figures 8.22 and 8.23) show you the results of asking any IDE drives found on the system to report what they are with the "Read Drive ID" command available with IDE devices.

Here we have our IDE hard drive and IDE CD-ROM drive baring their most intimate internal details.

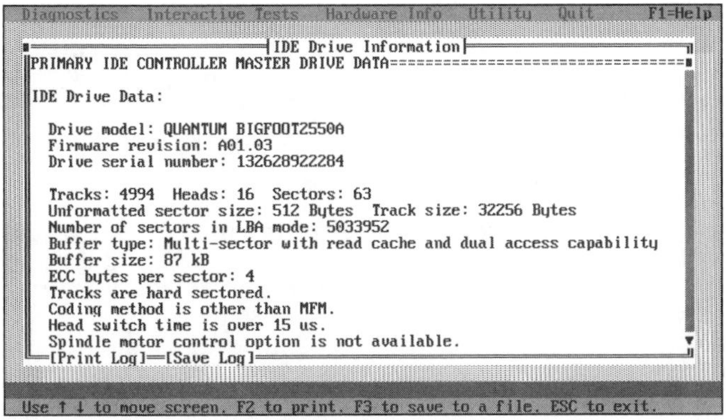

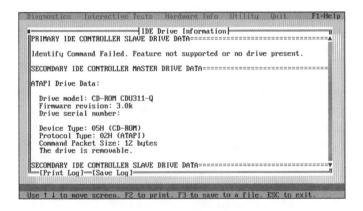

Figure 8.22 IDE Drive Info report, first page.

Figure 8.23 IDE Drive Info report, second page.

PCI Configuration

This selection within PC-Doctor provides basic information about the PCI bus and installed PCI components in your system. The PCI bus helps integrate a number of devices within the system board construction itself, reducing the need for a variety of add-in cards. Even though you may not have any PCI add-in cards plugged into your system, you may still have some PCI devices listed in this report. The information provided in this report (see Figure 8.24) is described below.

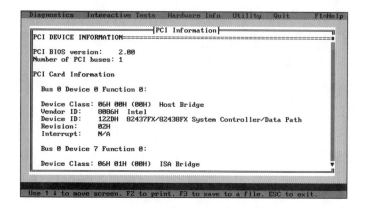

Figure 8.24 PC-Doctor PCI Information.

The first PCI information screen gives us the bare essentials of our PCI BIOS support, and begins to list PCI devices in the order they appear, the PCI chipset being a mandatory item for other PCI devices to exist.

The second PCI information screen (Figure 8.25) shows us a lot of detail, but most importantly the specific presence of the types of PCI devices in the system, starting with the integrated IDE drive adapter interface, then on to the add-in SCSI card.

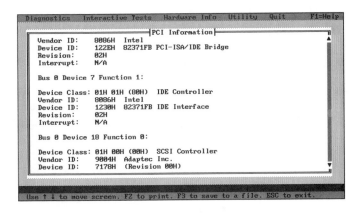

Figure 8.25 PC-Doctor PCI Information, second page.

The third PCI information screen (Figure 8.26) completes the SCSI information and shows us the PCI video card information.

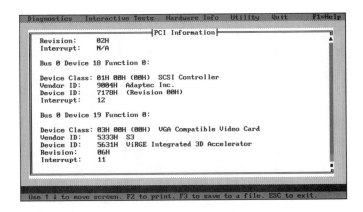

Figure 8.26 PC-Doctor PCI Information, third page.

NOTE

The latest evaluation and regular retail versions of PC-Doctor for DOS includes additional information reports covering PNP/ISA configuration, SMP (Symmetric Multi-Processor systems), and DMIBIOS (Desktop Management Information) support. Typical Plug and Play information can also obtained through PC-Doctor for Windows, as seen in Figures 8.31 through 8.34 below. The version available and distributed with this book may contain additional information options for which we did not provide screen shots. We hope this additional information is equally or more useful to you.

PC-Doctor for Windows

This section provides a brief overview of the system information available from PC-Doctor for Windows (Figure 8.27), another full-featured Windows 3.x and 95 diagnostic and information product.

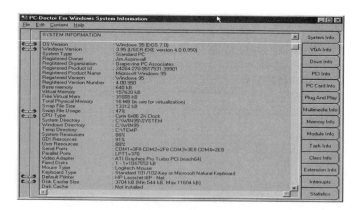

Figure 8.27 PC-Doctor for Windows System Info report.

PC-Doctor for Windows appears to know a lot more about your system than the DOS version in Figure 8.28 and subsequent screens, mostly due to the fact that there have to be so many device-specific drivers loaded and running for Windows to function.

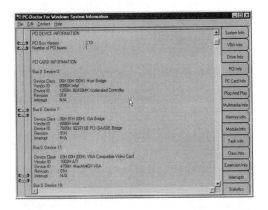

Figure 8.28 PC-Doctor for Windows VGA Info report.

Of course, one thing we don't see is a listing of our precious resources—IRQ, DMA, & I/O—but we will.

And the disk drive information looks pretty familiar.

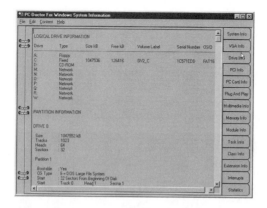

Figure 8.29 PC-Doctor for Windows Drive Info report.

As does the PCI information.

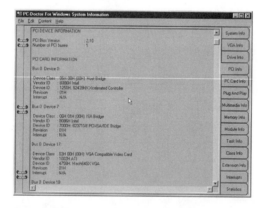

Figure 8.30 PC-Doctor for Windows PCI Info report.

Then we get to the "good stuff"—everything Windows 95 knows and can tell us about Plug and Play devices and resources. The inevitable IRQ and DMA assignments are shown in Figure 8.31.

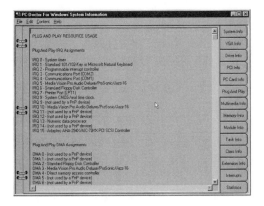

Figure 8.31 PC-Doctor for Windows Plug and Play Info report, showing IRQ and DMA assignments.

Then we see the addresses assigned to all the expected devices, from the bottom of memory on up (Figure 8.32).

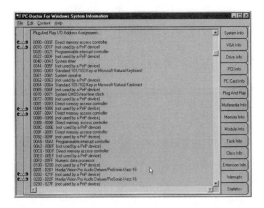

Figure 8.32 PC-Doctor for Windows Plug and Play Info report, showing memory address usage.

Then we begin to see the upper memory details, including video RAM and device BIOS regions (Figure 8.33).

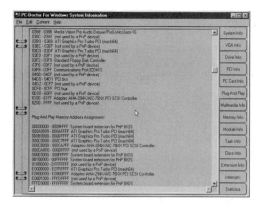

Figure 8.33 PC-Doctor for Windows Plug and Play Info report,
showing the upper memory area.

And while not finally (as there are more pages to this report),
we see details about each device that Plug and Play has
identified. Note that even a legacy ISA device is reported.
Whether or not a device is specifically PnP-compatible or
–supported, PnP must still identify it and the resources used,
before it can configure the real PnP devices.

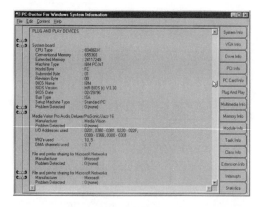

Figure 8.34 PC-Doctor for Windows Plug and Play Info report,
showing Plug and Play and legacy device information.

Rosenthal Conflict Resolver

Doren Rosenthal found the first edition of "IRQ, DMA & I/O" in the course of his work in creating his conflict detection and resolution software, RCR. I'm sure I didn't help him, a programmer, technically, but certainly provided some validation to the work at hand. He was kind enough to mention the book in the document file for his utility program. We've been comparing a lot of notes ever since. The results of the tests I've done with his programs, and how they operate, convinced me that they deserve more than a little mention in this book.

The highlight of Doren's utilities for me is RCR, or the Rosenthal Conflict Resolver program (**RCR.EXE**) and his System Monitor, **SYSMON.EXE**, both of which are on the diskette at the back of this book, with some of his other works.

RCR

RCR runs and functions like no typical DOS utility program, and it performs two functions. First, it is designed to run as part of the boot, or perhaps as a pre-boot operation, so that it can absolutely track all system IRQ and DMA activity. It does this by working off of a special diskette that the program will create for you, which is then used to pre-boot the system; thus, it does not interfere with your hard drive in any way.

The big difference here is that RCR is actively monitoring IRQ and DMA incidents as they happen, as you use your system, regardless of what device caused the signals to happen. This is significantly different from most diagnostic and information programs, which merely inspect any devices found in the system and tickle them to see what activity they generate.

At least one of the benefits here is that Plug and Play devices, and even some of those elusive soft-configured sound cards we mentioned before, can change their configuration as different programs use them. A game program may set up and use a sound card in very different ways than the card's drivers might set the card up for use under Windows. As you use the system and devices under any and all imaginable conditions, you will likely discover that a device uses more resources than you thought. Still more configuration mysteries unraveled all the time!

The second function of RCR is a real-time indicator of IRQ and DMA activity. You can start and use this real-time indicator at any time (provided you've booted with that special diskette) as a TSR in your **AUTOEXEC.BAT** file if you wish, or later on (but it is most useful in TSR mode). In its real-time display mode, it shows you when an IRQ or DMA line goes active, and leaves an indication turned on if any of the lines has ever been activated (should you happen to blink and miss the real-time activity).

Even without the TSR portion running, RCR logs all IRQ and DMA activity to a file for later inspection, also by the RCR utility program. The point here is to have the pre-boot activity monitor running and logging activities while you merrily exercise any and all parts of your system to their fullest.

Finally, after you've done all of your tests, run games, run network applications, used the CD-ROM drive and sound card, etc., you can inspect the **RCR.DAT** logfile that the program created to see what activity happened, or run RCR to display the file contents itself.

RCR and the techniques used above are intended for troubleshooting and tracking down mysteriously active conflicts you can't find any other way—or finding the easy problems easier. It is not intended for every day use.

System Monitor

SYSMON is intended to be used every time you start your system. It runs once to get a profile of the system, which it logs to your disk drive. It can be run again at any time to log if anything has changed since the last time it was run.

It is a perfect daily configuration tracking tool that can be used to log the system before and after software or hardware installations, so you can review the log to look for any changes in the configuration. You never know when adding a sound card may rearrange your network card or how software handles these changes unless you have this kind of information. Even changing the order in which you load drivers and resident programs can be detected and give clues as to why something suddenly doesn't work right.

This is a great tool for system installation and technical support people who want to get a snapshot of how they left the system, then come back and compare the configurations for any changes that may have happened, and gain clues as to why the system crashed.

The logfile is fairly technical and extensive, so it's not exactly for the average user to enjoy, but a technician looking for the mysterious "bug" will enjoy the details that are recorded.

Using RCR and System Monitor Together

RCR and System Monitor also work together to form a very comprehensive record of system configurations and activities, combining the configuration report with the IRQ and DMA activity report. Using them together makes a very powerful troubleshooting tool set. Here's how I do it:

1. First you run the RCR program (in DOS, or in a DOS box) and allow it to make a special boot diskette.

2. Next you put **SYSMON.EXE** into the beginning of your **AUTOEXEC.BAT** file—edit the file so it looks something like this:

```
C:\RCR\SYSMON (first line of AUTOEXEC.BAT
ECHO OFF (the rest of AUTOEXEC.BAT)
CLS
PROMPT $p$g
SET PATH=......
```

3. Reboot the system with the special RCR diskette in place, allowing it to load the piece of code that does the IRQ and DMA monitoring processes. The bootup then progresses normally through loading boot information; **CONFIG.SYS**, DOS, and **AUTOEXEC.BAT**.

4. Run your system through all of its normal paces: play games, run Windows, surf the Web, play a CD-ROM, etc.

5. When you think you've done enough exercising your mouse, video card, disk drives, sound card, network card and modem, and even run Windows (3.x or 95), it's time to get out of Windows (do a **Shutdown** or **Restart** under Windows 95), stopping at a DOS prompt if you can, to manually run the SYSMON program again. Or you can run SYSMON at any later time to see the log file, or view **SYSMON.DAT** with a text editor.

Also unlike other DOS-based utilities, Doren's program survives quite nicely and does not disturb Windows 3.x or Windows 95, to the extent that opening a DOS-window under Windows 95 shows you the RCR on-screen activity monitor as you're working away. Thus, my **AUTOEXEC.BAT** file ends up looking something like:

```
SYSMON
RCR
ECHO OFF
CLS
LH C:\WINDOWS\COMMAND\DOSKEY /INSERT
```

With this **AUTOEXEC.BAT** file, SYSMON is logging all of the activity that's going on with the system; I get the RCR activity monitor during any DOS sessions I call up.

RCR and SYSMON report the software interrupts in use by various programs and drivers, giving you some further clues as to what program or device might be causing the unknown interrupt activity.

The real value here is that RCR is not just looking for and testing the IRQ and DMA lines of known, detected I/O devices. It detects and records any and all IRQ and DMA line activity that occurs as you use the system, making sure you know if an IRQ or DMA line was in use, even if you don't know what device may have caused it. Just the trick for those elusive conflicts you either didn't know you had, or couldn't find otherwise.

Doren's other utilities are equally as innovative and interesting to work with, as you'll see if you spend any time with them. He's also got a hardware-based IRQ and DMA indicator card available, which will give you a real-time visual indication of what's going on with the system as you're poking around. It's a lot cheaper and simpler than using an oscilloscope or logic analyzer, and you can see all of the signals happening at once.

The best part about Doren's tools is that they are *shareware*, meaning they are freely available and quite inexpensive (though he does have to charge a reasonable fee if you want to order the hardware IRQ/DMA indicator card separately). For the latest news and files from Doren, check out his Web site at **http://slonet.org/~doren/**.

Managing the Configuration of Microsoft Windows

There are at least two major hassles when dealing with Windows in any version or configuration: managing its configuration, and adding or removing installed programs. The tools we'll be looking at in this section provide a tremendous amount of support for you and your Windows configurations.

The following sections are only brief highlights of some exceptional tools to help you with Windows woes, as we don't intend to cover the vast realm of Windows configurations. These highlights should give you some incentive to consider these tools for your own use. After all, once you have your system hardware configuration perfected, it may be time to do something about the on-screen environment you work with.

Adding and Removing Software

As you may know, simply deleting a desktop object or a program icon from Windows does not remove that program or all of the files it added to your system. After upgrading or changing to a new program, or trying to delete an old one, you don't always know which files it installed onto your system, or what changes were made to your **WIN.INI** or **SYSTEM.INI** files. Removing an old program can be tedious work, and may leave behind several megabytes of unused files. The Remove-It utility from Vertisoft helps you manage this situation.

In Versions 2 and 3 of Remove-It, anticipating the upgrade to Windows 95 that many of us will be making, Vertisoft provides an Upgrade Assistant utility to inventory your current Windows configuration, and makes a migration record to carry the essential and upgradeable portions of your Windows 3.x configuration into Windows 95. Run the Upgrade Assistant again under Windows 95, and ta-da! Your old Windows 3.x groups are all setup for you.

Remove-It

There are a lot of uninstall utilities around for Windows. These utilities keep track of all of the files, Windows program groups, and subdirectories that are placed on your system when a new application is installed. If you later decide to remove a particular program, the uninstall utility remembers everything that was installed and can delete it from your system. This process prevents a lot of disk drive clutter left by program files that are no longer needed.

Since installing a program under Windows, especially Windows 95, involves more than just copying some files to your hard disk and creating a desktop icon, we could all use a little help monitoring the process and getting out of it if we don't like the software later on. Many software packages provide their own uninstall routines—which is good, since they know what they installed where in the first place, and the chances are that we don't and won't. Windows 95 will also track a lot of software installations, but this is the environment we might also be a little suspicious of, so we'd like some third-party validation of what's going on.

I've spent more than a little time working with Remove-It from Vertisoft Systems, Inc., and I believe it's at the top of its class for utilities of its kind. Remove-It is not just a utility to track and help you remove software installations. It also tracks almost every file on your system for use, or lack of it, and for duplications and mixed versions of files which may be causing a variety of obscure conflicts on your system. This tracking activity will tell you what files are junk or excess, and if they can be deleted, without impairing the operation of your system.

Ideally, a utility that tracks software installations and system changes should be installed and used immediately after you have done a fresh Windows installation and before installing all of your applications, so that you have an installation log of everything on your system. If you've decided to use one of these utilities on an existing and fully loaded Windows installation, some of these programs can still survey your disk drives to locate the bits and pieces of installed applications.

The Remove-it screen is shown in Figure 8.35.

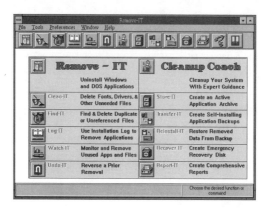

Figure 8.35 Remove-It's main screen.

Remove-It provides the basics of what an uninstall utility can do, and has a lot of additional features, including keeping track of whether or not certain device drivers and font files are used. If you want, you can remove files that are historically never used. Why waste precious disk drive space? The benefits do not stop here. If you would rather not completely uninstall a seldom-used application, you can have Remove-It instead do an archived removal of an application by compressing and backing up all of an application's files, making them available for later use, but saving some disk space in the meantime. See Figure 8.36.

As with any resident program that works in the background on your system, such as Microsoft's own FindFast disk content indexing program, utility software that monitors your system for changes and records what's going on is admittedly going to use up a little CPU time and disk space. Just like backups, defragmenters, disk and file system testers, and anti-virus scanners, Remove-It needs a little time of its own to survey and log your current system and software installations. Let it do so. The power of this program to keep track of your system's software configurations, and cleanly remove excess bits you don't want is well worth the few minutes you let the program run to do its job.

WARNING

Users should read the readme files and manuals included with this and all similar utilities before deleting/archiving any files from Windows 3.x applications that you may still be running under Windows 95. **INI** files and many Windows 3.x **.VXD**, **.386**, **.DLL** and **.DRV** files may still be valid and necessary for your applications.

I know—reading the manual is a pain sometimes, but some are well written, informative and occasionally even educational. It's hard to know what level of user to write for or how much information to provide when doing product manuals and help files, but believe me, we do try!

One of the most interesting aspects of Remove-It is its Upgrade Assistant feature that can help you with that eventual installation of Windows 95. If you're like some of us, when you get Windows 95 you may not want to replace your existing Windows environment, preferring instead to install Windows 95 separately without affecting the currently installed version of Windows and test drive it first. Microsoft does not offer such an option. You must either replace your existing DOS and Windows installation with Windows 95, or replace DOS and install Windows 95 separate from the older version of Windows.

In the latter case, Windows 95 will not install your existing Windows program groups and applications in its configuration. To use your already installed Windows applications under a separate installation of Windows 95 you have to install or select each existing application separately, which is a *very* tedious and time-consuming task.

Another way to accomplish this "test drive" is to completely duplicate your existing Windows configuration into another subdirectory (\WIN95 works for me) and then install Windows 95 over this copy of Windows. This approach consumes a *lot* of disk drive space, as you end up with even more leftover, excess files that may never be used again. I don't know anyone who has *that* much disk space to waste.

Remove-It's Upgrade Assistant feature does all of this tedious work for you, in a lot less time, using a lot less disk space. First, it takes a separate survey of your existing Windows configuration, running within it, so that it has a log of the existing program groups, files, and other attributes to work with later. Then it surveys your DOS installation and evaluates your disk drive to see if you have enough free space to install Windows 95, either over the existing Windows installation or separately.

When this survey of the existing installation is complete, you are ready to install Windows 95. The survey process works even if you have already done a separate Windows 95 installation. The crucial aspect is to get a log of how Windows alone is configured. Once Windows 95 is installed and running, you invoke the Upgrade Assistant within Windows 95 and begin to migrate your previous configuration to the newly installed environment. This migration is done in detail including placing proper entries in Windows 95's system registry.

Once you have learned to use Windows 95 and decide to stick with it, the Upgrade Assistant can be used again to remove your old DOS and Windows files, completing the upgrade and migration process. See Figure 8.37.

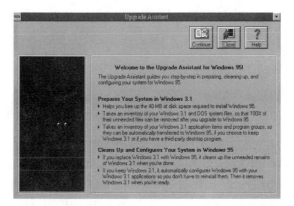

Figure 8.37 Remove-It's Upgrade Assistant screen.

So, now that you've got your software inventoried and logged, and have made the big upgrade step into Windows 95, let's look at the next level of utility we'll need.

Fix-It

Fix-It simply expresses the true nature of how many of us feel about diagnostic and utility software—it finds a problem and all we want it to do is "fix it!" Fix-It has five major features that should be of interest to any Windows 95 user:

- **Conflict Detector:** Checks for, compares, and reports software, driver, and DLL version problems, and offers to (you guessed it) fix them, or tells you what you need to do to get newer files and resolve the problem yourself.

- **Crash Defender:** Traps 16- and 32-bit program errors before they crash your entire system, and gets the annoyances out of your way so you can keep on working.

- **Preinstallation Inspector:** Finds potential conflicts before you install new software and end up creating problems. (That's the spirit!)

- **Change Remover:** Fix-It is nothing if not also polite. It gives you an "oops" feature so you can undo anything you let a software installation or configuration change do to your system.

- **Problem Preventer:** Detects and corrects Windows environment issues in the Registry and other configuration files before you have problems.

When you start up and run Fix-It's conflict detector you see screens similar to Figure 8.38 below. The tests Fix-It does do take awhile, and you can dismiss this activity to the background if you're anxious to get back to work on something else. It summarizes its findings as shown in Figure 8.39.

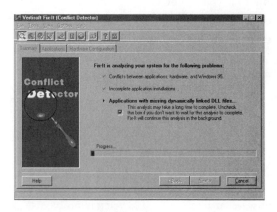

Figure 8.38 Fix-It checking for conflicts and problems.

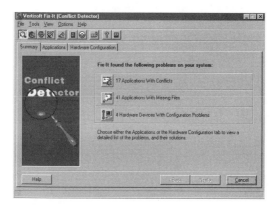

Figure 8.39 Fix-It conflict summary.

As we see in Figure 8.40, we do have a few hardware devices disabled that Fix-It found as problems, which may or may not be specific to the symptoms you're seeing on your system. Certainly if you have trouble using a hard drive or your USB port, Fix-It found the problem for you! In this case, I did turn off these devices in favor of others.

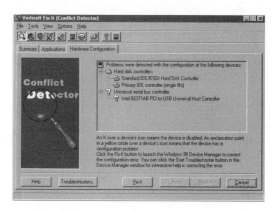

Figure 8.40 Fix-It Hardware Conflict detail.

If you're a do-it-yourself kinda person, but want to delve only so far into the system, Fix-It will take it from there.

TweakUI

TweakUI (Figure 8.41, is a free utility, available from Microsoft's Web site, alone or within the entire suite of Windows 95 add-ins called PowerToys. Its main purpose—or most popular use, anyway—is to let you turn off many of the annoying little features they've added to the shortcut icons and titles (you know, "Shortcut to..." and that ugly little arrow in the corner of the icon!) It also lets you control some of the desktop appearance, document and run history logs, and a few of the things about how Windows 95 boots up. Kudos to Microsoft for this handy little gem.

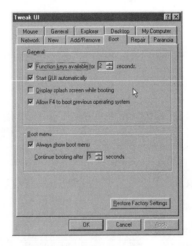

Figure 8.41 TweakUI Boot Features tab.

RegClean

For the timid or impatient (and I don't blame you one bit—the Windows 95 and NT Registry files are scary at best when you get into them), Microsoft now offers for downloading from their Web site a little application called RegClean (Figure 8.42). It seemingly miraculously scours your Registry data for duplicate and wrong entries and offers to remove them for you. It also saves what it removes into a unique file so you can merge the data back into the Registry at any time later if you want to. Pretty slick.

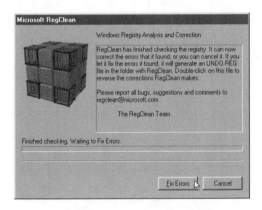

Figure 8.42 RegClean dialog after checking Registry for errors.

Preparing Information for Technical Support

Calling, e-mailing, or faxing for technical support may be something we have come to dread in our experience with PC hardware and software. It takes a lot of patience waiting through phone queues and time zones. The quest for technical support also requires a considerable amount of information exchange. Indeed, the lack of information—by lack of experience, awareness, or the proper tools—creates a technical support bottleneck at all stages of the process. If you are paying for technical support, by a pay-per-call service or a service contract, getting the best service for your money is critical. Books such as this one and well-chosen software tools can take a lot of pressure off of everyone along the way.

We expect technical support people to be familiar with almost every aspect of PCs, from hardware to software. Indeed, this is not very practical—or even possible—given the thousands of systems and programs in use. Those people who have become quite experienced and accomplished at providing technical support in one way or another are often elevated to design and development or management positions. The better someone is at technical support, the less time they spend doing it. Hopefully they will be able to share and promote greater expertise among others. Some of us even begin to write books to share what we know.

Technical support people, and perhaps all too often system and program developers, expect users to be more familiar with their PCs and software than they are or can be. Obviously, this is not always going to be the case, and may never be. Users should simply be able to use their systems and programs, through good design, planning, and training on these items, and not have to be able to design, build, or program them. (But if you try it, you might find it enjoyable and worthwhile!)

The burden of technical support—getting it and giving it—can be significantly relieved if all parties involved are adequately prepared and cooperative. The technical support person should be able to define the types of information needed in order to help resolve a problem. PCs are complex systems. A lot of aspects of them interact, and, yes, conflict at times. Sorting all this out, if you haven't been able to do it with the help of this book, takes you another level deeper into the system details. You can be prepared for this, which will save time and help you determine if you're getting the right help.

The information provided by the tools we've highlighted in this chapter, and the configuration details we've been discussing, are essential for effective technical support—even the support of software problems. Keeping your system inventory current and having a report of your current hardware and DOS and Windows configuration information will save you time in the technical support process. Being able to fax or e-mail this information to the support department may be even more effective. You'll find this type of transaction becoming more and more popular as technical support shifts to on-line electronic means.

In addition to all of this technical information, you should be able to reproduce the conditions under which a problem occurs, and be able to communicate this effectively as well. If your problem is that your printer "doesn't print," the support process takes longer than it has to. You'll be encouraged to check the basics: is the printer plugged in? turned on? connected to your computer? is your software configured properly? A little system information, and running a diagnostic program such as PC-Doctor or RCR and System Monitor, can help pinpoint the possible causes of your problem and get you on the right track to a solution much faster.

Certainly, the more you know about your PC, the more you'll be able to get from the services you request to support it. Your knowledge will help you determine if you're a satisfied customer, or if you need to seek out another service to help you. Since you picked up this book, you were obviously interested in becoming more familiar with your PC. You either want to support yourself directly or determine if you're getting the right support. When you know more, hopefully you'll share the information with others. You'll begin to find that users helping other users creates its own strong support network.

Summary

In closing our configuration management processes with this chapter, it's safe to say that we've covered a lot of ground in a short time. We've reviewed a lot of material that has taken many years for many people to accumulate, study, understand, and apply in daily practice, or through handy and essential software tools. We've seen how software and hardware can complement each other, and even how different types of software can be combined to make our PC configuration management quite complete, up to and including preparations for and transitions to new hardware and operating systems. Maybe you've learned something about this complex toaster and you're better prepared to "make toast" and enjoy the rest of your day.

As with everything else in this fast-paced PC market, you can expect new systems and software revisions to be available that may supersede some of the examples shown in this book. I'll try to keep pace with these developments and consider any and all input to the configuration process for future revisions to this work, perhaps even to some of the featured software tools. The PC business thrives on real-user ideas and needs. No idea, no conflict, no problem goes unheard if you make it known to the right people the right way.

Keep in touch, and *happy bits*!

APPENDIX A

SYSTEM CONFIGURATION DETAIL LIST

Update the following list, or keep a printed or file copy of the system information reported by a utility program such as PC-Doctor, Manifest, Norton's System Information, or MSD. This information is critical to any technical support needed.

Record the IRQ, DMA, and I/O address assignments, as well as the make, model, version, and type for each device in your system. Also record jumper and switch settings for the system board and each add-in board, disk drive, etc.

Configuration Item	Item Details
System BIOS:	
CPU:	
Math Chip:	
CPU Speed:	
Bus Type:	
Total RAM:	
External Cache Size:	
Diskette Drives:	
Hard Drive Adapter Type:	
Hard Drive #1:	
Hard Drive #2:	
SCSI Devices:	
Disk Compression:	
Video Adapter:	
Video BIOS Version:	
Operating System:	
User Interfaces:	
COM Port #1:	
COM Port #2:	
COM Port #3:	
COM Port #4:	
LPT Port #1:	
LPT Port #2:	
LPT Port #3:	
Mouse Type:	
Sound Card:	
Network Adapter:	
Modem:	
Other:	

Keep a backup file or printed copy of the following information and files:

- **AUTOEXEC.BAT**
- **CONFIG.SYS**
- **WIN.INI**
- **SYSTEM.INI**

APPENDIX B

STANDARDS AND PARTICIPATING ORGANIZATIONS

The listing below represents a majority of the official industry standards organizations that affect the PC industry. If you are a hardware designer or software programmer and need specific technical information about a technical specification or standard, these are the places to look. The information available from these organizations is exceptionally detailed and theoretical, and not generally useful for end-user tasks with PCs. These organizations do not maintain information about finished goods or vendor products.

If you are looking for less technical information, consult the bibliography references listed in Appendix C. If you are looking for vendor-specific information, you will find that most vendors provide direct end-user support on CompuServe, America Online, and the Internet, or are listed in many catalogs and magazines.

Organization	Type of Organization or Information	Electronic Information Resources
ANSI *American National Standards Institute* 1430 Broadway New York, NY 10018 212-354-3300 212-398-0023 (fax)	Computer, Electronic and other US standards	
ATA *AT-Attachment Committee/Small Form Factor Committee*	IDE disk drive specifications	subscribe to ATA mailing list through: Majordomo@dt.wdc.com
CCITT *International Telecommunications Union* Place de Nations Ch-1211 Geneva 20 Switzerland 41-22-99-51-11 41-22-33-72-56 (fax) *Information Gatekeepers, Inc.* 214 Harvard Avenue Boston, MA 02134 617-232-3111 617-734-8562 (fax)	Modem and telephony specifications	
DMTF *Desktop Management Task Force* JF2-51 2111 Northeast 25th Street Hillsboro, OR 97124 503-696-9300	DMTF/DMI workstation and network management specifications	ftp.intel.com (look in /pub/IAL) www.intel.com

EIA

Electronics Industry
Association
Global Engineering Documents
2805 McGaw Avenue
Irvine, CA 92714
714-261-1455
714-261-7892 (fax)
800-854-7179 (order info)

Computer and
Electronics standards

www.eia.org

EPA

Energy Star
Computers Program
(MC:6202J)
Washington, D.C. 20460
202-233-9114
202-233-9578 (fax)

Energy Star compliance

www.epa.gov.GODOAR/
EnergyStar.html

IEEE

Institute of Electrical
and Electronic Engineers
The Standards Department
445 Hoes Lane
P.O. Box 1331
Piscataway, NJ 08855-1311
201-562-3800
201-562-1571 (fax)

Computer and
Electronics standards

www.ieee.org

Intel Corp.

5200 NE Elam Young Parkway
Hillsboro, OR 97124-6497
503-696-2000

PCI, Plug and Play,
Advanced Power
Management specs

ftp.intel.com
www.intel.com

Microsoft Corp.

1 Microsoft Way
Redmond, WA 98052
206-882-8080

Plug and Play, PC95,
PC97, Advanced
Power Management
specs

ftp.microsoft.com
www.microsoft.com

PCI

(Peripheral Component Interconnect) PCI Special Interest Group M/S HF3-15A 5200 N.E. Elam Young Parkway Hillsboro, OR 97124-6497 503-696-2000	System bus, built-in and add-in card specifications	ftp.intel.com www.intel.com

PCMCIA (aka PC Card)

Personal Computer Memory Card Industry Association 1030 East Duane Avenue Suite G Sunnyvale, CA 94086 408-720-0107 408-720-9416 (fax)	Portable and desktop system add-in devices and cards	BBS: 408-720-9386 BBS: 408-720-9388 Internet news: alt.periphs.pcmcia CompuServe: GO PCVENF, Lib 12 www.pc-card.com

Plug and Play

	Plug and Play specifications	Compuserve: GO PLUGPLAY ftp://ftp.microsoft.com /developr/drg/Plug- and-Play/Pnpspecs

SCSI

Small Computer Systems Interface	SCSI, SCSI-2 and SCSI-3 specs	subscribe to SCSI mailing list through: scsiadm@witchitaks.ncr.com

Underwriters Laboratory Standards

Underwriters Labs Inc. 1655 Scott Blvd. Santa Clara, CA 95131 408-985-2400	Electrical and safety testing	www.ul.com

VESA

Video Electronics
Standards Association
2150 North First Street
San Jose, CA 95131-2029
408-435-0333
408-435-8225 (fax)

Video BIOS
Enhancements
(VBE), Local Bus

www.vesa.org

APPENDIX C

REFERENCE MATERIALS

You will find the following books most helpful in your pursuit of the operational and functional aspects of PC systems, including repair and upgrade techniques.

Title	Author(s)	Publisher
Troubleshooting Your PC	Aspinwall, Todd	MIS:Press
Inside the IBM PC	Peter Norton	Brady
Upgrading and Repairing PCs	Scott Mueller	Que
System BIOS for IBM PCs, Compatibles, and EISA Computers	Phoenix Technologies Ltd.	Addison-Wesley
Technical Reference, Personal Computer XT and Portable Personal Computer (see note) and *Technical Reference, Personal Computer AT* (see note)	IBM Corporation	IBM Corporation

Title	Author(s)	Publisher
DOS Programmer's Reference	Terry R. Dettman	Que
Hardware Design Guide for Microsoft Windows 95		Microsoft Press
Inside the Windows 95 Registry	Ron Perrusha	O'Reilly & Associates
The Windows 95 Registry	John Woram	MIS:Press
Windows 95 Registry Troubleshooting	Rob Tidrow	New Riders
PCI System Architecture	Tom Shanley, Don Anderson	Mindshare, Inc.
Plug and Play System Architecture	Tom Shanley	Mindshare, Inc.

NOTE

The technical reference manuals from IBM may be out of print, but available from a technical library or a friend.

APPENDIX D

FAVORITE SOFTWARE TOOLS, USER ASSISTANCE, MEMORY MANAGEMENT, AND MORE

If you want to explore the world inside your PC, or get more out of it—from the front-end to a virtual world without borders—the programs listed below are highly recommended and well worth having. Frankly, I like to brag about other peoples' products, especially the ones that help with PC use so much, and that might also make us look like we really have a handle on this PC stuff. The commercial programs, listed first, are available in most software stores or by phone or mail order from many sources.

PC-Doctor and PC-Doctor for Windows

In a pinch and with a twinkle of well-deserved opportunity in mind, the folks at Watergate Software have really helped out getting me the latest tools to further our quest for PC system information. While not your average, mainstream, glitzy retail product, the PC-Doctor programs are available to any PC user for the asking and at a fair price. I am incredibly impressed with the wealth of information and accuracy that these products have provided me with about my own systems. If they aren't calling or e-mailing me with good news about your response to their products, I'll be very surprised.

QEMM—Quarterdeck Corporation CleanSweep

Essential Utilities 97—Fix-It, Zip-It, Remove-It, Partition-It

Quarterdeck gets a billing here because I simply can't imagine using a PC without the tools and features they provide. Before many of us got dragged into the world of Microsoft Windows, we were users of DESQview, Quarterdeck's multi-tasking environment for DOS. DESQview led us to use QEMM as our memory manager, because no other memory manager of substance existed, and QEMM provides benefits with RAM that were unthinkable a few years ago. QEMM is simply faster, smarter, and easier to use than anything like it you might imagine. It's always been reliable, and the company has always been responsive to users and technology changes. If you need to get the most out of your system's memory, you need QEMM. With QEMM you also get MANIFEST, an excellent system information tool worth its weight as a stand-alone utility.

Remove-It, an innovative Windows configuration and installation manager, is an appropriate complement to anything you do in managing your PC hardware configuration. Once the hardware is set up correctly and working smoothly, you're probably not done managing your PC completely without keeping track of what Windows is doing, and being able to undo or uninstall the parts you don't want to use anymore. Just like getting your hardware in top shape before installing Windows 95, you should make sure that your Windows setup is under control, and this is the product to do it with. Install this package under Windows—you'll be glad you did. Thank you, Vertisoft!

Admittedly I've spent more than a 'normal' amount of user, test, consulting, and advisory time with the Remove-It and Fix-It products. A few readers out there may remember my presence on Vertisoft's CompuServe and AOL forums helping to support these gems. Since most folks just want me and others like me in their offices with broken PCs to "fix it," we can certainly relate to the incredible intuitive power it takes to simply figure out what's wrong with a PC and deal with it.

You can find Quarterdeck on the Web at **http:// www.qdeck.com.**

Norton Utilities–Norton/Symantec

If you're not already familiar with or using the popular Norton Utilities, I'd venture to guess that you've not had your system long enough to encounter a file or disk error more serious than DOS' **CHKDSK** or **SCANDISK** could fix. That's actually good news. Disk drives and system components are getting more reliable, but they aren't perfect yet. For all of the times I've intentionally tried to break the file structure on my disk drives, I couldn't find a problem short of actually erasing a few critical disk sectors at a low level that Norton's Disk Doctor (NDD) and/or DISKFIX programs couldn't fix. The UNERASE program is quick and easy to use. Not only are these must-have utilities for your disk and file system, but the other file utilities provide services to a DOS-based system that should have been a part of DOS since the beginning. Most of the utilities also run under Windows.

You can find Symantec on the Web at **http:// www.symantec.com.**

APPENDIX E

ON THE DISK

Some acknowledgments of and background about the programs provided on our diskette:

PC-Doctor from Watergate Software

PC-Doctor is a most complete source of information about PC system IRQ and DMA assignments and general system contents. It covers more hardware better than any other piece of independently developed software on the market.

Some very skilled, clever, imaginative, and just plain excellent people at Watergate create these products and continue their development on a regular basis to meet the demands of an ever-changing industry.

You can find Watergate Software on the Web at **http://www.ws.com.**

The Rosenthal Conflict Resolver

I almost can't thank Doren enough for not only validating this work, but for the kindred spirit discussions by phone and email about PC resource detection and troubleshooting. At the last minute he rushed me his hardware-based IRQ and DMA display board; I'm very impressed and thankful to have it in my PC-guru-arsenal of goodies. You can find Doren on the Web at **http://www.slonet.com/~doren.**

APPENDIX F

PC-DOCTOR PARALLEL PORT LOOPBACK PLUG

In order to accurately detect data and IRQ activity on parallel ports, most diagnostic programs require that a specially wired test connector be attached to all parallel (LPT) ports of interest.

This connector is very simple to make from commonly available parts: a male DB-25 data plug (male connector) and five short pieces of wire. Many computer stores and electronics stores such as Radio Shack carry these plugs in do-it-yourself form with small crimp-on pins that may be inserted into the connector body. More technical users will probably be able to dig into their "junk box" and come up with the necessary parts in a few minutes. If you have more than one parallel port in your system, make one loopback plug for each port so you only have to run the IRQ/DMA test once to detect the IRQs and any conflicts.

The wiring of the connector should be as follows:

- Pin 1 connected to Pin 13
- Pin 2 connected to Pin 15
- Pin 10 connected to Pin 16
- Pin 11 connected to Pin 17
- Pin 12 connected to Pin 14

GLOSSARY

8086

An Intel 8-bit external, 16-bit internal data bus microprocessor capable of addressing up to one megabyte of memory and operating at speeds up to 10MHz. Its companion numerical coprocessor or math chip is the 8087. The 8086 is found in the IBM PS/2 Models 25 and 30 and some clones.

8088

An Intel 8-bit internal, 8-bit external data bus microprocessor capable of addressing up to one megabyte of memory and operating at speeds up to 10MHz. This chip is used in the IBM PC, XT and compatible clone systems. Its companion numerical coprocessor or math chip is the 8087.

80286

An Intel 16-bit internal and external data bus microprocessor capable of addressing up to 16 megabytes of memory and operating at speeds up to 12 MHz. Some non-Intel equivalents may run at 16MHz. This chip's first use in PC systems was in the IBM PC/AT. Its companion numerical coprocessor or math chip is the 80287.

80386DX

An Intel 32-bit internal and external data bus microprocessor capable of addressing up to 4 gigabytes of memory and operating at speeds up to 33 MHz. Some non-Intel equivalents may run at 40MHz. This chip's first use in PC/AT-compatible systems was by Compaq. Its companion numerical coprocessor or math chip is the 80287 in some systems, otherwise the 80387.

80386SX

An Intel 32-bit internal and 16-bit external data bus microprocessor capable of addressing up to 32 megabytes of memory and operating at speeds up to 25 MHz. Its companion numerical co-processor or math chip is the 80387SX.

80486DX

An Intel 32-bit internal and external data bus microprocessor capable of operating at speeds up to 50 MHz. This processor contains an internal math coprocessor (floating point processor) and an 8 Kbyte internal instruction cache.

80486DX2

An Intel 32-bit internal and external data bus microprocessor capable of operating at speeds up to 66 MHz internally, due to a doubling of the external clock speed. This processor contains an internal math coprocessor (floating point processor) and an 8 Kbyte internal instruction cache.

80486DX4

An Intel 32-bit internal and external data bus microprocessor capable of operating at speeds up to 100 MHz internally, due to a

quadrupling of the external clock speed. This processor contains an internal math coprocessor (floating point processor) and an 8 Kbyte internal instruction cache.

80486SX

An Intel 32-bit internal and external data bus microprocessor capable of operating at speeds up to 25 MHz. It is equivalent to the 80486DX, but does not provide the internal floating point processor or the 8 Kbyte cache.

80486SX2

An Intel 32-bit internal and external data bus microprocessor capable of operating at speeds up to 50 MHz internally, due to doubling of the external clock speed. It is equivalent to the 80486DX, but does not provide the internal floating point processor or the 8 Kbyte cache.

Adapter

A hardware device, usually a set of connectors and a cable, used between two pieces of equipment to convert one type of plug or socket to another, or convert one type of signal to another. Examples are a 9-to-25 pin serial port adapter cable, a serial port to serial port null modem, and a PC printer interface to printer cable.

Adapter Card

A plug-in card used to exchange signals between the computer and internal or external equipment. See also Parallel Adapter, Serial Adapter, Video Adapter, Disk Controller.

Add-in Card

See Adapter Card.

Address

A location in memory or on a hardware bus, of either a specific piece of data or a physical hardware device.

ANSI

American National Standards Institute. A governing body managing specifications for the computer industry and other disciplines. In terms of computing, ANSI maintains a set of standards for the coding and displaying of computer information, including certain "ESCape sequences" for screen color and cursor positioning. A device driver file, ANSI.SYS, can be loaded in your PC's CONFIG.SYS file so that your screen can respond properly to

color and character changes provided by programs or terminal sessions between computers.

Application

A computer program, or set of programs, designed to perform a specific type or set of tasks in order to make a computer help you to do your work or provide entertainment. Typical applications are games, word processing, databases, or spreadsheet programs.

AT

A model series of the IBM PC family known as Advanced Technology. This series includes those systems that use the 80286 microprocessor chip. The AT classification has been applied to 80386- and 80486-based systems that offer basic compatibility with and enhancements over the original specification.

ATA

AT-Attachments. An industry-wide specification for the interfacing of devices, typically hard disk drives, to the PC/AT standard data bus.

AT-compatible

A description of a personal computer system that provides the minimum functions and features of the original IBM PC/AT system, and is capable of running the same software and using the same hardware devices.

AUTOEXEC.BAT file

An ASCII text file that may contain one or more lines of DOS commands that you want executed every time you boot your PC. Also known as just the "autoexec" file, this file is customizable, using a text editor program, so that you can specify a DOS prompt, set a drive and directory path to be searched when you call up programs, or load terminate-and-stay resident (TSR) programs that you want to have available all of the time.

Base address

The initial or starting address of a device or memory location.

Base memory

See DOS memory.

BATch file

An ASCII text file that may contain one or more lines of DOS commands that you want to execute by calling for one file (the name of the batch file) rather than keying them in individually. Also known as just a "bat" file, these files are customizable, using a text editor program, so that you can specify a DOS prompt, set a drive and directory path to be searched when you call up programs, or load and execute specific programs. Batch files are used extensively as shortcuts for routine or repetitive tasks, or those that you just don't want to have to remember each step for. These files always have the extension .BAT, as required by DOS.

BBS

Bulletin Board Service or Bulletin Board System. A public or private, local or remote computer system accessed by modem for message and/or file sharing between users. A BBS may be operated by anyone with the time, equipment, and software to do so. User groups, clubs, companies, and government agencies operate BBSes to share information. There may or may not be a charge for the use of some systems. BBS listings may be found accompanying some communications programs, in the back of PC journals, or in many phone book yellow pages. See also Online services.

BIOS

Basic Input/Output System. The first set of program code to run when a PC system is booted up. The BIOS defines specific addresses and devices and provides software interface services for programs to use the equipment in a PC system. The PC system BIOS resides in a ROM chip on the system board. BIOS may also exist on add-in cards to provide additional adapter and interface services between hardware and software.

Bootup

The process of loading and running the hardware initialization program to allow access to hardware resources by applications.

Bus

An internal wiring configuration between the CPU and various interface circuits carrying address, data, and timing information required by one or more internal, built-in, add-in, or external adapters and devices.

Byte

The common unit of measure for memory, information, file size, or storage capacity. A byte consists of 8 bits of information. There are two bytes to a word (16 bits) of information. 1000 bytes is referred to as a kilobyte or Kbyte, and contains 1024 bits of information.

CGA

Color Graphics Adapter. The first IBM-PC color display system, providing low-resolution (320x200) color graphics and basic text functions.

CMOS clock

A special clock chip that runs continuously, either from the PC system power supply or a small battery, providing date and time information.

CMOS RAM

A special memory chip used to store system configuration information. Rarely found in PC or XT models; usually found in 286 or higher models.

CMOS setup

The process of selecting and storing configuration (device, memory, date, and time) information about your system for use during boot-up. This process may be done through your PC's BIOS program or an external (disk-based) utility program.

Command line

The screen area immediately after a prompt, where you key in commands to the computer or program. This is most commonly the DOS command line, as indicated by the DOS prompt (C>, C:\> or similar).

CONFIG.SYS

An ASCII text file that may contain one or more lines of special DOS commands that you want executed every time you boot up your PC. Also known as the "config" file, this file is customizable, using a text editor

program, so that you can specify one or more items specific to how your system should operate when it boots up. You may specify device drivers (with DEVICE=) such as memory management programs, disk caching, RAM disks; the number of FILES and BUFFERS you want DOS to use; the location, name, and any special parameters for your command processor (usually COMMAND.COM), among other parameters. Refer to your DOS manual or device driver software manual for specific information.

Controller

See adapter.

Conventional memory

Also known as DOS memory, this is the range of your PC's memory from 0-640 kilobytes, where device drivers, DOS parameters, the DOS command processor (COMMAND. COM), your applications programs, and their data are stored when you use your computer. See Extended, Expanded, Video, High and Upper Memory.

CPU

Central Processing Unit. The main integrated circuit chip, processor circuit or board in a computer system. For IBM PC-compatible systems, the CPU may be either an Intel or comparable (AMD, Cyrix, IBM, or TI) 8088, 8086, 80286, 80386 (SX or DX), 80486 (SX or DX) or NEC V20 or V30 chips. Current PC system CPU chips include the Intel Pentium, Pentium II, Pentium Pro; AMD K5 and K6; Cyrix 5x86 and 6x86; and '586' variants from IBM and Texas Instruments.

Current directory

This is the subdirectory you or a program has last selected to operate from, and that is searched first before the DOS PATH is searched when calling a program. See also Current disk drive and Logged drive.

Current disk drive

The drive that you have selected for DOS and programs to use before searching the specified drives and directories in the DOS PATH (if any is specified.) This may also be the drive indicated by your DOS prompt (typically C> or C:\> or similar) or that you have selected by specifying a drive letter followed by a colon and the Enter key, as in A:<Enter>. This is also known as the "logged" drive.

DESQview™

A multi-tasking user-interface that allows simultaneous operation of many programs. DESQview uses Expanded Memory to create virtual DOS sessions and memory areas, and controls the amount of processor time given to each DOS session and the application using it.

DESQview/X™

A multi-tasking graphical user interface based on the MIT X-Window client/server standard. It allows simultaneous operation of many programs, on the local system and across other X-Window-based systems on a network. DESQview/X uses Expanded Memory to create virtual DOS sessions and memory areas, and controls the amount of processor time given to each DOS session and the application using it.

Device

An actual piece of hardware interfaced to the computer to provide input or accept output. Typical devices are printers, modems, mice, keyboards, displays, and disk drives. There are also some special or virtual devices, handled in software, that act like hardware. The most common of these is called NUL, which is essentially "nowhere." You can send screen or other output to the NUL device so that it does not appear. The NUL device is commonly used if the actual device to send something to does not exist, but a program requires that output be sent someplace. NUL is a valid place to send output to, although the output really doesn't go anywhere.

Device driver

A special piece of software required by some hardware or software configurations to interface your computer to a hardware device. Common device drivers are ANSI.SYS, used for display screen control; RAMDRIVE.SYS, which creates and maintains a portion of memory that acts like a disk drive; and HIMEM.SYS, a special device driver used to manage a specific

area of Extended memory, called the HMA. Device drivers are usually intended to be used in the CONFIG.SYS file, preceded by a DEVICE= statement.

Diagnostics

Software programs that test the functions of system components.

Directory

File space on disks used to store information about files organized and referred to through a directory name. Each disk has at least one directory, called the Root directory, which is a specific area reserved for other file and directory entries. A hard disk Root directory may contain up to 512 other files or directory references, limited by the amount of disk space reserved for Root directory entries. The files and directories referred to by the Root directory may be of any size, up to the limit of available disk space. Directories may be thought of as folders or boxes, as they may appear with some graphical user-interfaces, though they are not visually represented that way by DOS. See Root Directory and Subdirectories. All directories, except for the Root directory, must have a name. The name for a directory follows the 1-8 character restrictions that apply to filenames. See also Filename.

Disk

A rotating magnetic medium used for storing computer files. See also Diskette and Hard Disk.

Diskette

Also called a floppy diskette, this is a disk media contained in a cover jacket and which can be removed from a disk drive. The term floppy is synonymous with flexible, in that the disk medium is a magnetically-coated disk of thin plastic material.

Disk drive adapter or controller

A built-in or add-in card interface that provides necessary connections between the computer system I/O circuits and a disk drive.

DMA

Direct Memory Access. A method of transferring information between a computer's memory and another device, such as a disk drive, without requiring CPU intervention.

DOS Diskette

A diskette formatted for use with DOS-based PCs and file systems.

DOS memory

Temporary memory used for storage of DOS boot and operating system information, programs, and data during the operation of your computer system. DOS memory occupies up to the first 640k of RAM (Random Access Memory) space provided in your system's hardware. This memory empties out (loses its contents) when your computer is shut off.

DOS or Disk operating system

A set of software written for a specific type of computer system, disk, file, and application types to provide control over disk storage services and other input and output functions required by application programs and system maintenance. All computers using disk drives have some form of disk operating system containing applicable programs and services. For IBM-PC-compatible computers, the term DOS is commonly accepted to mean the computer software services specific to PC systems.

DOS System Diskette

A diskette formatted for use with DOS-based PCs and their file system, that also contains the two DOS-system hidden files and COMMAND.COM to allow booting up your system from a diskette drive.

Drive

The mechanical and electronic assembly that holds disk storage media, and provides the reading and writing functions for data storage and retrieval.

EGA

Enhanced Graphics Adapter. A color graphics system designed by IBM, providing medium-resolution text and graphics, compatible also with monochrome text and CGA displays.

EISA

Extended Industry Standard Architecture. The definition of a PC internal bus structure that maintains compatibility with IBM's original PC, XT, and AT bus designs (known as the ISA, Industry Standard Architecture), but offering considerably more features and speed between the computer system and adapter cards, including a definition for 32-bit PC systems that do not follow IBM's MCA (MicroChannel Architecture).

EMM

Expanded Memory Manager. The term is often given to software, or refers to Expanded memory chips and cards. See also Expanded Memory.

EMS

Expanded Memory Specification. The IBM-PC-industry standards for software and hardware that makes up Expanded Memory.

ENTER (<Enter>)

The command or line termination key, also known as return on your keyboard. There are usually two <Enter> keys on your keyboard. Under some applications programs these two keys may have different functions; the numeric keypad <Enter> key may be used as an "enter data" key, while the alphanumeric keyboard <Enter> key may be used as a Carriage Return.

Environment

An area of memory set up and used by the DOS software to store and retrieve a small amount of information that can be shared or referred to by many programs. Among other information that the DOS environment area could hold are the PATH, current drive, PROMPT, COMSPEC, and any SET variables.

ESDI

Enhanced Small Device Interface. A standards definition for the interconnection of newer high-speed disk drives. This standard is an alternative to earlier MFM, coincident applications of SCSI, and recent IDE drive interfaces.

Execute

The action that a computer takes when it is instructed to run a program. A running program is said to execute or be executing when it is being used.

Executable File

A program file that may be invoked from the operating system. DLLs and overlay files also contain executable program information, but their functions must be invoked from within another program.

Expanded Memory

This is an additional area of memory created and managed by a device driver program using the Lotus-Intel-Microsoft Expanded Memory Specification, known also as LIMS-EMS. There are three common forms of EMS: that conforming to the LIMS-EMS 3.2 standard for software-only access to this memory; LIMS-EMS 4.0 in software; and LIMS-EMS 4.0 in hardware. With the proper hardware, this memory may exist and be used on all PC systems, from PCs to 486 systems. Expanded Memory may be made up of Extended Memory (memory above 1 megabyte) on 386 and 486 systems, or it may be simulated in Extended Memory on 286 systems. LIMS-EMS 3.2, 4.0 (software) and 4.0 (hardware) are commonly used for additional data storage for spreadsheets and databases. Only LIMS-EMS conforming to the 4.0 standard for hardware may be used for multi-tasking. Expanded memory resides at an upper memory address, occupying one 64k block between 640k and 1 megabyte. The actual amount of memory available depends upon your hardware and the amount of memory you can assign to be Expanded Memory. The 64k block taken up by Expanded Memory is only a window or port giving access to the actual amount of EMS available. There may be as little as 64k or as much as 32 megabytes of Expanded Memory.

Extended Memory

This is memory in the address range above 1 megabyte, available only on 80286 or higher systems. It is commonly used for RAM disks, disk caching, and some applications programs. Using a special driver called HIMEM.SYS, or similar services provided with memory management software, the first 64k of Extended Memory may be assigned as a High Memory Area into which some programs and DOS can be loaded.

File

An area of disk space containing a program or data as a single unit, referred to by the DOS file directory. Its beginning location is recorded in the file directory, with reference to all space occupied by the file recorded in the DOS File Allocation Table (FAT). Files are pieces of data or software that you work with on your computer. They may be copied, moved, erased, or modified, all of which is tracked by DOS for the directory and FAT.

Filename

The string of characters assigned to a disk file to identify it. A filename must be at least one, and may be up to 8 leading characters as the proper name. A filename may be followed by a 3 character extension, separated from the proper name by a period(.). Allowable filename and extension characters are: A-Z, 0-9, !,@,#,$,^,&,_,-,{,},(,).'‚`,or ~. Also, many of the IBM Extended character set may be used. Reserved characters that cannot be used are: %, *, +, =, ;, :,[,], <, >, ?, /, \, |, " and <Space>. Filenames must be unique for each file in a directory, but the same name may exist in separate directories. Filenames are assigned to all programs and data files.

Filename extension

A string of 1–3 characters used after a filename and a separating period (.), with the same character limitations as the filename. The extension is often used to identify certain types of files to certain applications. DOS uses BAT, EXE, and COM as files it can load and execute, thought this does not preclude the use of these extensions for non-executable files. The extensions SYS, DRV and

DVR are commonly used for device driver programs that are loaded and used in the CONFIG.SYS file prior to loading DOS (as COMMAND.COM.) Refer to your software documentation for any limitations or preferences it has for filename extensions.

Fixed disk

See Hard disk.

Floppy disk

See Diskette.

Gigabyte (Gbyte or GB)

A unit of measure referring to 1,024 megabytes or 1,073,741,824 bytes of information, storage space, or memory. Devices with this capacity are usually large disk drives and tape backup units with up to 9 gigabytes or more of storage area.

Hard disk

A sealed disk drive unit with platters mounted inside on a fixed spindle assembly. The actual platter is a hard aluminum or glass surface coated with magnetic storage media. This definition also suits removable hard disks in which the hard platters are encased in a sealed casing, and mate with a spindle similar to the attachment of a floppy diskette to the drive motor. The platters are sealed to keep foreign particles from interfering with and potentially damaging the platters or the read/write heads that normally maintain a small gap between them during operation.

Hardware Interrupt

A signal from a hardware device connected to a PC system that causes the CPU and computer program to act on an event that requires software manipulation, such as controlling mouse movements, accepting keyboard input, or transferring a data file through a serial I/O port.

Hercules

A medium-resolution monochrome graphics and text display system designed by Hercules Technology, offering compatibility with IBM monochrome text. Hercules-specific graphics display was supported by many programs as a low-cost alternative and improvement to CGA displays before EGA was defined.

Hexadecimal

A base-16 numbering system made up of 4 digits or bits of information, where the least significant place equals one and the most significant place equals eight. A hexadecimal (hex) number is represented as the numbers 0-9 and letters A-F, for the numerical range 0-15 as 0-F. A byte of hex information can represent from 0 to 255 different items, as 00 to FF.

High Memory Area or HMA

A 64 Kbyte region of memory above the 1 megabyte address range created by HIMEM.SYS or a similar memory utility. The HMA can be used by one program for program storage, leaving more space available in the DOS or low memory area from 0-640k.

Host adapter

A built-in or add-in card interface between a device, such as a SCSI hard disk or CD-ROM drive, and the I/O bus of a computer system. A host adapter typically does not provide control functions, instead acting only as an address and signal conversion and routing circuit.

IBM PC-compatible

A description of a personal computer system that provides the minimum functions and features of the original IBM PC system, and is capable of running the same software and using the same hardware devices.

IDE

Integrated Drive Electronics. A standards definition for the interconnection of high-speed disk drives where the controller and drive circuits are together on the disk drive, and interconnect to the PC I/O system through a special adapter card. This standard is an alternative to earlier MFM, ESDI, and SCSI drive interfaces, and is also part of the ATA standard.

I/O or Input/Output

The capability or process of software or hardware to accept or transfer data between computer programs or devices.

Interrupt

See Hardware Interrupt, IRQ, and Software Interrupt.

IRQ

Interrupt ReQuest. This is a set of hardware signals available on the PC add-in card connections which can request prompt attention by the CPU when data must be transferred to/from add-in devices and the CPU or memory.

ISA

Industry Standard Architecture. The term given to the IBM PC, XT, and AT respective 8 and 16-bit PC bus systems. Non-32-bit, non IBM MicroChannel Architecture systems are generally ISA systems.

ISP

Internet Service Provider (such as Netcom, Best, Earthlink, iHighway.net, etc.). Commercial subscriber services offering home, SOHO, and small to big business connectivity to the Internet through a variety of connection options. Many ISPs are also Internet Access Providers to businesses (providing access to the Internet at-large for business that support their own internal WWW and e-mail servers, rather than using those provided by an ISP to end users).

Kilobyte (Kbyte, or KB)

A unit of measure referring to 1,024 bytes or 8,192 bits of information, storage space or memory.

LIMS (Lotus-Intel-Microsoft Standard)

See Expanded Memory.

Loading high

An expression for the function of placing a device driver or executable program in a high (XMS, above 1 megabyte) or upper memory area (between 640k and 1 megabyte). This operation is performed by a DEVICEHIGH or LOADHIGH (DOS) statement in the CONFIG.SYS or AUTOEXEC. BAT file. High memory areas are created by special memory manager programs such as EMM386 (provided with versions of DOS) and Quarterdeck's QEMM386.

Local Bus™

A processor to I/O device interface alternative to the PC's standard I/O bus connections, providing extremely fast transfer of data and control signals between a device and the CPU. It is commonly used for video cards and disk drive interfaces to enhance system performance. Local Bus is a trademark of the Video Electronics Standards Association.

Logical Devices

A hardware device that is referred to in DOS or applications by a name or abbreviation that represents a hardware address assignment, rather than by its actual physical address. The physical address for a logical device may be different. Logical device assignments are based on rules established by IBM and the ROM BIOS at boot up.

Logical Drive

A portion of a disk drive assigned as a smaller partition of a larger physical disk drive. Also a virtual or non-disk drive created and managed through special software. RAM drives (created with RAMDRIVE.SYS or VDISK.SYS) or compressed disk/file areas (such as those created by Stacker,

DoubleDisk or SuperStor) are also logical drives. A 40 megabyte disk drive partitioned as drives C: and D: is said to have two logical drives. That same disk with one drive area referred to as C: has only one logical drive, coincident with the entire physical drive area. DOS may use up to 26 logical drives. Logical drives may also appear as drives on a network server, or be mapped by the DOS ASSIGN or SUBST programs.

Loopback plug

A connector specifically wired to return an outgoing signal to an input signal line for the purpose of detecting if the output signal is active or not, as sensed at the input line.

Lower memory

See DOS memory.

Math coprocessor

An integrated circuit designed to accompany a computer's main CPU and to speed floating-point and complex math functions that would normally take a long time if done with software and the main CPU. Allows the main CPU to perform other work during these math operations.

MCGA

Multi-Color Graphics Array. An implementation of CGA built-into IBM PS/2 Model 25 and 30 systems using an IBM analog monitor, and providing some enhancements for higher resolution display and gray-scale shading for monochrome monitors.

MDA

Monochrome Display Adapter. The first IBM PC video system, providing text-only on a one-color (green or amber) display. If you have one of these adapters, you own an antique!

Megabyte (Mbyte or MB)

A unit of measure referring to 1,024 kilobytes or 1,048,576 bytes of information, storage space or memory. One megabyte contains 8,388,608 bits of information. One megabyte is also the memory address limit of a PC or XT-class computer using an 8088, 8086, V20, or V30 CPU chip. A megabyte is 0.001 gigabytes.

Megahertz

A measure of frequency in millions of cycles per second. The speed of a computer system's main CPU clock is rated in megahertz.

Memory

Computer information storage area made up of chips (integrated circuits) or other components, which may include disk drives. Personal computers use many types of memory, from dynamic RAM chips for temporary DOS, Extended, Expanded and video memory, to static RAM chips for CPU instruction caching, to memory cartridges and disk drives for program and data storage.

MHz

See Megahertz.

Micro Channel™

Micro Channel Architecture. IBM's system board and adapter card standards for the PS/2 (Personal System/2) series of computers. This is a non-ISA bus system requiring the use of different adapter cards and different configuration information from that used on early PC, XT and AT compatible systems.

Microprocessor

A computer central processing unit contained within one integrated circuit chip package.

MIDI

Musical Instrument Device Interface. An industry standard for hardware and software connections, control, and data transfer between like-equipped musical instruments and computer systems.

MMX

Multimedia Extensions. Enhanced graphics and rendering features supplied within the micro-processor chip, to provide faster CPU support for games and other multimedia applications.

Modem

An abbreviation for MOdulator/ DEModulator. A hardware device used to convert digital signals to analog tones, and analog tones to digital signals used primarily for the transmission of data between computers across telephone lines.

Motherboard

The main component or system board of your computer system. It contains the necessary connectors, components, and interface circuits required for communications between the CPU, memory, and I/O devices. Also known as the system board.

Multi-tasking

The process of software control over memory and CPU tasks, allowing the swapping of programs and data between active memory and CPU use to a paused or non-executing mode in a reserved memory area, while another program is placed in active memory and execution mode. The switching of tasks may be assigned different time values for how much of the processor time each program gets or requires. The program you see on-screen is said to be operating in the foreground and typically gets the most CPU time, while any programs you may not see are said to be operating in the background, usually getting less CPU time. DESQview and Windows are two examples of multi-tasking software in common use on PCs.

Network

The connection of multiple systems, together, or to a central distribution point, for the purpose of information or resource sharing.

Network Interface Card

An add-in card or external adapter unit used to connect a workstation (PC system) to a common network or distribution system.

NIC

See Network Interface Card.

Online services

These are typically commercial operations, much like a BBS, that charge for the time and services used while connected. Most online services use large computers designed to handle multiple users and types of operations. These services provide electronic mail, computer and software support conferences, online game playing, and file libraries for uploading and downloading public-domain and shareware programs. Often familiar communities or groups of users form in the conferences, making an online service a favorite or familiar places for people to gather. Access to these systems is typically by modem, to either a local data

network access number, through a WATS/800 or direct toll line. Delphi, GEnie, America Online, Prodigy, and CompuServe are among the many online services available in the U.S. and much of the world. These differ from ISPs (Internet Service Providers) as they usually provide customized user-interface software for access to the service's features, and offer several predefined forums and topics within their systems that do not exist in the Internet's public domain.

Operating system

See Disk Operating System.

OS/2™

A 32-bit operating system, multi-tasking control and graphical-user-interface developed by Microsoft, currently sold and supported by IBM. OS/2 allows the simultaneous operation of many DOS, Windows and, OS/2-specific applications programs.

Page frame

The location in DOS/PC system memory (between 640k and 1 megabyte) where Expanded Memory is accessed.

Parallel I/O

A method of transferring data between devices or portions of a computer where 8 or more bits of information are sent in one cycle or operation. Parallel transfers require 8 or more wires to move the information. At speeds from 12,000 to 92,000 bytes per second or faster, this method is faster than the serial transfer of data where one bit of information follows another. Commonly used for the printer port on PCs.

Parallel Port

A computer's parallel I/O (LPT) connection, built into the system board, or provided by an add-in card.

Parameter

Information provided when starting or running a program, specifying how or when it is to run with which files, disks, paths, or similar attributes.

PC

The first model designation for IBM's family of personal computers. This model provided 64-256k of RAM on the System Board, a cassette tape adapter as an alternative to diskette storage, and

5 add-in card slots. The term generally refers to all IBM-PC-compatible models, and has gained popular use as a generic term referring to all forms, makes and models for personal computing.

PC-compatible

See IBM PC-compatible and AT-compatible.

PCI

See Peripheral Component Interconnect.

PCMCIA / PC Card

Personal Computer Memory Card Industry Association. An I/O interconnect definition, also called the PC Card, used for memory cards, disk drives, modems, network, and other connections to portable computers.

Pentium™

An 64-bit Intel microprocessor capable of operating at 90-233Hz, containing a 16 Kbyte instruction cache, floating point processor, and several internal features for extremely fast program operations.

Peripheral

A hardware device internal or external to a computer that is not necessarily required for basic computer functions. Printers, modems, document scanners, and pointing devices are peripherals to a computer.

Peripheral Component Interconnect

PCI. An Intel-developed standard interface between the CPU and I/O devices providing enhanced system performance. PCI is typically used for video and disk drive interconnections to the CPU.

Physical drive

The actual disk drive hardware unit, as a specific drive designation (A:, B:, or C:, etc.), or containing multiple logical drives, as with a single hard drive partitioned to have logical drives C:, D:, and so on. Most systems or controllers provide for two to four physical floppy diskette drives, and up to two physical hard disk drives, which may have several logical drive partitions.

Port address

The physical address, located within the computer's memory range, where a hardware device is set to decode and allow access to its services.

POST

Power On Self Test. A series of hardware tests run on your PC when power is turned on to the system. POST surveys installed memory and equipment, storing and using this information for boot-up and subsequent use by DOS and applications programs. POST will provide either speaker beep messages, video display messages, or both, if it encounters errors in the system during testing and boot-up.

Prompt

A visual indication that a program or the computer is ready for input or commands. The native DOS prompt for input is shown as the a disk drive letter and "right arrow" or "caret" character (C>). The DOS prompt may be changed with the DOS PROMPT internal command, to indicate the current drive and directory, include a user name, the date or time, or more creatively, flags or colored patterns.

PS/2™

Personal System/2. A series of IBM personal computer systems using alternative designs, bus, and adapter technologies. Early models did not support the many existing PC-compatible cards and display peripherals, though IBM has provided later models that maintain their earlier ISA expansion capabilities.

RAM

RAM stands for Random Access Memory, a storage area that information can be sent to and taken from by addressing specific locations in any order at any time. The memory in your PC and even the disk drives are a form of random access memory, though the internal memory is most commonly referred to as the RAM. RAM memory chips come in two forms, the more common Dynamic RAM (DRAM) which must be refreshed often in order to retain the information stored in it, and Static RAM, which can retain information without refreshing, saving power and time. RAM memory chips are referred to by their storage capacity and maximum speed of operation in the part numbers assigned to them. Fast Page Mode DRAM, EDO DRAM, and Synchronous DRAM are much faster and better suited to today's processors.

Chips with 16 Kbyte and 64 Kbyte capacity were common in early PCs, but 256 Kbyte and 1 MB chips were common until 4, 8, and 16 megabyte chips appeared. We now purchase RAM in SIMM (Single Inline Memory Modules) and DIMM (Dual Inline Memory Modules) that contain 16 or 32-bit wide RAM in increments of 8, 16, 32, or 64 megabytes per unit.

RETURN (<Return>)

See ENTER key.

ROM

ROM stands for Read-Only Memory. This is a type of memory chip that is preprogrammed with instructions or information specific to the computer type or device in which it is used. All PCs have a ROM-based BIOS that holds the initial boot-up instructions used when your computer is first turned on, or when a warm-boot is issued. Some video and disk adapters contain a form of ROM-based program that replaces or assists the PC BIOS or DOS in using a particular adapter.

ROM BIOS

The ROM-chip-based start-up or controlling program for a computer system or peripheral device. See also BIOS and ROM.

Root directory

The first directory area on any disk media. The DOS command processor, and any CONFIG.SYS or AUTOEXEC.BAT file, must typically reside in the Root directory of a bootable disk. The Root directory has space for a fixed number of entries, which may be files or subdirectories. A hard disk Root directory may contain up to 512 files or subdirectory entries, the size of which is limited only by the capacity of the disk drive. Subdirectories may have nearly unlimited numbers of entries.

SCSI

Small Computer System Interface. An interface specification for interconnecting peripheral devices to a computer bus. SCSI allows for attaching multiple high-speed devices, such as disk and tape drives, through a single 50-pin cable.

Serial I/O

A method of transferring data between two devices one bit at a time, usually within a predetermined frame of bits that makes up a character, plus transfer control information (start and stop or beginning and end of character information). Modems and many printers use serial data transfer. One-way serial transfer can be done on as few as two wires, with two-way transfers requiring as few as three wires. Transfer speeds of 110 to 230,000 bits (11 to 11,500 characters) per second are possible through a PC serial port, allowing up to 33.6k, 56k and even 128k (compressed) bits per second on-line rates

Serial Port

A computer's serial I/O (COM) connection, built-into the system board, or provided by an add-in card.

Shadow RAM

A special memory configuration that remaps/reallocates some or all of the information stored in BIOS and adapter ROM chips to faster, dedicated RAM chips. This feature is controllable on many PC systems that have it, allowing you to use memory management software to provide this and other features.

Software Interrupt

A non-hardware signal or command from a currently executing program that causes the CPU and computer program to act on an event requiring special attention, such as the completion of a routine operation or the execution of a new function. Many software interrupt services are predefined and available through the system BIOS and DOS, while others may be made available by device driver software or running programs. Most disk accesses, keyboard operations, and timing services are provided to applications through software interrupt services.

Subdirectory

A directory contained within the Root directory, or in other subdirectories, used to organize programs and files by application or data type, system user, or other criteria. A subdirectory may be thought of as a file folder in a filing cabinet, or an index tab in a book.

SVGA / Super VGA

A newer high resolution text and graphics standard supporting original VGA capabilities and enhanced displays, providing up 1600 × 1200 pixels display resolution of over 64 million color variations.

TSR (Terminate-and-stay-resident program)

Also known as a memory-resident program. A program that remains in (RAM) memory to provide services automatically, or on request through a special key sequence (also known as hot-keys). Device drivers (MOUSE, ANSI, SETVER), disk caches, RAM disks, and print spoolers are forms of automatic TSR programs. SideKick, Lightning, and assorted screen-capture programs are examples of hot-key controlled TSR programs.

UAR/T

Universal Asynchronous Receiver/ Transmitter. This is a special integrated circuit or function used to convert parallel computer bus information into serial transfer information, and vice versa. A UAR/T also provides proper system-to-system online status, modem ring, and data carrier detect signals, as well as start/stop transfer features. The most recent version of this chip, called a

16550A, is crucial to high speed (greater than 2400 bits per second) data transfers under multi-tasking environments such as DESQview, Windows 3.x, 95 and NT.

Upper memory and Upper Memory Blocks (UMB)

Memory space between 640k and 1 megabyte that may be controlled and made available by a special device driver (EMM386.SYS, QEMM386, 386Max, etc.) for the purpose of storing and running TSR programs and leaving more DOS RAM (from 0-640k) available for other programs and data. Some of this area is occupied by BIOS, video, and disk adapters.

USB (Universal Serial Bus)

A new (circa 1997) high-speed interface port providing serial data connections for computer peripherals.

Utilities

Software programs that perform or assist with routine functions such as file backups, disk defragmentation, disk file testing, file and directory sorting, etc. See also Diagnostics.

V20

An NEC clone of the Intel 8088 8-bit internal and external data bus microprocessor capable of addressing up to one megabyte of memory and operating at speeds up to 10MHz. NEC has optimized several of the internal microcode commands so this CPU chip can perform some operations faster than the Intel chip, which it can replace. Its companion numerical coprocessor or math chip is the 8087. This chip can generally be used in any PC or XT system that uses an 8088 chip.

V30

An Intel 16-bit internal, 8-bit external data bus microprocessor capable of addressing up to one megabyte of memory and operating at speeds up to 10MHz. NEC has optimized several of the internal microcode commands so this CPU chip can perform some operations faster than the Intel chip it can replace. Its companion numerical coprocessor or math chip is the 8087. This chip can only be used in IBM PS/2 Models 25 and 30, and some clones.

Variable

Information provided when requested by or within a program, specifying how or when it is to run, with which files, disks, paths, or similar attributes. A variable may be allowed for in a BATch file, using %1 through %9 designations to substitute or include values keyed in at the command line when the BATch file is called.

VGA

Video Graphics Array. A high resolution text and graphics system supporting color and previous IBM video standards using an analog interfaced video monitor. Original VGA capabilities have been superseded by Super VGA specifications. See also Super VGA.

Video Adapter Card

The interface card between the computer's I/O system and the video display device.

Video memory

Memory contained on the video adapter dedicated to storing information to be processed by the adapter for placement on the display screen. The amount and exact location of video memory depends on the type and features of your video adapter. This memory and the video adapter functions are located in upper memory between 640k and 832k.

Windows™

A Microsoft multi-tasking and graphical user interface allowing multiple programs to operate on the same PC system and share the same resources.

Windows 95™

A Microsoft multi-tasking operating system and graphical user interface, an upgrade from the Windows 3.1 and 3.11 versions.

Windows NT™

A Microsoft 32-bit multi-tasking operating system and graphical user interface.

XMS

Extended Memory Specification, a standard that defines access and control over upper, high, and extended memory on 286 and higher computer systems. XMS support is provided by loading the HIMEM.SYS device driver or other memory management software that provides XMS features.

XT

The second model of the IBM PC series, provided with "eXtended Technology" allowing the addition of hard disks and eight add-in card slots. The original XT models had between 64 and 256k of RAM on board, a single floppy drive, and a 10 megabyte hard disk.

INDEX

How to Use the Files on the Disk

PC-Doctor and The Rosenthal Utilities are best run on a system booted to a DOS-prompt only, not within a DOS-box/window or Windows 95 system restarted into MS-DOS mode. The raw system information and resources are more accurately determined this way, without Windows (or OS/2) device drivers impacting the results.

In certain cases you may also need to load any SCSI adapter, sound card, network card, or mouse drivers in order to detect and record information about these items—but again—only in DOS.

The files on the diskette are in ready-to-run, uncompressed formats. They may be used directly from the diskette, but may be handier if copied to your hard disk to avoid risking any corruption of the diskette.

Please refer to the README files on the diskette for complete installation instructions.

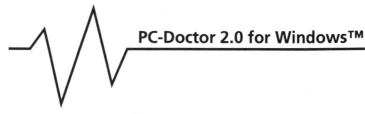 **PC-Doctor 2.0 for Windows™**

by Watergate Software, Inc.™ is a dynamic system information and diagnostic tool that can test your computer, determine its cofiguration, and even perform low-level DOS testing! Used by leading PC manufacturers, this one software package provides more than 250 professional-level hardware diagnostic tests in a modular, easy-to-use format. These extensive tests detect failures in system components from the CPU to SCSI devices, CD-ROM drives, and PCMCIA cards, as well as providing IRQ and DMA usage and complete system and hardware information. Plus the handy help screens and an on-line manual keep you well-informed of the diagnostic process!

Includes:

- *Comprehensive Windows System Information*
- *Intel® Pentium™ Statistics*
- *More than 20 Interactive Tests and Utilities*
- *Includes PC-Doctor for DOS*
- *Maximum System Load Test*

Watergate Software, Inc.
2000 Powell Street, Suite 1200
Emeryville, CA 94608 USA
Tel: (510) 596-1770 Fax: (510) 596-2092
Internet: http://www.ws.com